WHOSE AMERICA?

JONATHAN ZIMMERMAN

WHOSE AMERICA?

Culture Wars in the Public Schools

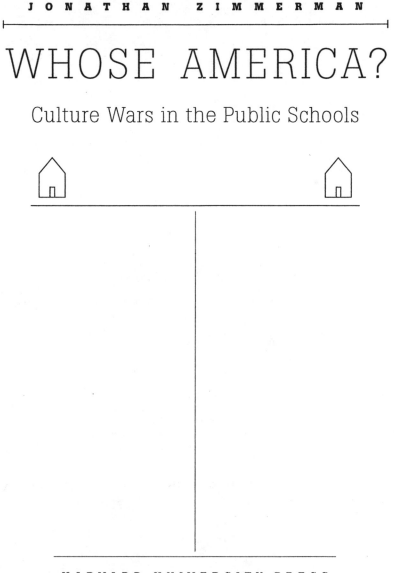

HARVARD UNIVERSITY PRESS

Cambridge, Massachusetts, and London, England

Library of Congress Cataloging-in-Publication Data

Zimmerman, Jonathan, 1961–
Whose America? : culture wars in the public schools /
Jonathan Zimmerman.
p.   cm.
Includes bibliographical references and index.
ISBN 0-674-00918-5 (alk. paper)
ISBN 0-674-01860-5 (pbk.)
1. Educational sociology—United States.
2. Textbooks—United States.
3. United States—History—Study and Teaching.   I. Title.
LC191.4 .Z56 2002
306.43'2'0973—dc21   2002190204

Designed by Gwen Nefsky Frankfeldt

For Sarah and Rebecca,
and Coming Home

Contents

WHOSE AMERICA?

Beyond Dayton and Chicago

In 1928 America's foremost political journalist published a book on the perils of popular efforts to alter the public school curriculum. Walter Lippmann entitled the book *American Inquisitors* and focused most of his attention on recent campaigns against teaching about evolution and against so-called New History textbooks in the schools. Following a circus-like trial in Dayton, Tennessee, a local court had upheld the state's anti-evolution law and levied a small fine against the young teacher who challenged it, John T. Scopes. In Chicago, meanwhile, Mayor William H. Thompson—a.k.a. "Big Bill"—led a successful drive to stop the use of texts by Charles Beard, David Muzzey, and other leading scholars. There were key distinctions between these two movements: whereas anti-evolutionists were mainly old-stock evangelical Protestants, for example, the Chicago campaign drew most of its support from Irish and German immigrants. But both attacks stemmed from America's grassroots, raising the danger of a perpetual conflict in its schools. "You may feel that I am making too much of the spectacles at Dayton and Chicago," Lippmann noted,

> and that I am wrong in taking them as symbols and portents of great significance. May I remind you, then, that the struggles for the control of

the schools are among the bitterest political struggles which now divide the nations? . . . It is inevitable that it should be so. Wherever two or more groups within a state differ in religion, or in language and in nationality, the immediate concern of each group is to use the schools to preserve its own faith and tradition. For it is in the school that the child is drawn towards or drawn away from the religion and the patriotism of its parents.[1]

Lippmann's argument neatly foreshadowed much of our contemporary discussion of cultural politics in America. Especially in its schools and universities, we are told, the nation is "wracked" by "culture wars."[2] These conflicts typically concern "religion" or "patriotism," just as Lippmann predicted. The issue of evolution continues to divide countless school boards and communities, which now face a host of other religion-related controversies: prayer, sex education, drug education, and so on. In history and the social studies, critics allege that an emphasis on America's racial diversity—and particularly on its racist deeds—erodes students' reverence for their country. These battles reflect not just differences over specific educational policies, it often seems, but different ways of seeing the world. After two students gunned down thirteen of their peers at a Colorado high school in April 1999, some commentators were quick to blame the massacre on the lack of prayer or the teaching of evolution in the school. Other observers, pointing to the two students' racist statements, complained that the curriculum had failed to imbue the murderers with knowledge and appreciation of the diverse cultures surrounding them.[3]

In this book I tell the story of culture wars in twentieth-century American schools. I investigate how successive generations of Americans have addressed the thorny issues of religion and nation—and race—in the public school curriculum. Despite the huge outpouring of writings in social history during the past four decades, we know very little about how ordinary Americans conceived of—and engaged in—these conflicts. An able historian himself, Lippmann realized that he could not narrate the conflict about public school curriculum without examining "the public." Following his lead, I explore the myriad and mostly unknown Americans who have struggled over the school curriculum for the past hundred years.

In one significant respect, my work departs from Lippmann's legacy. To Lippmann, the disparate conflicts over religion and patriotism in the schools—"Dayton and Chicago," in his geographical shorthand—reflected a single phenomenon: the "wide conflict" between "scholarship and popular faith" in American political life.[4] In our own day, likewise, commentators on the "culture wars" routinely collapse religious and patriotic controversies into a unitary, all-encompassing battle. But I will show that the two conflicts have two separate histories, belying the common frame that we use to analyze them. When I began to work on this book, I imagined mapping a single highway from Dayton and Chicago to the Colorado shootings—from the "culture wars" of Lippmann's day into our own. Instead, I discovered a pair of roads, one from Dayton and the other from Chicago. Often intersecting but nevertheless distinct, the roads follow sharply different paths between the past and the present.

The road from Chicago—our conflict over patriotism and nationalism in the schools—is a fairly straight line, reflecting one constant theme: the progressive inclusion of more and more Americans in the grand national story. Lippmann cast a jaundiced eye on this development, because the immigrants he examined often ignored or even disdained modern canons of historical scholarship. My own view is more sympathetic, because I focus largely upon a group Lippmann ignored: African-Americans. Invoking the very standards of scholarship and objectivity that Lippmann prized, black citizens removed a vicious array of racist slurs from school textbooks. Most of all, they won a part—or, sometimes, a starring role—in the texts' larger narrative. Thanks to several generations of grassroots black activists, students of every color now learn as much (if not more) about Frederick Douglass, Booker T. Washington, and Martin Luther King Jr. as they do about Andrew Jackson, Theodore Roosevelt, or John F. Kennedy. Given the neglect or outright denigration of African-Americans for most of our history, this achievement must rank as one of the great triumphs of that same history.

To be sure, the victory has never been complete. Jealously guarding their own dominant position in the American narrative, old-stock white conservatives worked to block immigrant and black voices from school textbooks. Eventually most parties to the dispute reached a rough compromise: each racial and ethnic group could enter the story, provided that none of them questioned the story's larger themes of freedom, equality, and opportunity. For Americans who could not wait for or abide by such an accord, the nation's educational system offered a built-in safety valve: local control. Impatient with racist history textbooks, for example, blacks across the segregated South promoted and adopted their own books and courses. After World War II, when many history texts started to lose their bigoted cast, publishers continued to produce so-called mint julep editions—all-white books—for the white southern market. But these episodes were exceptions, proving the overall rule of increasing diversity in the standard history curriculum. By 1973 even Governor George C. Wallace of Alabama would proclaim the second week of February African-American History Week.[5]

By contrast, America's road out of Dayton—its struggle over religion in the public schools—has been marked by sharp bends and curves, not by a straight path. Countering Lippmann's prediction of a war between "religious fundamentalism" and secular values, the nation's diverse faiths reached a fairly harmonious *modus vivendi* with the public schools during the three decades after *Scopes*. The key once again was America's tradition of local discretion, which allowed communities as well as individual families to determine both the type and the amount of religious instruction that children would receive in the schools. Under the system known as "released time," students could select instruction in the faith of their choice—or, if they preferred, they could opt out of the subject entirely. This arrangement sparked a spirited competition between certain mainline religions and self-avowed "fundamentalist" groups, each aiming to lure as many children as possible to its classes. Contrary to many historical accounts, the fundamentalists did not go "underground" after *Scopes;* instead, they fought tooth and nail to control religious instruction in the public schools. But they usually failed. Most religious instruction was controlled by liberal Christians, who used released-time classes to promote racial integration, poverty relief, and other progressive causes.[6]

In the early 1960s the Supreme Court's bans on organized prayer and Bible reading brought the "choice" system—and its liberal character—to an abrupt halt. Rather than ceding religious exercises to local jurisdictions and families, states and school districts now issued flat prohibitions against all such practices. Liberals quickly retreated from the arena of religious education, fearful of eroding the Court's authority on questions of race. But conservative and fundamentalist Christians continued to press their claims upon the schools. Across the country, advocates of school prayer revived older notions of a "Christian America": since the nation was founded and sanctified "under God," they argued, its public schools should respect the biblical injunction to worship God. Other Christian conservatives targeted sex education, which they saw as undermining the scriptural dictate of abstinence outside marriage. Born as a liberal effort to promote social justice for America's diverse races and classes, religious instruction quickly became a conservative campaign to impose a single morality on all of them.

In the 1980s the road from Dayton took yet another sharp turn. Instead of asking schools to tailor curricula to their values, Christian conservatives began to demand "equal time" for their views. The switch was most clearly evident in the revived battle over evolution, where conservatives called upon science teachers to present biblical accounts of creation alongside Darwinian ones. Likewise, they said, schools should present "Christian" instruction about sexuality to complement the allegedly atheistic messages in regular sex education classes. Lest devout believers suffer "discrimination," finally, conservatives pressed schools to restore organized prayer in the classroom.

In many ways these claims returned the debate over religion to its original, liberal roots: since Americans practiced a wide array of faiths, schools should provide the widest possible "choice" among them. Yet the new demands for religion in schools also echoed modern multiculturalism, with its emphasis on identifying and compensating the victims of social prejudice. Just as textbooks opened their pages to the distinct cultures of racial minorities, the argument went, so should classrooms open their doors to "oppressed" religions and *their* cultures—including the culture of prayer.

By the early 1990s, then, the roads from Chicago and Dayton seemed to merge into a single, unifying "culture war." But a closer inspection dispels this impression, highlighting the huge differences that still separated the battles over religion and patriotism in the public schools. Despite shrill warnings by a wide range of polemicists, the inclusion of racial and ethnic minorities in textbooks did not dilute America's majestic national narrative. Instead, these fresh voices were folded into the old story, echoing a century-long pattern of challenge, resistance, and co-option. On the religion front, compromise proved far more elusive. Reflecting Americans' essential beliefs about God and the universe, religious principles simply could not be reconciled in an additive, come-one-come-all fashion. Conflicts over history textbooks generally occurred within a shared set of assumptions about American civic tradition. But religious disputes often lacked this common language, a lack that accounts for their vehemence as well as their persistence. More than a decade after George C. Wallace welcomed black history into Alabama schools, for example, he continued to press for prayer in those same schools. More to the point, he also endorsed a campaign to remove "humanistic" literature textbooks, contrasting their content to the God-centered, "Judeo-Christian" worldview of his constituents.[7]

This book is a work of history, not of contemporary social commentary. But I live in the present, and the book was very much motivated by my personal, modern-day concerns. As a public school history teacher in the 1980s, I was struck by the bland, hackneyed quality of the textbooks that were issued to my students. Since then, many scholars have confirmed my initial impression: although texts have added welcome material about formerly neglected Americans, they have retained their mawkish and triumphal tone about "America" itself.[8] All the while, strangely, a range of critics—mostly conservatives, but some liberals as well—have berated history instruction for *denigrating* the nation.[9] In part, I wrote this book to discover how this loud, confusing debate had come about. Along the way, I hoped, I could also suggest some peace treaties—or at least a cease-fire—for the country's "history wars."

But what I found was that the history wars are vastly exaggerated. In the rarefied atmosphere of universities and think tanks, admittedly, theorists joust angrily over the proper balance of unity and diversity in the public school curriculum. Out in the schools themselves, however, this battle was settled long ago. Throughout the twentieth century, campaigns to diversify history instruction almost always served to enhance—not to erode—its "patriotic" quality. For blacks and immigrants, especially, the constant goal has been a place at the table—that is, a voice in the curriculum—rather than a new set of furniture. From our comfortable multicultural armchairs, it is easy to forget how much resistance these groups encountered to the simple proposition that every American belonged in American history. But we should also remember that these prior struggles concerned the roster of eligible patriots, not patriotism itself. "America" was a talisman, a sacred entity that none could sully or even contest. The only issue was whom it would include.

Here the contrast to religious "culture wars" could not be sharper. Several scholars have suggested that these religious conflicts are also exaggerated or even mythical: that in the educational arena, for example, staunchly conservative Christians evince far more interest in class size, school safety, and other prosaic matters than in red-flag cultural questions like prayer and sex education.[10] The point is well taken, but we should not take it too far. The vast majority of present-day citizen complaints to school boards concern religious issues, not racial or ethnic ones.[11] Inasmuch as these conflicts do divide America, moreover, they do not allow for easy truces. A citizen who views fornication as an abomination before the Lord may have little to share—or even to discuss—with a sex educator who wishes to teach children about contraception. "What have you been reading?" a flustered New Jersey resident asked her state school board in 1980, blasting sex education. "I don't understand you. I can't even hold a conversation with you."[12]

Her comment highlights the central moral and intellectual dilemma portrayed in this book. As I began to study America's history wars, I discovered that the combatants rarely subjected America itself to analysis: even as different groups struggled to insert their own heroes into the national story, they rarely challenged that narrative's broader contours and themes. As I will argue, the infusion of "diversity" into American textbooks—however laudable in its own right—actually delayed rather than promoted the critical dialogue that a healthy democracy demands. Yet given the frequent *absence* of dialogue in America's religious conflicts, readers might ask, shouldn't we celebrate our consensus on history? All nations—not just the United States—construct narratives that are partly "untrue" or mythological.[13] But these narratives provide a common discourse of understanding, something that has been sorely missing in America's wars over religion in the schools. How can I denounce these shared assumptions when it comes to history, then decry the *lack* of such assumptions about religion?

These are difficult questions, and I do not pretend to have all the answers. But I do think that a close examination of America's dual culture wars can clarify the origins of the conflicts, the nature of our current dilemma, and the decisions that lie ahead. In the end, that is probably all that any good history can do. I have done my best to map the roads from Dayton and Chicago to the present. Wherever they go next, I hope this book will help others navigate them.

PART ONE

HISTORY WARS

"I will never rest until the histories in use in the Chicago public schools are purged of their pro-British propaganda." The speaker was Chicago's mayor, William H. Thompson, who charged that textbooks maligned the American Revolution and its multi-ethnic heroes. Cartoonists and reporters linked Thompson's campaign to the 1925 *Scopes* trial surrounding the teaching of evolution in Dayton, Tennessee: in each case, they claimed, ignorant hordes had assaulted America's citadels of knowledge. But in the end, one publishing executive wrote, knowledge would win out: "The general current of historical writing cannot be swerved by such ridiculous charges. In Dayton and then Chicago, some little group gets out brooms and endeavors to sweep back the books they do not themselves like, but the current is too strong for them and science and art and history go on."[1]

The executive badly misjudged the breadth and strength of both campaigns. The *Scopes* trial would cast a pall over American schools into the 1960s, sharply restricting instruction about the theory of evolution. The effect of Thompson's crusade was more complicated. On the one hand, his attacks led to the insertion of more and more ethnic groups—or at least of their leading figures—into the grand national narrative; on the other, he blocked any critical discussion or evaluation of this same narrative. Over the next seventy years textbooks would open their pages to a diversity of races and ethnicities. But the texts did not question the overall principles of liberty, prosperity, and equality that supposedly bound Americans together. Books that contested these rosy themes rarely thrived. Waves of protest in the early 1940s swept away Harold Rugg's series of social studies texts, which emphasized America's economic inequality as well as its ethnic diversity. Weaned on the very gospel of private enterprise that Rugg denounced, Americans rejected any suggestion that poverty might prevent them from sharing in the nation's birthright of freedom.

Most of all, this birthright stopped at the color line. Even as history textbooks celebrated freedom and equality, they neglected or denigrated the nation's black citizens. Throughout the century blacks fought to remove these distortions and to insert their own achievements into general American history texts. At the same time, they demanded separate textbooks and courses about their distinctive past. Both campaigns would reach their zenith in the 1960s, exposing sharp tensions between them. Black activists and their white allies successfully "integrated" American textbooks, which continued to portray the nation as beacon of hope and liberty to the world. To a younger, more militant generation, however, only special "black studies" courses could expose the racism and oppression beneath this cheerful veneer. Nowhere were students of any color asked to decide how much liberty—or how much racism—characterized their shared history.

Perhaps it must always be so. Schools across the globe teach the glories of nationhood, linking children to a set of transcendent events and ideals. Yet our own triumphal narrative places a special emphasis on personal liberty: in America, we are told, individuals are uniquely free to decide their values, beliefs, and attitudes. If we applied that principle to instruction in history, we would encourage our children to develop their own interpretations instead of foisting a single view upon them. Since William H. Thompson's textbook campaign in Chicago, the American ideal of equality has helped bring many racial and ethnic groups into a heroic national narrative. One day, we might hope, the American ideal of liberty will help each of us to narrate the nation on our own.

Ethnicity and the History Wars

To the philosopher Horace M. Kallen, America faced two alternative futures in the early twentieth century. One was "Kultur Klux Klan," the "social and intellectual conformity" symbolized by the Klan's hooded hoodlums. The other was "Cultural Pluralism," a term Kallen coined in 1924 to celebrate "variations of racial groups" and "spontaneous differences of social heritage, institutional habit, mental attitude, and emotional tone." Nativist sentiment dominated the United States in the 1920s, Kallen admitted, citing drives for immigration restriction and "100 percent Americanism." Yet, he emphasized, this impulse "has never existed unopposed." Beneath America's "compulsions toward conformity" lay a more liberal tradition of ethnic tolerance, respectful of "differentiated communities" and "the free flow . . . of spiritual values between them."[1]

A few months before Kallen's essay appeared, the New Jersey legislature debated a bill that would have barred so-called treasonous history textbooks from the state's classrooms. The bill's sponsors targeted authors like David S. Muzzey and Charles A. Beard, whose "new methods" of socioeconomic analysis seemed to diminish the Founding Fathers. Invoking the liberal tribune John Dewey, Kallen condemned measures like the New Jersey bill as the epitome of America's homogenizing heritage. "The fact is, the genuine American, the typical

American, is himself a hyphenated character," wrote Dewey, in a passage that Kallen quoted. "And this means at least that our public schools shall . . . enlighten all as to the great past contributions of every strain in our composite make-up." Rather than capitulating to the narrow demands of Anglo-Saxon patriots like the American Legion and the Veterans of Foreign Wars, Kallen concluded, schools should highlight the talents and achievements of America's entire ethnic panoply.[2]

Unbeknownst to Kallen, however, the same ethnic minorities that he celebrated often *supported* the school history laws that he despised. In New Jersey, for example, backers of the textbook bill included not just the Legion and the VFW but also the Steuben Society, the Knights of Columbus, and the Jewish Alliance. To these ethnic groups, any diminution of America's grand national story would erode—not enhance—their special contribution to it. After all, one Newark citizen reasoned, a text that downplayed the heroic deeds of George Washington would effectively discount the "German, Polish, and French generals" who assisted him. It would also place their English enemies in a far more favorable light, as a German activist emphasized. "Friends, there has never been a dearth of Tories in our midst," he warned, "of men who regret the great achievements of the past and would bring us back to the British fold."[3]

The ethnic dimensions of this episode—and of countless other "history wars" throughout the decade—suggest a revision of our own historical narrative about American culture and education in the 1920s. Most accounts of the era follow roughly the same terms that Kallen laid down in 1924, pitting hard-edged Americanizers against ethnic groups and their liberal advocates.[4] In public schools, especially, nativists like the Ku Klux Klan fought to remove foreign-language instruction, Catholic teachers, and the other "perils of pluralism," to borrow David Tyack's memorable phrase.[5] During the struggle over history textbooks, however, ethnics joined hands with Anglo-Saxons to block more critical, complicated readings of

America's origins. Ethnic groups did manage to insert new heroes like Crispus Attucks and Thaddeus Kosciusko, adding a few fresh hues to the monochromatic national story. At the same time, though, they reinforced its bland, triumphal message of English tyranny and American righteousness. The result was a history of many colors but one idea, culturally diverse yet intellectually static.

Ironically, ethnic groups often embraced so-called Progressive interpretations of the Civil War, industrialization, and the Progressive era itself. But they refused to apply this socioeconomic analysis to the Revolution, insisting that America's conception and birth remain immaculate. In large part, their effort reflected a defensive response to discrimination within the United States: ethnic groups must protect their Revolutionary heroes from the taint of "material interests," one activist argued, lest these groups suffer further waves of "racial and religious ostracism."[6] Outside America, meanwhile, revised accounts of Britain's colonial past threatened to buttress its imperial claims in the present. For if England had brought the American colonies certain advantages, as recent histories suggested, its contemporary control of Ireland and Palestine might seem similarly benign. Hence ethnic activists balked at any fresh interpretation of the Revolution, uniting with their erstwhile Anglo-Saxon enemies to block the "new" history from America's textbooks.

To be sure, tensions often racked this fragile coalition of "patriotic societies and Gaelic politicians," as one annoyed historian called it.[7] While welcoming the support of Irish and German groups in the textbook struggle, old-stock patriotic organizations scorned their anti-British biases. Ethnic groups battled one another, too, crowding a curriculum that could not possibly accommodate them all. And whereas most ethnicities fought for simple recognition, African-Americans also had to combat textbooks' expression of active prejudice against them. Yet all these groups rallied behind hero worship in history, challenging any text that dared to question the courage or conduct of America's multi-ethnic founders. In the history skirmishes of the 1920s, then, Horace Kallen's two alternative pathways merged into a single road. Hardly a brake upon "intellectual conformity," as Kallen imagined, cultural pluralism helped speed it along.

The "New History" and Its Critics

In 1911 the historian James Harvey Robinson wrote a flattering preface for a textbook by his former student David Saville Muzzey. Completing his now-classic account of the "New History," published the following year, Robinson praised Muzzey for adopting vital trends in modern scholarship. Whereas traditional texts stressed "the tactics and casualties of military campaigns," Robinson wrote, Muzzey's *An American History* probed deeper changes in the nation's economy, politics, and population. The textbook went through four more editions in the next fourteen years, each prefaced by Robinson's same laudatory statement. Muzzey added his own introduction to the 1925 edition, highlighting its "added emphasis on social and economic factors" and its updated discussion of recent historical events.[8]

In its treatment of the American Revolution, however, Muzzey's 1925 textbook actually included *less* "social and economic" analysis than had appeared in earlier versions. At the beginning of a chapter entitled "British Rule in America," his 1911 text emphasized the complex divisions and dilemmas on both sides of the Atlantic:

> This great event has too often been represented as the unanimous uprising of a downtrodden people to repel the deliberate, unprovoked attack of a tyrant upon their liberties; but when thousands of people in the colonies could agree with a noted lawyer of Massachusetts, that the Revolution was a "causeless, wanton, wicked rebellion," and thousands of people in England could applaud Pitt's denunciation of the war against America as "barbarous, unjust, and diabolical," it is evident that, at the time at least, there were two opinions as to colonial rights and British oppression.

By 1925, however, the same chapter started with a simplistic statement of British malfeasance and American resistance:

This great event marked the entrance of the United States into the family of nations. It was the armed protest against the invasion by the British Parliament of rights long cherished by the American colonies.[9]

The 1925 edition pared away several other nuanced passages, including a comment that historians held "differences of opinion" regarding the causes of the Revolution. Meanwhile, it added rich descriptions of American valor on the battlefield. The Battle of Bunker Hill—summarized in a single sentence in the original text—now received two pages of fulsome detail.[10] Even as his mentor praised him for elevating social analysis over military heroics, it seemed, Muzzey was busily inverting them.

Many years later Muzzey recalled that he had only revised his textbooks to correct minor errors, such as "a date or the initial of a man's name." Yet texts by Muzzey and other "new" historians reveal much more substantive changes, spurred not just by right-wing patriotic societies—as subsequent chroniclers have suggested—but also by ethnic critics. In 1922 the New York City municipal official David Hirshfield—a self-proclaimed "101 percent American"—conducted five public hearings about texts that supposedly "belittle[d] illustrious American patriots." Hirshfield's first witnesses hardly fit the mold of the "pure" Anglo-Saxon nativist, however. Joining speakers from veterans' and hereditary societies were the black spokesman William Pickens and the Jewish leader Julius Hyman, who bemoaned the absence of their own ethnic heroes in recent history texts. "There is no good reason why American histories should not be fair to the great men and women of the past who made the present America possible," a Jewish magazine editorialized in praise of Hirshfield's efforts. "Justice should be done to all, regardless of race, creed, or color."[11]

Splashing across the national press, New York's text inquiry generated a wave of similar activity beyond the Empire State. By 1923 at least twenty-one legislatures were considering measures to regulate the content of "new" history textbooks. Countless school districts and municipalities also moved to bar the offending books, culminating in a lengthy "textbook trial" convened by Chicago's Mayor William "Big Bill" Thompson in 1927—actually a dismissal hearing for Superintendent William McAndrew, whom Thompson accused of imposing "treasonous" and "un-American" texts on the schools. From Boston and Baltimore to Seattle and San Francisco, meanwhile, a wide range of ethnicities rallied against these "treasonous" texts. "All the important national groups of which we are composed have their eye on the schools," observed Walter Lippmann in 1928. "In fact, it almost seems as if there were hardly an organization in America which has not set up a committee . . . to rewrite the textbooks."[12]

Following Lippmann, historians likened these "anti-British inquisitors" to the nation's flourishing anti-evolution movement: in both cases, the argument went, popular passions and prejudices had corrupted the curriculum.[13] Yet many of the same historians had altered their own textbooks during World War I to reflect—and to reinforce—the public's *pro-British* sentiments, as Lippmann also noted. "There is nothing I would not do to help bring about the warmest relations between the English speaking peoples," declared the historian Claude Van Tyne in 1918. "To my mind, the whole future of the democratic world depends upon that factor." Written with Andrew C. McLaughlin, another prominent scholar, Van Tyne's *History of the United States for Schools* epitomized this Anglophilic impulse. According to a wartime promotional leaflet, the textbook showed "that the real leaders of English thought sympathized with America and were bitterly opposed to the Autocratic policies of King George III and his hired Hessians." Other texts emphasized the king's own Germanic heritage, attributing the provocations that led to the Revolution to "junker aristocrats" in the House of Hanover while exonerating their British subjects.[14]

To further cement "good understanding" with England, textbook authors also inserted more material about "economic and social development" during the Revolutionary era, as the historian David Matteson admitted. Typified by Charles A. Beard's masterpiece, *An Economic Interpretation of the Constitution of the United States* (1913), this approach was frequently associated with contemporary "Progressive" reforms like railroad regulation, the income tax, and direct primaries. In foreign affairs, however, it could just as easily serve to bind America to its former ruler. By complicating the old story of a venomous England and a virtuous America, scholars believed, the "new" history would help heal old wounds between them. Yet by tailoring textbooks to "the political necessities of 1917," Lippmann warned, historians also set a dangerous precedent for the ensuing decade: "It was made plain that history is something that can be cut and shaped to suit the purposes of the moment."[15]

In many ways, as another observer noted, ethnic attacks on textbooks in the 1920s reflected a natural "backwash" of the "waves of propaganda" that had preceded them. "We should remember that what is good fare for the goose is also good fare for the gander," a journalist added, recounting Anglophilic text revisions during the war. "As long as one part of the country insists upon singing 'Rule, Britannia,' another part is going to continue their 'Deutschland, Deutschland uber Alles.'" Book companies moved quickly to meet the new demands, even enlisting ethnic leaders as editors on occasion. "The matter is of serious commercial importance to the authors and to us," one publisher wrote privately. "We [will] make such changes in the text as may appear to be justifiable and reasonable." Some publishers simply removed controversial sentences, such as "British pluck triumphed" or "King George III alone was to blame." Others revised their accounts of the Revolution completely, while still others released new texts that stressed the traditional interpretation. Even Charles and Mary Beard's *History of the United States,* first published in 1921, scanted economic analysis in favor of lavish battle scenes and biographies.[16]

These changes help explain the continued popularity of books like the Beards' text and especially of Muzzey's *An American History,* which remained on the bestseller list into the 1930s. In New Jersey, for example, ethnic societies withdrew their complaints about the Muzzey text after Muzzey deleted descriptions of Stamp Act demonstrators as a "mob" and of the Boston Massacre's victims as "ruffians." But other ethnic spokesmen deemed such revisions insufficient, insisting that "new" history books still bore an Anglo-Saxon bias. Chicago activists even prevailed upon their school board to publish a supplementary pamphlet celebrating "distinguished Patriots from Europe" who assisted the Revolution, because none of the city's textbooks gave these heroes appropriate attention. "The poison," one critic insisted, "is still there."[17]

Indeed, some ethnic groups charged, the "poison" had been laid by England herself. Behind the scenes, they claimed, British officials conspired to sway American historians through a clever fusion of flattery and perfidy. According to one widely circulated story, Muzzey and other "new" historians were corrupted by a sumptuous London dinner held in their honor in 1921. (Surely, an amused historian retorted, this theory represented "one of the most impressive tributes to British cooking ever made by an American.") Others charged that scholars had received actual bribes—"British gold"—from the Carnegie Foundation, the Rhodes Scholarship Fund, and other sinister pro-English sources. *"Americans, Wake Up!"* screamed a leaflet by the Knights of Columbus, America's largest Catholic organization. *"Our History is being distorted and polluted and our children thereby de-Americanized. The achievements of the many different races—Irish, German, Italian, French, Scandinavian, Slavik, Polish, Spanish, etc. in founding, developing, and maintaining the institutions of this country are treated with contempt to the glory of England—the age-long, implacable foe of America."*[18]

Under this syllogism, any censure of the Founding Fathers weakened the Revolution; weakening the Revolution elevated England; and elevating the English belittled America's other ethnicities. "New" historians scoffed at the charge, noting their own pleas for *greater* scholarly attention to non-English peoples. For example, Arthur M. Schlesinger's collection of essays *New Viewpoints in American History*—a target of Big Bill Thompson's attack—began with a detailed, flattering chapter entitled "The Influence of Immigration on American

History." Yet Schlesinger's own viewpoint was essentially social: like other leading scholars, he tended to stress broad demographic and economic developments rather than "heroes of racial origin," as one journalist observed. Although they frequently shared historians' overall liberal views, ethnic groups resented this perceived slight upon their heritage. "All nationalities are entitled to a place in the sun," Thompson proclaimed, "and our national heroes are the stars in the firmament of our patriotism."[19]

Whereas "new" historians frowned on nativist movements like the Ku Klux Klan, then, ethnic activists tended to equate the two: whatever their other differences, revisionists and nativists both diminished non-British achievements. "Assimilation of the various races living in the United States is not, and cannot be synonymous with their anglicization," averred Edward F. McSweeney, chair of the historical commission of the Knights of Columbus. "Each racial group [has] made a substantial contribution." Besides fighting to bar "treasonous" texts, McSweeney's commission sponsored a series of historical monographs about Irish, German, Jewish, and black achievements in America. McSweeney labeled this effort an "honest plea for Americanization," contrasting it to the "pro-English" version promoted by "new" historians and 100 percent nativists alike. The Anglophiles were the *real* "super-hyphenates," he insisted, because they exaggerated the exploits of a single ethnic group over all the others.[20]

Activists from many ethnic groups helped "twist the Lion's tail," the era's euphemism for anti-British agitation. But Irish-Americans took the lead. Convening in Philadelphia in 1919, delegates to America's first "Irish Race Convention" resolved to press for three goals: U.S. recognition of the Irish Republic, rejection of the League of Nations treaty, and revision of "the British propaganda which is falsifying and misrepresenting the facts of American history." A subsequent flyer by the "Friends of Irish Freedom" boasted that thirteen signers of the Declaration of Independence, seven members of the Constitutional Convention, and fully one-third of the Revolutionary Army had been of Irish heritage. During the League of Nations debate in Congress, meanwhile, one senator provoked howls of protest by suggesting that most Irish soldiers in the Revolution fought on the British side. Indeed, America's history wars were so closely related to the Irish freedom struggle that some observers predicted parallel dénouements for both. "This agitation was begun . . . to stir up anti-British feeling," declared the New York state historian James Sullivan in February 1922. "Now that the Irish free state is established I do not anticipate very much of a continuance."[21]

As Irish activism declined, however, other ethnic groups accelerated their own attacks on textbooks. Still stinging from their persecution during World War I, German-Americans were especially vocal in demanding recognition for their achievements. "I am in favor of getting our message across by the revision of these text books," a spokesman proclaimed in 1927, "and I believe [in] digging up the stories of heroism wherever the hero is a German." The previous year a Steuben Society pageant at New York's Madison Square Garden had highlighted the central characters whom Germans hoped to insert into the nation's historical drama. The first figure was Peter Minuit, governor of New Netherland but a German by birth. Then came Daniel Pastorius and the settlers in Germantown, Pennsylvania, bearing the first antislavery petition on American soil. The last character to reach the stage was Molly Pitcher, "nee Maria Ludwig," who proceeded to vanquish a slew of mock British soldiers. Nevertheless, Steubenites charged, few of these "fellow racials" ever entered American textbooks. Examining six texts in his school district, one activist complained that twice as many lines were devoted to a single Frenchman—Lafayette—than to five German heroes combined.[22]

Even as they condemned "pro-British" books, then, ethnic groups often competed with one another to revise them. During the textbook "trial" in Big Bill Thompson's Chicago, for example, Italians and Norwegians fought over who had discovered America: Christopher Columbus or Leif Eriksson. "At first it seemed as if the solution of the momentous Thompsonian question was to have a composite history wherein each 'race' could have its heroes sung," one editorialist observed. "But the Italian-Norwegian campaign in Bigbilldom shows the fallacy of that supposition . . . The fight is no longer against England alone. It is civil war." Poles complained that Chicago's special textbook supplement identified Pulaski as "the son of a Lithuanian patriot"; Lithuanians, in turn, protested that it called Kosciusko "a Pole of noble birth." Dutch parents charged that textbooks emphasized other ethnic settlements over New Amsterdam; but Germans claimed this colony should be credited to *them,* in recognition of the Hapsburg influence in Holland. Surveying these debates, a Steuben Society chapter resolved to seek "an end of race conflicts among the white citizens of America." Even as they celebrated their own heroes, different "racials" could unite behind a shared European ancestry—and a shared enmity for England.[23]

Significantly, nonwhite activists also joined the assault on history texts in the 1920s. In Chicago the Grand Council Fire of American Indians complained that the schoolbooks neglected Pocahontas, Tecumseh, and Chief Joseph. Such heroes embodied a "*real* 100 per cent Americanism," the council continued, since Indians predated all white migration to the United States. Attacks on textbooks by other ethnic groups also galvanized Chicago's African-Americans, who sensed that "there is no better time than now for us to place our claim for recognition," as a black newspaper argued. Since Thompson had proposed adding sixteen white ethnic heroes to the city's texts, the newspaper added, African-Americans should receive an equivalent apportionment. It even offered to send him the names of sixteen black luminaries, along with "biographical sketches" of each. "Are we content to take a back seat as the parade of boasting passes by?" a black Chicagoan asked. "I tell you No! a thousand times, No! A different Negro is now coming to the front."[24]

Yet textbooks took little account of the achievements of black or Indian Americans, instead harping on their alleged inferiority. Indeed, both groups had to combat not just historical neglect—the common plight of white ethnics—but also "base untruths," a black spokesman complained. Texts routinely depicted Native Americans as barbaric savages, scalping white settlers and slaying white heroes like George Custer. Even so, a black observer hastened to add, textbooks "have done worse by the Negro than by the Indians." Whereas Indians were merely deemed warlike, he noted, texts portrayed blacks as childlike; they were cheerful and affectionate, to be sure, but also fearful and superstitious. "The laziness, shiftlessness, and irresponsibility of the Negro [are] part of his racial heredity," a textbook used in Philadelphia flatly asserted in its discussion of slavery. "Most [slaves] accepted their fate stoically, for their moral ideals were low and their conceptions of family life undeveloped." Worst of all were the textbooks' accounts of the Reconstruction era, when rude and licentious blacks supposedly looted—or, even worse, raped—an innocent white South.[25]

Praising Mayor Thompson as a "champion of all the oppressed races," a black newspaper in New York urged African-Americans across the country to support his campaign in defense of the nation's multi-ethnic patriots. Thus far, the paper acknowledged, Thompson had failed to include blacks in his roster of the historically neglected. Since blacks had backed his recent election bid in overwhelming numbers, however, they might induce him to grant their race "due credit for the heroes and patriots it has produced." Often denounced for pandering to African-Americans, Thompson seems to have ignored their appeals. He did meet with Indian textbook critics, by contrast, assuring them of his full cooperation. (Ever the showman, Thompson donned an Indian headdress of eagle feathers and performed a "war dance.")[26]

Even when they prevailed in the textbook wars, racial and ethnic groups also had to worry about their putative allies: white patriotic societies. In the same breath as he applauded Thompson, for example, a black journalist fretted that the Sons of the American Revolution (SAR), the United Daughters of the Confederacy, and even the Ku Klux Klan had also backed Thompson's crusade. Such groups used patriotism as a "cloak of convenience," the journalist continued, hiding a host of "sins and inconsistencies" against African-Americans.

Likewise, patriotic societies feared that Irish, German, and black activists would make their own crusade look "ludicrous," as one leader of the SAR complained. Most concerned of all was the KKK, which welcomed Thompson's barbs against "pro-British propaganda" but warned that a far more nefarious foreign agent was at work. "During the last few years an influx of pictures, stories and garbled accounts of Roman Catholic heroes has found its way into these textbooks," a KKK editorial charged. "This Thompson attack . . . did not touch this vast evil."[27] As the 1920s wore on, in fact, increasing numbers of Protestant nativists *supported* the "new" history as a way of *stemming* immigrants' influence. Bigots backed critical readings of the past, that is, not to open more minds to history but to shut ethnic Americans out of it.

Cracks in the Coalition

William Morris was bitter. Surveying a decade of conflict over history textbooks, the New York newspaperman shuddered at the inaccuracies and exaggerations that still pervaded them. At the universities, he conceded, professional historians had revised simplistic, black-and-white accounts of the American Revolution and other central events in the nation's past. Yet too many schoolbooks still indulged in an old-fashioned "fairy tale," depicting Revolutionists as "demigods" and every British leader as "a deep-dyed scoundrel." They also inflated the deeds of non-English heroes, capitulating to the whims of a polyglot citizenry. "Americans of Polish, German, Irish, Negro, Jewish, Hungarian, and Dutch origin all demanded that they be given credit in the making of America," Morris wrote in 1930. "Only two sides were ignored, the British and the historians." In Chicago, most of all, Mayor Thompson and his cronies promoted books that "flattered the national vanity" of ethnic voting blocs. "There is no bloc of English voters," Morris tartly claimed.[28]

Of course, this claim was an exaggeration. Despite a huge influx of Eastern and Southern Europeans prior to the Immigration Restriction

Act of 1924, Morris and his fellow citizens of British descent still made up a sizable plurality of America's population. For members of patriotic and hereditary societies, then, the textbook controversy of the 1920s was fraught with ambivalence. Fearful of any movement that might erode faith in the nation's founders, groups like the SAR and the American Legion united with ethnic societies to keep more critical interpretations out of textbooks. But they also feared that these same ethnics might erode their own white Protestant superiority, throwing out the Anglo-Saxon baby with the pro-English bathwater. "Our textbooks need not be anti-British," the SAR's president-general declared hopefully in 1922, "to be truly American." The trick, it seemed, was to venerate the Founding Fathers without maligning the Mother Country.[29]

Often these tensions remained veiled from the general public. In Wisconsin, patriotic and ethnic societies eagerly locked arms to win a 1923 law barring any text "which falsifies the facts regarding the War of Independence" or "defames our nation's founders." The measure required a public hearing upon the complaint of five citizens, "be they Daughters of the American Revolution, or Irish-Americans," as one critic pointedly warned. Back East, however, these two groups were already feuding. In a speech to commemorate the tercentenary of the Pilgrims' arrival, the DAR's president-general told a Massachusetts audience that Americans were "English in our history and tradition"; other ethnic groups had contributed to the nation's greatness, she acknowledged, but they had also "become Anglicized in the end." The response from the Bay State's large Irish community was swift and irate. The Pilgrims were themselves rebels from England, one Irishman argued, deriving their ideas from the "Dutch Republic" of the Renaissance and—even more venerably—from the "Hebrew Commonwealth" of scripture. Their DAR patron was simply a "Tory," he added, hardly worthy of her own Revolutionary heritage.[30]

Meanwhile, ethnic and patriotic groups also clashed over textbook accounts of more recent American history. Even as he condemned class-based interpretations of the Revolution, the Knights of Columbus leader Edward F. McSweeney maintained that subsequent events had been powered more by "greed" and "the accumulation of wealth" than by "spiritual impulse" or "moral urge." Indeed, text critics admitted, they *needed* a sacred Revolution if they were to critique the profane social inequality that followed it. "I have known reformers to do many foolish things, but nothing else so foolish as . . . the discrediting of the American Revolution," wrote Charles Edward Russell, a socialist muckraker and a founder of the National Association for the Advancement of Colored People. "If they have merit they consciously or unconsciously seek to complete [its] ideals." Without those ideals, an Irish-American activist asserted, no one could attack "Big Money" and its contemporary corruption of national life. Little wonder, he argued, that leading industrialists feared the simple, unadorned message of the Revolution: all men are created equal. It might undermine their own power, just as it had helped topple George III.[31]

Here ethnic groups frequently joined hands with labor unions, which also demanded that history texts address modern "social and economic matters" like unemployment, collective bargaining, and workmen's compensation.[32] Yet any such text material drew fire from Anglo-Saxon patriotic leaders, who feared its "anti-American" or even "socialist" implications. Too often, they charged, textbooks exaggerated the problems and perils of the Industrial Revolution; by the same token, the books seemed too friendly toward "Progressive" measures aimed at correcting its consequences. In Idaho the SAR blasted one text for its "one-sided" discussions of the income tax, the direct primary, and the "labor question." Written by the popular "new" historian Willis Mason West, the book devoted more pages to the exploits of three Progressive legislators—Robert La Follette, Hiram Johnson, and "the almost forgotten William Uren"—than to "the entire military history of the Revolutionary War," an enraged Idahoan noted.[33]

Significantly, even left-leaning ethnic critics echoed the Idahoan's anger: for ethnics and Anglos alike, the Revolution trumped every other concern. In Wisconsin an Irish activist and self-proclaimed "LaFollette Progressive" joined with American Legion leaders to condemn several "treasonous" texts—including West's *History of the American People,* the very book that patriotic societies deemed too friendly to La Follette. Its introductory pages seemed to "malign the nation's founders," the Irish critic argued, thus "poison[ing] the well where the children drink"—and polluting any positive features of West's later chapters. Elsewhere a Legion official ridiculed the widespread ethnic accusation that Muzzey, West, and other scholars had conspired with England to slant school histories. But in the same breath he blasted these books for underscoring "the blunders, foibles and frailties of prominent heroes." Whatever the source of text bias, he concluded, Legionnaires should work to bar the biased texts.[34]

Outside the large patriotic societies, by contrast, ethnic considerations caused many white Protestants to *support* "new" history books. Some advocates were openly Anglophilic, praising Muzzey and other authors for placing Great Britain in a better light.[35] More commonly, however, they celebrated the new scholarship for the same reason that immigrants censured it: by reinterpreting the Revolution as a clash of socioeconomic forces, it promised to diminish non-English heroes who had aided the cause. "Put none but Americans on guard when we make up our histories," warned a New Jersey nativist, "or . . . they will have George Washington either an Irishman or a German." A Boston newspaper published a satirical "Declaration Av Indipindense," which argued that "the Oirish did all the foighting" in the Revolutionary War. In a similar spirit, a Dallas editorial mocked German-American efforts to claim Abraham Lincoln as one of their own: "The German origin of Honest Abe clashes with the Italian theory. Lincoln under this theory becomes L'Inchiostro, meaning "the ink" . . . The Chinese theory proves direct descent from the famous Lin family, Lin Kong being as perfect Chinese as you could expect to find in a month of Sundays. Abraham Llyncollyn was Welsh beyond a doubt, and the origin of Abraham Linsky-Cohen needs no further explanation."[36]

Other white Protestants sported a much harsher brand of bigotry, condemning ethnic text activists as "Sinn Fein agitators," "hyphenates," and "so-called Americans." They added jabs at Anglo-Saxons who continued to ally with the ethnics, thereby allowing "distorted historical facts" to enter the classroom. "Patriotic organizations should protect the children . . . from the efforts of these turbulent unassimilated immigrants," an anonymous New York teacher wrote, "and should protect our sacred history." A Massachusetts correspondent congratulated the textbook author Claude Van Tyne for shredding "the whole fabric of Hibernian political philosophy," which was premised upon the "unmitigated tyranny" of English rule. The most vicious attack came from Dr. M. M. Yates, a cranky bigot in Santa Barbara, California. "Roman catholic–Vatican conspirators . . . are rushing events along, to dispossess all Americans—and destroy all History," Yates wrote to Van Tyne. "Even now, our Traitor politicians are abetting and comforting the reptiles to make a Catholic History—leaving out all facts of their damnable assassinations and wrecking of laws!"[37]

Such expressions of nativist support placed historians in a difficult spot. On the one hand, they welcomed any assistance they could get in defending their beleaguered textbooks. But they also feared that aid from the wrong quarters could further alienate ethnic constituencies. Most historians fashioned themselves as liberal on issues of race and ethnicity, moreover, so they bridled at any outward identification with anti-immigrant sentiment. Indeed, they tended to dismiss both ethnic hero worship *and* white nativism as functions of a "boastful, intolerant nationalism," as the historian Carleton Hayes wrote in 1926. Traditionally, Hayes noted, white Protestant patriotic societies had led the drive for a "100 percent American" history curriculum. But now other ethnicities were getting in on the act, all aiming to impose their own "special group-loyalties" upon the schools: "Every religious group and every racial group and every sub-national group contends with others for official recognition of its distinctive status as 'American.' The time may come when, by the spirited stirrings of ultra-nationalists, the American melting-pot will be a seething cauldron of fiery nonfusible nationalisms."[38]

The following year a prominent ethnic spokesman celebrated the same enduring affiliations that Hayes maligned. Addressing the "Concord Society," named after the ship that brought the first Germans to America, John Andrew Russell praised the society's efforts to enshrine its heroes in statues, holiday celebrations, and especially school textbooks. Without such activity, he argued, America's rich fabric of race and ethnicity would lose its special texture: "Our country is a composite country, and some people, whose rhetoric is drawn from the science of metallurgy, like to think of our civilization as being the result of a melting pot. I cannot believe that literature and culture and spirituality are things that are gross, like copper, iron and lead, to be brought together by the destructive action of fire. I rather like to think . . . of each and every race drawing its own beautiful design upon the common background of humanity."[39]

Here, perhaps unwittingly, Russell echoed the pluralist philosophy developed by Randolph Bourne, Horace Kallen, John Dewey, and other liberal theorists of the era. Denouncing the melting pot's homogenizing tendencies, Bourne described America as a complex tapestry of distinct—but interwoven—threads. Kallen preferred the image of an orchestra, with each instrument contributing its own unique pitch to the grand national concert. Such views found little currency in the 1920s, Dewey acknowledged, when a mean-spirited, monotonal nationalism swept the land. In schools, then, children should study—and celebrate—America's "different racial elements." Only then, Dewey believed, would the nation rediscover the "natural, old-fashioned toleration" and the "unified social consciousness" that a truly democratic polity required.[40]

In a similar vein, historians of the 1920s have depicted a clash between an ascendant Protestant nationalism and a more tolerant, poly-ethnic tradition. But nationalism won, the historians add, stamping out America's glorious pluralist heritage. The victory was never complete, of course; ethnic Americans, as Gary Gerstle notes, continued their dogged quest to "turn . . . cultural policy in a more liberal direction." But this was a rear-guard action, stalled and then quashed by a newly energized state and its henchmen in right-wing citizen groups. By the Great Depression, if not earlier, "the forces of social control and conformity" had overwhelmed most vestiges of "pluralism and individualism" in the United States.[41]

As the controversy over school history textbooks reveals, though, cultural pluralism itself could reinforce ideological conformity. Across the country, racial and ethnic groups successfully inserted colorful new characters into American history textbooks. But at the same time they blocked a more critical, sophisticated analysis of the nation's founding narrative. Indeed, the inclusion of new groups in textbooks helped shape a cheerfully banal, even jingoistic version of this narrative. Diversity and critical history both remain worthy goals. But we should resist the easy presupposition that one will spawn the other.

In 1924 Irish-Americans blasted a peace activist's "insidious attempt" to eliminate the most violent stanza of "The Star Spangled Banner" from New York textbooks. The revision, they argued, would bolster Great Britain, devalue America's cause in the War of 1812, and degrade the Irish martyrs who died in that war. Other ethnic groups joined in the attack, claiming that any critical investigation of the war would cheapen their special contribution to it.[42] No ethnic leader asked why the United States entered the conflict, how it was conducted, or whether American schoolchildren should celebrate it. Each "race" could have its heroes sung, it seemed, but no race could question the underlying melody that united them all.

Struggles over Race and Sectionalism

"American children are being taught a conception of the character, capacity, history, and achievements of the Negro utterly at variance with the facts, and calculated to arouse against him feelings of aversion and contempt." So declared the newly established Committee on Public School Textbooks, forged by the National Association for the Advancement of Colored People in 1932. Just a decade earlier, committee chair Charles Edward Russell recalled, ethnic and patriotic societies had blocked textbooks' supposedly pro-British interpretations of the American Revolution. Now the NAACP would organize a comparable attack on the books' anti-Negro bias, focusing especially on their flawed analyses of the Civil War and its aftermath. "We fought them to a standstill about the Revolution," Russell averred, "and we can do the same here."[1]

South of the Mason-Dixon Line, however, many white critics charged that these very texts maligned *them*. Just a few days before the NAACP's first textbook salvo, the United Daughters of the Confederacy (UDC) and the Sons of Confederate Veterans (SCV) began their own effort to bar David S. Muzzey's *An American History* from schools in Virginia. A frequent target of black complaints, Muzzey combined a gentle criticism of southern slavery and secession with a rank condemnation of "Negro rule" during Reconstruction. To Dixie's die-hard white defenders, even a mild rebuke of the South was one rebuke too many. As outraged Virginians told their state legislature, Muzzey deemed the Confederacy a "rebellion" and Abraham Lincoln the South's "savior." ("Saved," an SCV officer quipped, "by invasion and coercion.") Indeed, the UDC leader Anne V. Mann insisted, the entire episode highlighted the need for so-called homemade books—that is, for texts produced by southern authors and publishing houses. "North is North and South is South," Mann proclaimed, "and I don't think the twain ever shall meet, at least not in a history textbook."[2]

No such split marked the battle against "pro-British" textbooks in the 1920s, when African-Americans locked arms with other ethnic groups to inscribe their heroes—Thaddeus Kosciusko, Haym Solomon, Crispus Attucks—in accounts of America's struggle for independence. Even southern veterans joined the multicultural cavalcade, successfully inserting—or inflating—the Revolutionary exploits of Patrick Henry, Richard Henry Lee, and other regional notables.[3] Yet the issues surrounding America's great internal conflict could not be settled in this additive, come-one-come-all fashion. Narrating the Civil War, Americans did not just contend over which heroes to include; they contested the narrative itself. Especially in the South, citizens sensed the difference. "History!" exclaimed a South Carolina newspaper in 1914, blasting "lopsided" northern texts. "Whose History? Written by Whom?"[4]

Similar questions reverberated across the American South well into the 1940s, challenging what historians have described as a new national synthesis surrounding the Civil War. Galvanized by the conflict with Spain in 1898, North and South reached a "negotiated settlement of sectional differences," as Peter Novick argues. Southerners conceded that secession was unconstitutional and slavery was wrong, although its evils had been widely exaggerated by sly Yankee historians; northerners tempered their criticism of slavery but accelerated their attacks on Reconstruction. Captured in countless textbooks as well as in monographs, movies, and novels, this devil's bargain dominated mainstream interpretations for at least a half-century.[5] But accounts of this agreement tend to neglect two important groups who dissented from it: African-Americans and white Confederate societies. While black intellectuals like W. E. B. Du Bois led the scholarly struggle for a nonracist history, southern black classrooms were already *teaching* that history: from Maryland to Mississippi, black high schools adopted special textbooks by African-Americans and offered special courses about them.[6] At the other end of the spectrum, neo-Confederates promoted a distinct, rigidly pro-southern set of texts for white students. Refusing to concede even a scintilla of Dixie honor to the invading Yankee horde, these orthodox books dominated white schools for at least forty years.[7]

Three important differences separated the neo-Confederate and African-American textbook campaigns. The first was the astounding success of the former. Whereas African-Americans influenced a single course in a subset of black schools, Confederate loyalists controlled the entire history curriculum in thousands of white ones. As early as 1913 the historian William Dodd could report with horror—and with only slight hyperbole—that "two distinct histories are taught in the schools": one above the Mason-Dixon Line, and one below it.[8] Exiled from Dixie for his deviations from Confederate dogma, Dodd also emphasized white southerners' open disdain for the modern, "scientific" history that he practiced. Whereas most black activists tried to wrap themselves in this mantle, neo-Confederate groups often invoked a perspectivist—even relativist—argument to counter it. Views of the past depended on where you stood in the present, southerners argued; and they stood in Dixie, repository of a culture and wisdom that Yankees could never comprehend. Finally, the Confederate movement engaged women far more frequently than any other American textbook campaign, including the black one. Into the 1940s, southern white women policed the unyielding sectional orthodoxy of southern white textbooks.[9]

The Neo-Confederate Challenge

Barely three decades after the Civil War concluded, America's two largest veterans' groups both called for a unified schoolbook that would bind them together. "We are a single nation and have a single history," intoned the New York commander of the Grand Army of the Republic in 1897. "There need be no diversity of views." In the South, similarly, a United Confederate Veterans official demanded "a true national history" for all U.S. classrooms. "There shall not be one history for Massachusetts and another for South Carolina," declared the Mississippi war hero Stephen D. Lee, chair of the UCV's history committee, "but Americans everywhere shall read the same books." The following year Lee predicted that the Spanish-American War would link North and South "at home"—that is, in their textbooks—as well as "on the field of battle." He was echoed by no less a personage than Woodrow Wilson, scion of Old Virginia and president of Princeton University. "I have long desired to prepare an impartial school history of the United States, especially for the use of Southern schools," Wilson wrote to the UCV in February 1898. "I know how dissatisfied the Southern schools are with histories written with a decided Northern bias."[10]

Meanwhile, each side pressured textbook companies, school boards, and legislatures to create—or adopt— products to their liking. Publishers did their best to placate both camps, removing red-flag terms like "rebel" and inserting passages that described the Civil War from northern and southern perspectives. By 1904 the Grand Army of the Republic was satisfied enough to disband its school history committee. But the United Confederate Veterans—and particularly their burgeoning sister society, the United Daughters of the Confederacy—were not so easily appeased. Stepping up their textbook campaigns, southerners especially targeted so-called neutral or balanced histories "on the order of . . . 'we thought we were right,' rather than 'we were right,'" as one Virginia veteran wrote. "We did know we were right then, and we do know it now . . . And we *have the right, therefore, to insist that our children shall be told the truth about it, and we should be content with nothing less."* So much for Woodrow Wilson's dream of an "impartial" history, uniting both halves of America. For white southerners, indeed, the very term came to imply almost the inverse of what Wilson intended: since southern truth *was* impartial, they argued, any trace of Yankee sentiment reflected sectional bias. "I have written *forty five* letters in regard to school histories," wrote a Kentucky UDC official, detailing her efforts to bar "balanced" textbooks. "We must have Southern histories, non-partisan."[11]

By 1911, the "Golden Jubilee" of the Civil War's first crossfire, the UDC had become the leading enforcer of textbook orthodoxy in the American South. Text agitation by the UCV and other male veterans' groups declined, reflecting these groups' overall decrease in size as well as their dampened "feelings of sectional recrimination," the historian Cecelia O'Leary writes. Within the UDC, by contrast, membership multiplied and sectionalism continued to swell. Quadrupling in membership between 1900 and 1920, the UDC appointed hundreds of state and local "historians" to demand school texts that vindicated "the South's right to self-determination," as the Virginia UDC historian Mary Carter declared in 1925. Although she was not a "real historian," Carter added, she had personally distributed thousands of pieces of "pure" southern literature to schools and educational officials.[12]

At the helm of this campaign stood Mildred Lewis Rutherford, the UDC's historian-general from 1911 to 1916 and its leading textbook critic until her death in 1928. Principal of a female academy in Athens, Georgia, the indefatigable Rutherford sent out reams of circulars and personal letters imploring UDC women to monitor their local school texts. Most important, "Miss Millie," as she was affectionately called, wrote and distributed at least twenty-nine books and pamphlets to help these field workers define and defend "true" southern history. "Do not reject a textbook because it omits to mention your father, your grandfather, your personal friend," Rutherford warned in her best-known work, *A Measuring Rod to Test Textbooks* (1919). "But reject a book that speaks of the Constitution other than

[as] a Compact between Sovereign States . . . that calls the Confederate soldier a traitor or rebel, and the war a rebellion . . . that says the South fought to hold her slaves . . . that speaks of the slaveholder of the South as cruel and unjust to his slaves . . . that glorifies Abraham Lincoln and vilifies Jefferson Davis."[13]

For Rutherford and her followers, these propositions formed the basic pentagon of southern textbook orthodoxy. As in any geometric figure, the sides were connected. Since the Constitution bound states into a federal government—*not* into a "national" one—the southern states had every legal and moral right to secede; and the North, not the South, violated America's founding principles. ("There was a rebellion," Rutherford told her state and local UDC aides, "but it was north of Mason and Dixon's line.") Once under attack, the South fought back—but only to defend these constitutional principles, not to maintain the bondage of African-Americans. Slavery required no such protection, because it was benign: slaves, Rutherford insisted, "were the happiest set of people on the face of the globe, free from care or thought of food, clothes, home." Why, then, did the North invade? The South's answer had two simple words: Abraham Lincoln. "The war between the States was deliberately and personally conceived" by Lincoln, a UCV committee resolved in 1922, quoting a pamphlet that Rutherford distributed, "and he was personally responsible for forcing the war upon the South." Hardly a suitable model for young children, Rutherford added, Lincoln used foul language and once even denied the divinity of Christ. By contrast, the South's own president was a paragon of probity. Jefferson Davis "never stood for coarse jokes, never violated the Constitution, never stood for retaliation," she noted. "Lincoln stood for all of these."[14]

Yet wherever southerners looked, "false" textbooks predominated. Almost all major turn-of-the-century textbook companies were headquartered in the North, critics stressed, and their wares reflected the bias of their region. In Richmond local veterans complained in 1895 that one text depicted the Emancipation Proclamation as "patriotic and proper" rather than as "a palpable violation of the Constitution."

Nine years later outraged members of Maryland's UDC found that one of their state texts still described Lincoln as "one of the wisest and greatest men of history." Nor were other subjects in the curriculum immune to this Yankee infection. New Orleans schools taught music from a book containing both "The Battle Hymn of the Republic" ("intense in its Northern sentiment," Louisiana veterans snarled) and an updated version of "The Star Spangled Banner," which celebrated black Americans as "the millions unchained." In Texas, meanwhile, a local UCV chapter discovered children using an arithmetic text that required them to calculate Ulysses S. Grant's age on the day he captured Vicksburg. After veterans petitioned the governor to remove the text from the state's list of approved texts, its publisher promised to issue a new edition. The revised text would replace its "Yankee word problem" with a more sectionally appropriate question, asking students to determine the amount of time between Texas's independence from Mexico and its annexation by the United States.[15]

The Texas episode exemplifies the most common pattern of southern textbook development: Confederate groups complained about a text, then the publisher altered it. "The mist of error is rapidly passing away," boasted one Virginia veteran in 1897. Textbook houses, he added, "are now apologizing to the South, saying they will revise, correct, and republish." At least one company even solicited the UCV's feedback before its books went to press, offering to make "any corrections or changes" that the veterans suggested. By 1904 a UCV text committee in Louisiana proudly reported that the worst snubs against the South—especially charges of "treason" and "rebellion"—had been excised from its state texts. Other Confederate groups bragged that they had successfully pressured publishers to discard or replace entire chapters, including one textbook's discussion of the causes of the Civil War.[16]

To many white southerners, however, these changes were insufficient. Publishers frequently removed some objectionable passages but retained others, leaving Dixie's loyal defenders with half a loaf.[17]

Other companies released special "southern" or even distinct state editions, complying with most of the Confederates' wishes but spiking suspicions all the same. As one Missouri UDC woman argued, any author who would revise his textbook "to suit the fancy and desire of each State and community" was "unworthy of belief"—and might be persuaded to revise again in the opposite direction, if the price was right. Moreover, critics warned, even a separate southern version of a northern book was bound to embody Yankee biases, publishers' pious assurances aside. A special Alabama edition of Muzzey's *An American History* still condemned the South for slavery and secession, for example, albeit in far gentler terms than the northern version did.[18]

Across the former Confederacy, then, activists devised other means to uphold orthodox Dixie history. The most common tactic was the student essay contest, which encouraged children to collect their own material—and to contest their northern textbooks. Mississippi's UDC offered a prize for the best essay that drew on interviews with ex-slaveholders, who would presumably help students perceive the justice and prudence of human bondage in the Old South. "Today we are resting under the shadow of the New England version of slavery," a UDC official wrote in 1912, in a letter to Mississippi high schools announcing the contest. Yet, she emphasized, "the best testimony can be gathered from the actual witnesses of the institution now fast disappearing. This would be REAL history." Award-winning entries left little doubt about what version of veracity the UDC desired. In Virginia's Pittsylvania County the high school pupil Elise Dodson received a five-dollar gold medal for an essay that deemed slavery "the happiest time of the negroes' existence." Basing her conclusions on Confederate memoirs as well as on "conversations with elderly persons," Dodson acknowledged that a tiny minority of slaveowners had abused their bondsmen. For the most part, however, interracial harmony had pervaded the southern plantation: "The slave was a member of the family, often a privileged member. He was the playmate, brother, exemplar, friend, and companion of the white man from cradle to grave."[19]

Here the Virginia schoolgirl unwittingly echoed the emerging defenses of slavery by a handful of younger historians, especially the Georgia-born scholar Ulrich B. Phillips. Yet Phillips's outright praise of southern bondage reflected a minority perspective within the profession, where a mildly censorious view of slavery still held sway. Rather than seeking allies among the rising coterie of so-called scientific historians, Confederate groups often challenged the entire concept of science—indeed, of objectivity—in history. In a 1917 exchange with the Harvard historian Albert B. Hart, Mildred Rutherford cited a long list of memoirs and monographs in defense of the Old South. When Hart dismissed these accounts as relics of the "dark ages," Rutherford invoked the authority of her *own* advanced age and the memories that accompanied it. "With great respect for your ability and learning, and with no desire to question your research, I do know, Dr. Hart, *you are wrong*," underlined Rutherford, who had been almost ten years old when the Civil War started. "I lived in those early days and I know whom of I speak."[20] Unlike Hart and his fellow Yankees, a Dallas bookseller added, southerners had actually experienced slavery and its aftermath. "Why don't these New England Negro-lovers let us alone?" J. T. Jenkins asked:

We *know* that the Negroes are an inferior Race of people, We *know* that we have been taxed Millions of Dollars to educate him during the last 40 years, and we *know* that you can count on your fingers the men of a Race of Nine Millions of people who have dome [*sic*] or said anything to impress itself on the reader of History fifty years from now . . . Let the learned Doctor [Hart] go into the Blackest of the Black belt, and stay there two or three years, and when he goes back to the people who originally sold us the Negroes— the New Englanders—he will be better qualified to write of our troubles.[21]

Echoing northern patriotic societies, meanwhile, other southerners feared the methods of "scientific" history more than its supposed Yankee bias. Even in textbooks that shared their views of slavery and secession, critics claimed, too much concern with impersonal "causes" and "forces" would sap children's faith in their forefathers.

"No child can really understand the vastly complex relations of historical events," a panel of Virginia veterans argued, "but any child's imagination . . . may be fired by the recital of great deeds." Well into the 1920s, southern loyalists joined with their erstwhile Yankee enemies to stop—or at least to slow—the entry of "new" history into American schools. Like any marriage of convenience, the union suffered periodic strains. Patriotic groups attacked southern veterans for brushing over the Confederacy's crimes; Dixie activists condemned the "Roman Catholic-Irish group" in the North for its "Kaiser-phile" assault on textbooks' alleged pro-British spirit, as UCV's historian-in-chief Arthur Jennings reported in 1923. Still, Jennings stressed, the two regional campaigns faced the same small set of foes: David Muzzey, Albert Hart, and other "new" historians. So he held out an olive branch to ethnic text critics in the North, holding his nose all the while.[22]

In the early 1930s, however, southerners unearthed two unlikely allies in the groves of "scientific" history: Charles and Mary Beard. Ever since the appearance of Charles Beard's *Economic Interpretation of the Constitution* (1913), text critics in both regions had blasted the Beards' class-based analysis of America's birth and early development.[23] But when the Beards applied this lens to the nation's sectional conflict, especially in their bestselling *Rise of American Civilization* (1927), Dixie die-hards seized on it. By reinterpreting the Civil War as an essentially economic clash—northern capitalists versus southern planters—the Beards minimized its moral dimensions, particularly those surrounding slavery. Less than a decade after reviling "scientific" history, then, some southerners began to invoke it. In 1938, for example, the national commander of the Sons of Confederate Veterans urged schools to embrace "the modern scientific trend" of "politico-economic" explanation. Too many textbooks still depicted the Civil War as a "moral" struggle, he complained, pitting freedom-loving Yankees against slave-driving southern aristocrats. Since "the seeds of sectional dissension were sown and grown in the field of economics," texts should stress the two regions' distinctive patterns of industry and agriculture rather than their respective claims of Right and Wrong.[24]

For at least one American critic, though, this effort at moral distancing represented an egregious moral disaster. As a scholar with strong socialist sympathies, W. E. B. Du Bois endorsed the Beards' concern for America's "'poor down trodden' common people"; indeed, one of Charles Beard's earlier textbooks listed Du Bois as a reference, sparking loud objections among southern whites. Yet in their *Rise of American Civilization,* Du Bois complained, the Beards had omitted any mark of concern for the most downtrodden Americans of all. "Our histories tend to discuss American slavery so impartially, that in the end nobody seems to have done wrong and everybody was right," Du Bois wrote in *Black Reconstruction* (1935), citing the Beards and several other scholars. "The difference of development, North and South, is explained as a sort of working out of cosmic social and economic law." No textbook explained the evils of slavery, the courage of the abolition movement, or—most of all—the freedman's struggle for dignity and democracy. "Can all this be omitted or half suppressed," Du Bois asked, "in a treatise that calls itself scientific?" Even as southern whites began to embrace "scientific" history, it seemed, African-Americans had started to assail it.[25]

The Struggle for Negro History

Next to Du Bois, the best-known scholar of black history in the United States was Carter G. Woodson. The founder and longtime leader of the Association for the Study of Negro Life and History (ASNLH), Woodson wrote textbooks for special "Negro history" courses in all-black schools. But some African-Americans opposed these courses, arguing that Negroes should be integrated into the regular curriculum. "True enough," Woodson retorted, "but how can it be done when the Negro is either omitted entirely from the texts used or mentioned only to be condemned?" One day, Woodson hoped, Americans would chronicle the achievements of all races "as one record." Until then, black Americans would have to rely on "devices"—special courses and texts—to "get the neglected truth before the youth." Historical truth *required* a separate history, at least for the foreseeable future.

But at the same time, Woodson complained, other African-Americans promoted a history that was separate but not true. Here he took aim at amateur black historians and their acolytes, who "would increase the volume of Negro history by identifying as Negroes 'white persons' who had any imperceptible infusion of Negro blood." To these polemicists, the roster of famous blacks included the Queen of Sheba, King Solomon, Mohammed, Socrates, and even Christ. Woodson had little patience for such "pseudo-historians," whose fulsome fantasies betrayed their ignorance of blacks' actual achievements. "The story of the Negro is too brilliant to be neglected for such trifles played up frequently by writers who are not scientifically trained," he insisted. "This is an unnecessary effort to make history to order."[26]

Together, Woodson's remarks encapsulate blacks' two crucial internal debates in the struggle to insert their past into the American curriculum. As a host of present-day historians have shown, scholars like Woodson and Du Bois challenged whites' interpretations of slavery, the Civil War, and Reconstruction.[27] But blacks differed sharply among themselves, too, debating the best means of spreading their story—separate courses versus "integrated" ones—and even the meaning of "black" itself. From the turn of the century until World War II, the separationists held sway: like white neo-Confederate groups, blacks sought and often won special textbooks and classes for their children in the segregated South. Unlike Dixie's white loyalists, however, African-American leaders also aimed to dress their separate past in the modern, professional garb of "scientific" history. Here they provoked attacks from black polemicists, not just from white bigots. For if African-Americans should rule their own history, black critics asked, *which* African-Americans should write it? And why not lay-people, who understood blacks' true sorrow and triumph much better than any self-touted "expert" scholar did?

Born to ex-slaves in Virginia, Woodson inherited the popular black credo that history should promote "race pride." But he fused this ethos with the modern drive for scientific history, which he absorbed during his graduate study at Harvard under Albert B. Hart. Condemned by white southerners as a "Negro lover," Hart actually believed that blacks were an inferior race. Yet he imbued Woodson with a deep reverence for the techniques of professional history, especially its emphasis on documentary evidence. Throughout his career, Woodson never wavered from these dual commitments; indeed, he never discerned a conflict between them. "Of course, the racial motive remains—legitimately compatible with scientific method and aim," one supporter wrote in 1925, neatly summarizing Woodson's approach.[28]

Woodson promulgated his views via the ASNLH, which he founded in 1916 and directed until his death in 1950. Composed mainly of teachers and other black professionals, the ASNLH did not develop the grassroots breadth of white southern organizations like the United Daughters of the Confederacy. But its sway far exceeded its size, especially after Woodson inaugurated Negro History Week in 1926. Spurred by the ASNLH's relentless leafleting, black schools across the South sponsored pageants, speeches, and artwork commemorating notable African-Americans. The following year a Virginia newspaper reported "unprecedented" demand for Negro history. Primary schools introduced the subject into their reading lessons, while black groups across the South attacked racist history texts in their high schools. Already, Woodson boasted, several districts had ordered "the disuse of undesirable textbooks" and "the removal of the most glaring faults of certain others by careful revision." Other victories were sure to follow.[29]

Within the next few years, however, Woodson's strategy shifted. Rather than simply removing offensive texts, he argued, blacks should aim to replace them with books—and eventually courses—of their own. Woodson himself had written a college textbook, *The Negro in Our History,* which a handful of black high schools adopted in the 1920s. He also published an elementary school version *(Negro Makers of History)* and later a more specially tailored high school edition *(The Story of the Negro Retold)*. For other subjects, moreover, a growing range of black-oriented textbooks were available. As early as 1929, for example, pupils in Washington, D.C., studied a book on "Negro Poets" in English class as well as a biography of the Haitian patriot Toussaint L'Ouverture in French class.[30]

Before any child received a black-oriented text, of course, white school officials would have to approve it. Since most blacks still lived in the South—and since most southern school systems centralized their textbook adoptions—the ASNLH first petitioned state educators below the Mason-Dixon Line for their imprimatur. Woodson feared that these officials would rebuff him, but his worries proved groundless: across the South, white educational leaders expressed nearly unanimous praise for his textbooks. Visiting North Carolina in 1930, Woodson's aide Lorenzo J. Greene got a "splendid" greeting from school officials, "as cordial as a Negro could expect to receive from any Northern white man and, if anything, more genuine," Greene gushed. Tar Heel educators quickly agreed to adopt two of Woodson's books, provided that the publisher slashed prices to bring the texts "within the buying power of the Negro family." By the end of the decade at least three other states—Delaware, Oklahoma, and South Carolina—had adopted special texts about black history or literature for their black public schools.[31]

Elsewhere in the South, states placed several black history texts on their "approved" lists and let school districts decide whether to adopt them. Just like state officials, meanwhile, local white school boards embraced black history—for black students. As early as 1931, Atlanta, St. Louis, and Tulsa had all adopted Negro history texts; by 1935 New Orleans and Birmingham had done the same. Black history also spread into rural regions, where the majority of African-Americans still resided. The roster of southern towns adopting black history texts reads like an old train map connecting hundreds of tiny whistle-stops. From Boley, Oklahoma, to Bessemer, Alabama; from Gonzales,

Texas, to Goldsboro, North Carolina; in one-room shacks and newly consolidated high schools, black children read black history from special black-oriented textbooks. Moreover, white school boards encouraged them to do so.[32]

Indeed, these same boards often approved separate history courses for African-Americans. Occasionally the classes were compulsory: in Atlanta students could not graduate from Booker T. Washington High School without passing its famous Negro History class. More commonly, though, black history was provided as an elective. In a 1933 survey 50 of 174 southern black high schools offered such a course; just eight years earlier only eight of them had done so. The electives proved most popular in the Deep South, where blacks were "more concentrated" and "race consciousness [had] reached a fairly high degree of development," according to the survey's director. Nearly all of Mississippi's black high schools offered Negro history; in Alabama more than three hundred students in the state's largest black school elected to take it. In the Southwest, too, white school boards approved the course. "Negro boys and girls should know the outstanding and commendable people of their race," asserted a Houston principal after persuading his school board to permit a black history class. "Other schools will be granted this added feature to their curriculum only for the asking."[33]

As Carter G. Woodson often complained, however, far too many Negroes still refused to ask for it. To Woodson, the struggle for black history was "the most important effort . . . in behalf of the Negro" since Emancipation. When large fractions of blacks ignored or eschewed it, Woodson could only conclude that they were still shackled by the slave driver's chains. Borrowing from the cult of Freud that swept interwar America, a 1929 ASNLH round table agreed that "the Negro was suffering from an inferiority complex"—and that "the best means of combating such was to inoculate him with a virus of the achievements of his own race." But how could physicians assist a patient who declined the cure? The same dilemma haunted textbook activists of every stripe, from Irish and German groups in the North to white Confederate societies in the South. But it proved particularly difficult for African-Americans, who confronted the most pernicious litany of stereotypes and lies. As Woodson often noted, blacks who had embraced these falsehoods could hardly be expected to back a course that indicted them. "I am trying to sell the Negro to Negroes," lamented an ASNLH field secretary in 1932. "I find it a very difficult task . . . Negroes must learn to believe in themselves."[34]

The blame for this situation lay not with black children, whose minds remained relatively open to "race interest and appreciation," as one Washington, D.C., observer noticed. Instead, Woodson placed primary fault with their instructors, "the Negro teachers who believe that nothing should be said about Negroes." The worst offenders were often the best-educated blacks, he claimed, college graduates who had been "miseducated" to prize white history over their own. Across the South, ASNLH activists heaped ridicule and resentment upon these alleged racial renegades. "Most [black] teachers assume a know-it-all attitude," a Houston critic charged, "while the children who come under them . . . are crushed by the vicious propaganda and theories circulated about Negroes in the textbooks." Until a new set of teachers learned true Negro history, Woodson argued, schools would never establish it; but until true Negro history was established, of course, teachers would never learn it. The dilemma remained.[35]

Up north, meanwhile, another set of activists proposed a very different remedy: rather than adding black history textbooks, as Woodson envisioned, they resolved to remove or change "regular" ones. Convening in New York in 1932, the NAACP's new textbook committee called on local branches to examine their history, literature, and civics schoolbooks—and to protest the most offensive texts. It repeated this recommendation in 1938 and again in 1939, releasing a pamphlet entitled *Anti-Negro Propaganda in School Textbooks* to assist community activists. Other NAACP officials visited publishers to demand revision of their texts, while still others pleaded with young people—the most direct victims of bigoted books—to take up the fight. "Why is it that you find in the North today the doors of opportunity slammed in your faces, and why do you find prejudice still rampant?" Charles Edward Russell asked the NAACP's youth councils in 1938. His answer was simple: school textbooks. Russell urged the councils to review the books, write to school boards, publish newspaper articles, go on the radio—anything to rid their schools of racist texts.[36]

Northern blacks did succeed in forcing some publishers and school boards to delete racist slurs from the books, especially the terms "savage" and "nigger."[37] Nevertheless, anti-black errors and stereotypes continued to mar nearly every American history text. If anything, a series of NAACP-sponsored studies suggested, texts were getting worse. Critics reserved their sharpest ire for texts' exaggerated accounts of black violence, incompetence, and corruption during Reconstruction. Gloria Oden, a black high school student who visited the NAACP's New York headquarters in 1939, was outraged by the following description of a "Negro" statehouse in the 1870s from a U.S. history text:

> We enter the house of Moses, the speaker looks down upon the members mostly black and brown, some of the type rarely seen outside the Congo . . . A cozy atmosphere, too, with the members' feet upon the desks, their faces hidden behind their soles. Chuckles, guffaws, the noisy crackling of peanuts, and harsh voices disturb the dignity of the scene. Mingling with the Negroes we see the ferret-faced carpet-baggers, eager for the spoils.

As Oden learned from the NAACP's literature, the textbook was approved for use in several large school systems. "With this drilled into the minds of growing children," she wrote, "I see how hate and disgust is motivated against the American Negro."[38]

Indeed, NAACP leaders argued, the hate would continue so long as any American child—of any region or race—read such textbooks. After all, they observed, history texts in the South were even more bigoted than their northern counterparts. Hence any "race pride" that black children developed in a special Negro-oriented course would be quickly quenched by their regular U.S. history textbook, which still besmirched them as hapless clowns or ruthless thugs. Perhaps worse, they added, white students across the country would imbibe the same odious slurs. More than separate texts in black schools, then, America needed new, nonracist books in white ones. "I do not say that a change in our anti-Negro text-books will kill prejudice, but I am convinced it is a major step in that direction," a black Kansas City newspaperman wrote. "The white youth [who] grows to maturity learning the truth will not be disposed to impart the old myths to his offspring." Already, he noted, white children who "actually rubbed shoulders" with blacks in mixed classrooms displayed less racism toward African-Americans. If they learned about black heroes like Frederick Douglass and W. E. B. Du Bois, a Los Angeles activist believed, the same happy result would ensue.[39]

Ironically, Du Bois himself voiced strong skepticism about this strategy in the early 1930s. Gradually rejecting the NAACP's commitment to racial integration, particularly in public schools, he also doubted whether "integrated" textbooks could temper white racism. By contrast, Carter Woodson maintained a steadfast devotion to mixed-race schools *and* to special Negro history courses in black ones. One day, he fervently hoped, all children would study alongside one another from fair, multi-racial books—"one classroom, one curriculum," as integrationists proclaimed. Until then, African-Americans needed to take care of their own. "Is it advisable to wait for that indefinite time when the writers of textbooks will become broad enough to mention the Negro humanly?" Woodson asked rhetorically in 1938. "We have already waited for this three centuries." To be sure, he added, blacks should never refrain from denouncing bigoted textbooks—or from demanding replacements. In the long journey to racial justice, however, this elusive "negative" goal had to take a back seat to a more "positive"—and attainable—one: winning Negro history in Negro schools.[40]

Across the American South, meanwhile, black supporters echoed Woodson's basic dictum: segregated curricula now, integrated curricula tomorrow. Eventually, a Washington, D.C., educator wrote, he wanted his son to appreciate "all the makers and sustainers of civilization," whatever their race—especially inspirational figures like St. Francis of Assisi. For the moment, however, the boy should study "some modern saints who bear a more intimate relation to his experience": famous black Americans. "We are simply looking out for our own," explained Margaret Washington, wife of the famed Tuskegee educator and chair of a small women's network promoting Negro history in Negro schools. "The first law of nature is Self-preservation." Even a few northern voices began to demand special textbooks and courses for the African-American. "Negro history should be a daily topic in his childhood; he should digest it as he does his dinner," editorialized New York's *Amsterdam News*. Lest they go to bed hungry, the *News* declared, black youngsters must learn that "Negro blood" had "flowed in the veins" of the Pharaohs and the Queen of Sheba as well as of Crispus Attucks and Peter Salem.[41]

The editorial's last point highlighted a final thorn in the side of Carter G. Woodson: Afrocentrism.[42] Even as some blacks blasted his goal of a distinct African-American curriculum, it seemed, others were arguing that its content should be more African and less American. In 1924, for example, the black activist and author George Wells Parker circulated a set of "Questions and Answers in Negro History," generated by queries from black readers across the country:

Was Mohamet a black man?—R.S.P., Dayton

Mohamet was a brown-skinned Arab of Negro descent.

Were any Negro races concerned in the Trojan War?—B.L.Y., Boston

All the major peoples concerned in the Trojan War were Negro and of African descent. The Greeks were led by Agamemnon, a king of Mycennae, the royal house of this kingdom having been founded by Africans. Priam, King of Troy, was a brother of Tithonus, King of Ethiopia.

Was Hiram, King of Tyre, a Negro?—C.P.D., Des Moines

He most certainly was. And had it not been for Hiram, the Temple of Solomon would never have been built. Solomon was ignorant of the craft discovered and perpetuated among Negro kings, therefore [he] was forced to call upon Hiram to aid him.[43]

Foreshadowing contemporary scholars like Martin Bernal, Parker argued that much of so-called Western civilization had its roots in Africa. Other polemicists emphasized Egypt as the more specific cradle of black history, culture, and intellect. Throughout the interwar period a burgeoning cottage industry of authors claimed that "Egyptian Pharaohs were Negro Kings"—and that whites had conspired to suppress this fact. "Historians and scientists . . . have been smart enough to eliminate, almost entirely, the Negroid people who have really been the founders of this present-day civilization," asserted the black New Yorker James Patten in a letter to a Chicago newspaper in 1927. Endorsing Mayor "Big Bill" Thompson's attack on allegedly pro-British textbooks, Patten encouraged African-Americans to mount a similar assault on "anti-Egyptian" ones. "We have been so busy getting filled up with lies from the pens of white writers that we are blind to our own greatness," Patten wrote. "The idea has always been to keep the Negro peoples down."[44]

In many respects, Woodson embraced this tradition of Afrocentric thought. In the second volume of his *Journal of Negro History*, for example, he published an article by Parker proclaiming the "African Origin of Grecian Civilization." He also championed the popular black claim that African explorers had visited America before Columbus, including it in his textbooks and other literature. Most generally, Woodson insisted that Africa belonged at the core of every Negro history course—and textbook—in America. He devoted the first five chapters of his most popular text to blacks' African origins; he edited a compilation of African folktales to give "children in the lower grades" an "understanding of their past"; and he published dozens of articles about the continent in the *Negro History Bulletin*, the ASNLH's monthly periodical for teachers. "Our record in the Western Hemi-sphere does not compare with that in Africa," Woodson declared in 1936, citing African achievements in art, philosophy, science, and lit-erature. Only by studying their ancestral homeland, then, could young black Americans perceive "the proper place of the race" in world history.[45]

At the same time, though, Woodson insisted that any claims for ancient African prowess pass modern, "scientific" muster. Many of them failed to do so, starting with the dubious propositions that cer-tain "white" figures from antiquity were actually "black." Besides lacking sufficient historical evidence, Woodson argued, such state-ments bore an ugly resemblance to the real enemy: white racism. "The blatant Caucasian . . . has in turn bred his Ethiopian counter-part," wrote the black book collector and ASNLH stalwart Arthur Schomburg in 1925, "the rash and rabid amateur who has glibly tried to prove half the world's geniuses have been Negroes and to trace the pedigree of nineteenth-century Americans to the Queen of Sheba." Ten years later, a worried Woodson observed, Italy's invasion of Ethiopia lent these fallacies a new vogue. Welcoming the rejuvenated black American interest in Africa, Woodson also cautioned against "pseudo-historians" whose polemical tracts would "exploit a gullible public." Here he took a thinly veiled swipe at the prolific journalist J. A. Rogers, who reported on the Ethiopian conflict for the black American press. The author of popular books like *World's Greatest Men of African Descent,* Rogers published long lists of allegedly Negro nota-bles—ranging from ancients such as Aesop to more recent luminaries like Beethoven.[46]

Yet as Woodson recognized, the most important promulgators of Afrocentric doctrine were Marcus Garvey and his Universal Negro Improvement Association. Woodson admired Garvey's grassroots efforts to promote black pride and "Africa for the Africans," as the UNIA's first international convention resolved in 1920. The same convention demanded that "instructions given Negro children in schools include the subject of 'Negro History,'" exactly as Woodson wished. But Garvey also aimed to alter the content of this subject, arguing that blacks should construct a history every bit as racialist as the society they inhabited. To Garvey, Woodson's goal of a neutral or "scientific" history was deeply flawed: *all* history "is written with prejudices, likes and dislikes," so all races should transmit their own. "The white man's history is his inspiration," Garvey wrote, "and he should be untrue to himself and negligent to the rights of his posterity to subordinate it to others." By the same token, blacks would be remiss if they failed to teach children to "lionize our own celebrities"—including Socrates and St. Peter, both deemed "Negro" by the UNIA.[47]

Here Garvey almost perfectly echoed white organizations like the United Daughters of the Confederacy. Across the American South, the UDC and other Dixie loyalists taught children the beauty of slavery, the glory of the Ku Klux Klan, and the overall superiority of their race. Rather than condemning these activists for their bigotry, however, Garvey congratulated them for their honesty. "If I were of your race, I would have written with the same force and probably with prejudice," Garvey wrote to the white author Earnest Cox, who maintained that all great civilizations were Caucasian. *"Our only differences are in history and that is not so material in view of the fact that yours couldn't be ours and ours couldn't be yours.* We lay respective claim to what we believe in that respect without affecting the main issue."[48]

For America, "the main issue" was always race. Garvey's comment provides a convenient epigraph for the country's textbook wars, in which southern whites used the same argument—you have your past, we have ours—to promulgate neo-Confederate history. African-Americans struggled valiantly to repel racist interpretations, winning special courses in some schools and slightly revised general history textbooks in others. But they could not overcome America's united front of white opinion, which sought to placate—if not always to satisfy—southern concerns. Even First Lady Eleanor Roosevelt—perhaps the country's leading white race liberal—argued that textbooks should call the Civil War the "War Between the States" lest they offend Dixie's delicate opinions on the subject. "I find in the south they like that term better," Roosevelt told the NAACP's Charles Edward Russell in 1939, "and I think that sensitive people should always be catered to if possible."[49] Naturally, this formulation took little account of blacks' sensitivities; instead, it catered only to racist whites. Not until the 1960s would black Americans rise up en masse against racist history, compelling the rest of the country to take heed.

Social Studies Wars in New Deal America

In 1941 the beleaguered textbook author Harold Rugg published an impassioned defense of his fourteen-volume series of social studies texts, Man and His Changing Society. Immensely popular for most of the 1930s, Rugg's books had come under heavy fire from patriotic and business groups near the end of the decade. As Rugg stressed, however, these attacks were only the latest salvoes in a much longer right-wing war on American textbooks. Indeed, Rugg insisted, the campaign against his series was "almost an exact replica" of the assault on "new" history texts in the early 1920s. In each case, "self-appointed censors of the schools" had sought to eliminate "anything that presents negative aspects of American history and development." But the "new" history had survived this onslaught, Rugg noted, suggesting at least a ray of hope for his own books. Just as David S. Muzzey and Charles A. Beard had rebutted charges of "subversion" in their texts—and retained their dominant positions in the schools—so might Rugg's social studies series repel the conservative challenge.[1]

Several months earlier, however, a veteran of both text battles had stressed the differences—not the parallels—between them. A former director of the army's chemical warfare division, Amos A. Fries, had spearheaded an unsuccessful drive to remove Muzzey's *An American*

History from Washington, D.C., schools in 1925. Ten years later he led a second quest to bar textbooks by Rugg and Carl L. Becker—another "new" historian—from the nation's capital. By then, though, the rationale for the attacks had altered dramatically. Whereas Muzzey was maligned for his allegedly pro-British interpretation of the American Revolution, Fries blasted Rugg and Becker for their "class-based" or even "socialist" views of the Constitution, industrialization, and especially the Great Depression. To conservatives like Fries, most 1930s textbooks read like campaign briefs for Franklin D. Roosevelt and his New Deal. Like Roosevelt, critics claimed, textbooks denounced private enterprise—or "privileged enterprise," as the President mockingly called it—and demanded wide government controls upon it. Rugg happily acknowledged his texts' obvious mimicry of FDR, who had recently won an unprecedented third term in the White House. "The conflict with [conservatives] is irreconcilable, but we have no such conflict with the bulk of the American people," Rugg wrote in 1941. "Their own voice in elections and the acts of their chosen representatives are proof of the side upon which they stand."[2]

This boast sat uneasily next to Rugg's oft-repeated claim that his texts depicted "both sides" of every public question, including the New Deal itself.[3] Most of all, though, his eager embrace of Roosevelt ignored the shift in the President's own program during the late 1930s. Abandoning the critique of capitalism that had marked its birth, the New Deal increasingly addressed broad economic trends like inflation, employment, and consumption. Less and less would FDR seek direct regulation of corporations and the "plutocrats" who ruled them; instead, he aimed to enhance America's overall economic "health" via remote levers of fiscal policy.[4] In this new ideological climate, Rugg's continued denunciations of "free enterprise"—and his demands for "social controls"—began to sound dated or even dangerous. The Rugg texts were "seemingly too liberal for the times," a sympathetic New Jersey newspaper summarized in August 1940; "people just don't want them around." More specifically, the conservative columnist George E. Sokolsky wrote, *parents* detested the books: "Do [parents] have no rights? Are they to have no voice as to what their children should be taught? . . . If the parents believe in the capitalist way of life, if they earn their living and their children's living by that way, should teachers indoctrinate them with Socialism and Communism? I say that I have the right to withdraw my child from a school in which the teacher tells him that the Supreme Court is a tool of the rich."[5]

Sokolsky's remarks captured three central dimensions of the right-wing attack on social studies, all sharply different from the "new history" conflict that preceded it. Whereas earlier battles had focused almost solely on America's War of Independence, Depression-era struggles frequently encompassed the nation's entire social, economic, and political culture—its "way of life"—and the proper role of free enterprise within it. Insofar as history entered the new dispute, controversy most often surrounded the drafting of the Constitution and the development of the Supreme Court, which 1930s conservatives came to regard as the last bastion of laissez-faire capitalism.[6] Finally, the social studies debate reignited the perennial question of popular control of American public schools. The issue was largely muted in the 1920s, when groups as disparate as the Knights of Columbus and the American Legion sought to enlist "expert" historians behind their respective points of view. Critics like Sokolsky mounted a much more populist campaign, openly ridiculing text writers and insisting on their own ability to judge the past. "I might as well pack my bags for Alcatraz," wrote another textbook foe in a typical jibe at historians' "expert" authority. "Not only am I no historian, I am one of that negligible minority who do not even hold a doctor's degree."[7]

The social studies controversy was also distinguished by what it *excluded:* questions of race and ethnicity. Such issues lay at the heart of the "new history" battles of the 1920s, when a wide array of immigrants joined hands with veterans and patriotic societies to block allegedly pro-British readings of the Revolution. By the Great Depression, however, ethnic and racial controversy had largely disappeared from America's textbook wars (the NAACP's campaign against racist history texts was an important exception; see Chapter 2). Historians have attributed such silences to liberals' overall neglect of race and ethnicity in the 1930s, when a "preoccupation with class division" trumped all other concerns.[8] To be sure, social studies textbooks placed heavy emphasis on economic problems like poverty and unemployment. But they also devoted new attention to ethnic minorities, replacing slurs and stereotypes with fresh material about immigrants' myriad contributions to American life.[9] A critical component of Roosevelt's electoral coalition, immigrants themselves seem to have welcomed the textbooks' paeans to the New Deal and to their own cultures and achievements.[10] The economic focus of Depression-era text controversy came from conservative critics, who concentrated their bile on the books' supposed fondness for New Deal "collectivism" over free-enterprise "capitalism." In America's textbook wars, indeed, the right did far more than the left to shift debate onto an "economic" field. Hardly the exclusive province of liberals, a "preoccupation with class division" characterized the entire political spectrum.

From Ethnicity to Economics

The late 1920s bore little hint of this shift toward economic issues. In 1927, for example, patriotic and ethnic groups blasted the supposedly "pro-English" biases of *Modern History,* a textbook by the historians Carleton J. H. Hayes and Parker T. Moon. In New York the Veterans of Foreign Wars claimed that the book snubbed America by attributing its Revolution to John Locke: "The inspired men . . . who startled the world with their new conception of human rights are charged with having plagiarized it all from England." In "Big Bill" Thompson's Chicago, meanwhile, Irish and German critics condemned Hayes's alleged disparagement of the Liberty Bell and the Stars and Stripes. Hayes "may be a professor at Columbia," the city's school board chairman declared, "but the president of this board says he is a cad." Others suggested that Hayes was a propagandist for the "English-Speaking Union," which hoped to return America to its colonial master.[11]

Just three years later, however, an Episcopal priest suggested that the book *denigrated* many Americans' European heritage. Plastering New York City school officials with letters and petitions, the Reverend Lefferd Haughwout complained that Hayes and Moon—both converts to Catholicism—had maligned Calvin, Luther, and Henry VIII. Even as the text "persistently criticized" these Protestants, Haughwout added, it "deliberately defended" the Roman Catholic Church. Less than a month after Haughwout's initial attack, Superintendent Harold G. Campbell quietly removed the book from New York's list of approved texts. In a meeting with its authors, however, Campbell distinguished his own objections from the cleric's complaint. To school officials, a Campbell aide bluntly explained, "the most serious thing was along economic lines" rather than religious ones. Specifically, the Hayes/Moon textbook treated capitalism "as the cause of all human woes." Better to "emphasize the benefits of it," the aide added, lest students fall into the hands of "Bolshevist" agitators.[12]

Here school leaders cited the text's forthright assertion concerning social stratification in modern industrial nations: "When one man comes into the world penniless while another inherits a million, there can be no real equality of opportunity." As Campbell's aide noted, such comments suggested that "capitalism might be improved." Surely, Hayes retorted, that was true; no economic system was perfect. But to Campbell it was also irrelevant. The issue "was not a question of historical facts," he told the astounded authors; instead, "it was a question [of] whether all the true statements in the book ought to be taught to school children." Several days later Campbell expanded this argument in a prepared statement for the press. The textbook "might easily give to children the impression that many, if not all, of the cries raised against . . . the present economic structure are true," he warned. "The schools of New York are interested in historical accuracy, but they are far more interested in Americanization."[13]

The Hayes/Moon episode marked a critical shift in textbook controversies across the country, mirroring larger changes in the meaning of "Americanization." Haughwout's "pro-Catholic" claim reflected a final gasp of ethnic politics from the 1920s, when the Ku Klux Klan and other nativist groups had demanded strict adherence to a white Protestant version of "100 percent Americanism." Immigrants had fought back by inserting their own heroes into the grand national narrative, condemning anyone who questioned this story—even cultural pluralists like Hayes and Moon—as "pro-British." To textbook assailants in the 1930s, however, "Americanism" became defined less by ethnicity than by an economic system: capitalism. Any mention of the system's failures might undermine children's commitment to the nation, making them easy prey for "communist" seduction. During these same years, indeed, anticommunism replaced ethnic xenophobia as the central theme of American text activism. Periodic "Red Scares" had rocked the country since World War I, often merging with attacks on Germans, Russians, and especially Jews.[14] But the attack on communism did not enter America's textbook wars until the 1930s, when it lost most of its nativist cast. Except for a few far-right anti-Semites, text critics eschewed the ethnic vituperation that had suffused the 1920s. Instead, they focused their wrath on allegedly Red books and the Americans—of every ethnicity—who embraced them.

During these same years, right-wing groups also stepped up their hunt for communist instructors in public school classrooms. Across the country, attacks on "Red" teachers and "Red" textbooks often went hand in hand. Passed by more than twenty states, laws requiring teachers to take loyalty oaths provided the most common touchstone for these controversies. A few months after Congress required all Washington, D.C., instructors to swear that they would not "teach or advocate" communism, for example, right-wing groups charged that three textbooks did precisely that. Led by the ubiquitous Amos A. Fries, critics trained most of their fire upon a world history text by the historian Carl L. Becker. Deeming Becker a "well-known communist writer," conservatives especially reviled his account of the Bolshevik Revolution and its critique of private property. "The Russian revolution aims to effect a complete transformation of society," Becker concluded in a passage that foes often cited to illustrate his "pro-Soviet" bias. "That is why it is, of all the events of our time, the most interesting and perhaps the most important." Critics also demanded the removal of two books by Harold Rugg, who alluded to Russian "accomplishments" in public health and recreation.[15]

From his home in upstate New York, Becker organized a telegram campaign to defend his textbook in Washington. "Of course I don't personally give a damn what these nit-wits think of me," he wrote to Arthur M. Schlesinger, "but the school authorities and teachers need what help they can be given." District of Columbia school officials eventually received cables in support of Becker from more than twenty prominent figures, including Schlesinger, Felix Frankfurter, and Charles Beard. "Only a blind partisan can see communism in [Becker's] writings," Beard's telegram declared. "If the schools are to teach truth, they must fairly present both sides of every important question that appears in the course of any historical period." Beard's brief defense actually embodied two very different claims. In point of fact, Beard wrote, Becker was not a communist; but he had a duty to present communism factually so students would develop the capacity to judge it. In his own communiqués to newspapers and school officials, Becker invoked the same two-pronged argument. Noting his personal antipathy to "Russian Communism," he nevertheless insisted that pupils should evaluate it on their own.[16]

To Washington conservatives, however, these dual claims were mutually contradictory. If the "American system" was truly superior to the Soviet one, they asked, why should schools let students "choose" between them? "Children have unformed, plastic minds; they are sent to school to have their minds and morals shaped according to American standards," one text critic wrote. "They should be instructed in our constitutional form of government and taught respect for that government which has made this Nation the greatest on earth." Others argued that Becker and Rugg had selected facts "slyly favoring communism," depriving students of the very "choice" that the authors claimed to prize. If the textbooks were as neutral as advertised, finally, "treasonous" teachers would easily twist them toward their own "diabolical" point of view. To ensure a truthful depiction of communism, the conservative firebrand Alexander Sidney Lanier concluded, the Washington schools would have to produce a booklet for instructors to read in the classroom "without comment," just like the Bible. Carefully chosen quotations from Lenin and Trotsky would effectively illuminate the "impractability and undesirability" of communism, Lanier suggested. Or, if school officials preferred, they might also draw upon "the writings and speeches of Mr. Tugwell, and several other prominent officials of the present Administration."[17]

Penned near the end of Roosevelt's first term, Lanier's closing barb at FDR's adviser Rexford G. Tugwell signaled the next important development in Depression-era textbook wars: the attack upon Roosevelt and his New Deal. Right-wing opposition to the President coalesced during his reelection campaign in 1936, when FDR intensified his own offensive against greedy "economic royalists" in America's corporate kingdoms. Led by the newspaper titan William Randolph Hearst, angry foes charged that Roosevelt was actually a communist; his New Deal was a "Red Deal," a Soviet-inspired perversion of American political tradition. Critics also skewered FDR's so-called Brain Trust of expert aides, reserving special scorn for the brilliant but prickly Tugwell. One prominent foe called him "Comrade Tugwell, Brain Truster No. 1"; others suggested that this handsome economics professor was the Lenin of the New Deal, secretly masterminding a communist coup d'état. A September 1936 cartoon in the Hearst-owned *Chicago Tribune* pictured a cardboard cut-out of Roosevelt propped up by "Tugwell Plotter No. 1." To a bearded Bolshevik looming menacingly in the background, Tugwell whispered, "Shh-h-h, keep down until after the election."[18]

When conservatives began to critique the New Deal biases of American textbooks, then, they quite naturally turned to an economics text by Rexford G. Tugwell. Cleveland, Kansas City, and Los Angeles all dropped Tugwell's *Our Economic Society and Its Problems* in 1935, citing the book's "New Deal views." On the eve of Roosevelt's reelection bid, Delaware's state board of education did the same. Like Carl Becker, critics charged, Tugwell and his co-author Howard C. Hill showed far too much solicitude for the Soviet Union. But the central complaint concerned the authors' analysis of contemporary America, which emphasized economic inequalities and the need for state regulations to correct them. One illustration in the book depicted an elegant yacht costing, its caption claimed, "$100,000 per year to maintain—enough to support forty families in comfort." In another oft-quoted passage Tugwell and Hill decried "the unreasoning, almost hysterical attachment of certain Americans to the Constitution." Here they took a swipe at Roosevelt's enemies on the Supreme Court, who threatened to strike down much of the New Deal's pathbreaking legislation in the name of "economic freedom." To Tugwell and Hill such critics were simply spitting into the wind. "We continue to think in terms of individualism and competitive profit-seeking," the authors grumbled, "long after the conditions favorable to that economic philosophy have passed away."[19]

The last remark reflected the theory of "cultural lag," a staple of scholarly discourse—and often of school textbooks—in the 1930s. "Nearly all our social problems are due to cultural lags," a sociology text declared:

> The insecurity of the modern employee is the result of a lag in providing adequate unemployment insurance made necessary by the instability of modern industry. The instability of modern industry is due in part to the lag in curbing speculation and to the lag in adjusting buying power to producing power . . . The increasing occurrence of mental disease is [due] to excessive strains and worries suffered by individuals in a society that is

imperfectly aware of the need for guaranteeing work to everyone who wishes it. Social reform consists in discovering and overcoming each separate lag.[20]

In sum, the solution to "each separate lag" lay in New Deal–type regulation of private industry. In perfectly circular fashion, moreover, any resistance to such programs provided further evidence of the "lag" in question. Here textbooks echoed Roosevelt himself, who routinely mocked his foes' retrograde thinking. The New Deal's enemies wished to "take the country back to horse and buggy days," Roosevelt quipped; frustrated by modern life, they longed for an era of simple verities that were no longer true. In an October 1936 attack on left-leaning teachers and textbooks, however, a conservative critic employed the same metaphor for a very different purpose. "Our educational system is in control of *Socialists*," he insisted, "and 'horse and buggy' age common sense is beyond them." He singled out a small core of educators at Columbia University's Teachers College, proponents of a "new social order" and of a dangerous new subject: social studies. As the nation moved steadily to the right in the late 1930s, it would be these theorists—not their conservative opponents—who "lagged" behind.[21]

The Attack on Social Studies

"Daddy, was George Washington a big business man?" This question, posed by his fourteen-year-old son over dinner, shocked O. K. Armstrong, a prominent member of the American Legion. The boy went on: "Our teacher says the men who wrote the Constitution were landowners and business men." Flabbergasted, Armstrong investigated his son's history textbooks and discovered—to his horror—that they were not really "history" books at all. Instead, the texts were used in an omnibus course called "Democratic Living." Like other so-called social studies classes, Armstrong found, the course belittled the precious American heritage that schools had once celebrated. "Legionnaires are parents—most of us," Armstrong warned. "It's time we learned that our children are being taught, in the name of civics, social science, and history, doctrines so subversive as to undermine their faith in the American way of life."[22]

At the end of his article Armstrong named more than thirty allegedly "treasonous" texts. The list contained several history books from earlier controversies, including works by Carl Becker and Charles Beard. But the great majority of the tabooed texts came from social studies, with a single author, Harold Rugg, accounting for sixteen of them. Rugg, according to Armstrong, was one of the notorious "Frontier Thinkers" at Teachers College, a small clique of professors who had long functioned as a "Fifth Column" of un-Americanism in American public education. Adults most often encountered its theories through the work of George S. Counts, author of *Dare the Schools Build a New Social Order?* Yet within the schools themselves, Armstrong emphasized, Rugg's numerous textbooks provided children with their first glimpse of Frontier Thinker philosophy. Thanks mostly to Rugg, students like Armstrong's son regarded George Washington as a "land-grabber" and the Constitution as "a protector of the economic royalist." Even worse, Rugg's texts cast doubt on the entire "American system" of "private ownership and enterprise." In one book Rugg asked students whether the United States was "a land of opportunity for all people." His answer was succinctly stated in the teachers' guide: no. "There are great differences in the standards of living of the different classes of people," Rugg wrote in a passage that Armstrong quoted. "The majority do not have any real security."[23]

By 1941 dozens of other conservative groups had joined Armstrong and the American Legion in blasting the Rugg books. Several features distinguished their effort from previous attacks. The first and most obvious one was the assault on a supposedly "new" subject—social studies—and especially on a single author, Harold Rugg. Second, critics censured the texts for their supposedly subversive analysis of contemporary society and culture—the "American way of life," as Armstrong called it—rather than for their specific interpretations of the national past. The lone exception concerned the framing of the U.S. Constitution, which rapidly replaced the Revolution as the chief focus of historical controversy in American textbooks. Furthermore, whereas earlier attacks on textbooks had been almost purely local in origin and scope, the Rugg series generated the country's first coordinated, nationwide campaign. More than a million readers probably received Armstrong's missive against Rugg's books; the following year the Legion would distribute nearly half a million pamphlets reviling them.[24] Thanks to its breadth and publicity, finally, the Rugg dispute sparked a much wider debate about citizen control in American public education. Critics like Armstrong claimed that "the people"—and especially "the parents"—should govern school policy; despite their own paeans to "democracy," meanwhile, Rugg's defenders argued that selection of textbooks must remain a professional rather than a popular prerogative.

Throughout the 1930s, ironically, no American textbooks were more popular than the works of Harold Rugg. Starting three months before the 1929 stock market crash, Rugg released fourteen separate volumes of his series Man and His Changing Society and sold roughly four million textbooks, workbooks, and teachers' guides. Indeed, its publisher later recounted, the Rugg series was "largely responsible for keeping [us] in the 'black' during the depression." The texts capitalized on broad changes in the interwar American curriculum, when school districts steadily replaced history courses with electives and requirements in the social studies. Some of the new classes lay in traditional disciplines like economics, sociology, or government; others fused these disciplines into so-called combination courses like "Problems of Democracy," which was offered in twenty-eight states by 1930 and mandated by six of them. Within the history classes that remained, schools downplayed "military and political aspects" in favor of "social, cultural, and economic content," as one observer noted. All of these trends fit perfectly with Rugg's series, which focused explicitly on the "permanent problems of modern life" and drew upon a range of disciplines. By 1941 more than five million students in five thousand school districts had probably used a textbook by Harold Rugg.[25]

The attack on the Rugg books was swift and sudden, steamrolling across the country even more rapidly than the texts had done. As late as 1939 no prominent national voice had spoken out against the series. That August the publisher Bertie C. Forbes used the pages of his own magazine to blast Rugg's books as "viciously un-American." Forbes printed several more attacks over the next year in Hearst-owned newspapers, which echoed his position in their editorials. After the appearance of O. K. Armstrong's article in 1940, the American Legion officially condemned the Rugg series. Other large patriotic and veterans' groups quickly followed suit, presenting a nearly united front against the books by mid-1941. The business community also joined in the attack. The Advertising Federation of America distributed brochures against the books, quoting Rugg's negative remarks about newspaper and radio commercials. Led by the insurance executive Merwin K. Hart, the New York State Economic Council charged that Rugg had spread "collectivist theories" throughout the Empire State—and beyond. Finally, the National Association of Manufacturers published abstracts of social studies textbooks, laying particular stress on the Rugg series. Avowedly "neutral," the abstracts exposed the texts' supposed bias against "private enterprise philosophy."[26]

Reviewing these rapid-fire developments in 1941, a shell-shocked Harold Rugg concluded that the movement against his textbooks was a "manufactured conflict," engineered by a small circle of wily businessmen and overzealous patriots. But a closer look at the campaign reveals a much more popular pedigree than Rugg admitted.[27] Within the American Legion, for example, the anti-Rugg movement started in local posts and surged upward to the national leadership. In January 1938 the Legionnaire Augustin C. Rudd asked his community school board in Garden City, New York, to remove the Rugg books. He also wrote to Legion headquarters, urging a much more widespread and coordinated assault. "Our people don't know what is going on in the schools," Rudd told the national Legion commander, Stephen Chadwick. "That is why I suggest . . . the Legion bring it home to parents in every state of the Union." Rudd's school board quickly acceded to his demand, making Garden City the first known community to drop the Rugg books. But Legion leaders rejected Rudd's appeal to produce and distribute an "informational booklet" about Harold Rugg. "There may be many others whose views we do not share and to whose principles we do not subscribe," explained a Legion official, Homer L. Chaillaux. Hence the organization could not afford to attack a "single author," Chaillaux wrote, however reprehensible that author's philosophies or activities.[28]

Undeterred by this brusque reception from the Legion's top brass, Rudd sought allies closer to home. In rapid succession he persuaded his local and county Legion posts to denounce the Rugg books. Then he won a similar resolution from the Legion's New York State convention, which seems to have jolted national leaders out of their brief quiescence. A mere thirteen months after refusing Rudd's appeal for aid, Homer Chaillaux was only too eager to lend a helping hand. "You may be certain that we will be taking positive action," he wrote to Rudd privately in June 1940, "to defend our educational system against the Fifth Column sympathizers." By autumn Legion leaders were ready for a public declaration of war. Endorsing Armstrong's critique of "subversion" in Rugg's books, the *American Legion Magazine* promised many more fireworks to follow. "We have just begun to fight," it announced, "and we shall win."[29]

By the following spring hundreds of Legion posts were working to remove the texts from their schools. To Harold Rugg and his allies, this development simply confirmed their fears of a streamlined, centrally controlled opposition network. Just as some local posts took the lead in this movement, however, others dissented sharply from it. From Connecticut to Ohio to North Dakota, posts passed resolutions commending the Rugg books and condemning the national organization's assault on them. Individual Legionnaires also sent fervent complaints to its headquarters in Indianapolis. "I protest most vigorously against the senseless, damaging, inaccurate, unfounded, and un-American campaign," screamed a California veteran in November 1940, shortly after the Legion announced its "war" upon the Rugg texts. By endorsing a narrow and partisan interpretation of these books, the veteran claimed, the Legion put itself forward as "the final and only judge of what is and what is not Americanism." From Alabama another Legionnaire argued that the organization should defer to the proper "judges" of textbooks: trained educators. "Are we not coming very near being obnoxious meddlers when we insist upon throwing out books that WE do not like?" he asked. "I happen to know that textbooks are very carefully selected by very conscientious professional persons . . . Who are WE to take their place?"[30]

Within business organizations, likewise, members sometimes dissented from official denunciations of the Rugg texts. Shortly after the Advertising Federation of America leader Alfred T. Falk condemned the books, a retailer published a frank attack on *him*. "It would be very easy for the whole advertising profession . . . to become inflamed over these charges and to start a new kind of witch hunt," warned Earl Elhart in July 1939. Rejecting Falk's demand for a "wholly flattering portrait" of advertising, Elhart praised the Rugg books for showing "the business world as it is"—including its "abuses and evils." Six months later a business magazine blasted the hypocrisy and cowardice of Rugg's corporate critics, especially Bertie Forbes. Such men would never "assail and discharge" employees who exposed the inefficiencies and errors of their own companies, the *American Business Survey* argued. But these same executives now wished to remove Rugg for blowing the whistle on the nation's wide-ranging problems. "It is a strange spectacle when the physician is denounced for diagnosing the disease," the *Survey* intoned.[31]

Yet despite their internal divisions these patriotic and business groups "succeeded in stirring up unrest in hundreds of communities," as Rugg himself admitted. He was never able to square his view of the campaign as insular and autocratic—a "manufactured conflict"—

with the obvious fact that "hundreds of communities" embraced it. Nor could Rugg explain why so many of these communities decided to drop his books in so brief a span of time. In a confidential memorandum to Teachers College officials in June 1940, Rugg cited his texts' undiminished sales as proof that "this attack on our enterprise is not a popular protest." But the same logic would suggest that when sales did drop off the following year, "popular protest" was at least part of the cause. To be sure, some jittery school boards removed the books without any input from citizens; terrified of controversy, they sought to head it off before it started. Other boards were apparently swayed by rival publishers, who inundated school officials with anti-Rugg literature. Given the large number of school districts involved, however, the books could not have disappeared so suddenly without a strong popular animus against them.[32]

Indeed, this very fact became a vital component of the anti-Rugg movement. Invoking a venerable populist idiom, critics claimed that "the citizens"—not "experts," "intellectuals," or "professors"— should determine what their schools teach. "Why should not business men, members of the American Legion, or any other citizen, for that matter, have . . . the right to criticize what they believe to be wrong?" asked the Hearst-owned *Philadelphia Inquirer,* an important mouthpiece of the campaign against Rugg. "These people, after all, pay the taxes which support the school system." To protest the curriculum was "thoroughly in accord with old-fashioned American practice," added the *New York Sun,* another Hearst paper. "Let us have more of it!" Too many educators still viewed their profession as a "closed guild" and the classroom as their exclusive domain, a third critic noted. Beyond simply exposing a "subversive" series of textbooks, then, the campaign against the Rugg texts also promised to return public schools to their rightful owner: the public itself.[33]

At a still more basic level, other Rugg foes argued, the movement would also restore children to their parents. Like O. K. Armstrong, anti-Rugg leaders inevitably traced their efforts to a jarring exchange with their own children. In Cedar Rapids, Iowa, the newspaperman

Verne Marshall began attacking the Rugg books after his daughter asked him "why some people had to live in poverty"; in Haworth, New Jersey, police chief Albert Ettinger's son inquired whether World War I "was fought for the bankers"; and in New York, editor Fulton Oursler was censured by his daughter for accepting advertisements in his own magazine. Advertising was dishonest, the girl told Oursler, and it raised the price of goods. Oursler, the editor of the staunchly conservative journal *Liberty,* could not believe his ears—or his eyes: "I looked at April as if she were some other family's child, but there she was, my own eleven-year-old daughter, placidly peeling her orange." Oursler asked April if she had adopted this view on her own. "No, Daddy," she replied, "I learned it at school today." Even as textbooks denigrated "the will of the people," it seemed, they were also driving a wedge through the American family.[34]

To Harold Rugg, the latter charge was nothing short of laughable. "I had that child for five hours a day. You had him for 19," Rugg told Albert Ettinger in a tempestuous 1939 exchange. "If anyone's making him not love America, it's you, not I." But Rugg and his allies had much more difficulty dispensing with their foes' broader majoritarian argument: "Let the people decide." During the initial stages of the attack, Rugg simply retorted that "the people" stood with him; his opponents represented a tiny field of "business interests" dressed up as a grassroots movement. As more and more school districts began to drop his books, however, Rugg's defenders were forced to shift course. Rather than praising the public, they increasingly urged that it defer to experts. "We of the educational profession must insist upon our right to exercise final judgment in the selection of texts," asserted a panel of New York social studies teachers in a typical statement. From the American Historical Association to the National Education Association, other professional groups struck similar chords. "Judgment as to the merits of a textbook is the function of those most competent to form a judgment: the teachers concerned and professional scholars," the AHA resolved at the height of the Rugg battle.[35]

The most vigorous defense of the Rugg texts was launched by the American Committee for Democracy and Intellectual Freedom (ACDIF), a small group of eminent civil libertarians from the worlds of science, education, and journalism. Chaired by the economist Wesley C. Mitchell, the ACDIF's committee on textbooks encouraged "every citizen" to "take an active interest in the schools," especially in the books that children used. Under a "democratic approach to the problem of textbook selection," however, only those with "up to date knowledge of the subject treated, familiarity with school curricula and practical experience of teaching pupils"—that is, professional educators—would actually select texts. Amid the perennial storms of American politics, the ACDIF panel wrote, such experts would keep textbooks on an even keel: "Many of the problems presented by our past history and current practice are the subject of lively, sometimes bitter controversy. No youngster is properly prepared for life in a democracy who does not learn to weigh candidly opposing views on social problems." Rather than imposing a single "truth," in short, trained educators would make sure that textbooks presented a diversity of perspectives.[36]

Echoing earlier text critics, Rugg's foes responded to this defense with two separate, somewhat contradictory arguments: textbooks should not even try to present "both sides" of public issues, and Rugg had failed to do so. School texts must teach "personal morality" and "reverence for the Republic of the United States," Amos Fries stated in January 1941. "We want NOTHING ON THE OPPOSITE SIDE OF ANY of those questions." In high school, some critics conceded, students might be able to grapple with controversial social issues. But the Rugg books were intended for junior high school children or even older elementary pupils, who lacked that critical capacity. "What pupil of 12, 13 or 14 years does not take as 'gospel truth' what he reads in a school textbook?" asked an anti-Rugg newspaper in Burlington, Vermont. Rather than helping students develop their own viewpoint, the Rugg series would simply imbue them with Rugg's own.[37]

To the books' critics, there was no mistaking this perspective: the Rugg texts were "collectivist" and "New Dealish," supporting ever-expanding state regulation of American private enterprise. Even Rugg's allies sometimes admitted this bias, which contradicted their claims that the texts taught "several views" rather than a single one. "Dr. Rugg writes as a liberal who believes in . . . the broadening social control over property," the famous sociologist and ACDIF stalwart Robert S. Lynd acknowledged in a defense of the texts. To liberals like Rugg, Lynd explained, "the rise of the middle-class businessman to power . . . presents a major problem"; but to conservatives, "this development has been natural and unavoidable." Perhaps the battle over Rugg's textbooks was equally inescapable. The previous year Rugg had noted the yawning ideological divide between his censors and his supporters:

> Broadly put, the nub of our special conflict today is: What interpretation of "the American way of life" shall guide the study of civilization in the schools? More specifically, in the terms of [Merwin] Hart,]Augustin] Rudd and co., it is: *Which Brand of the American system of free enterprise shall be taught?* They have one emphatic answer: it shall be that concept which guarantees government's hands off all business, old-fashioned laissez-faire . . . My colleagues and I have a different answer, hence the irreconcilable conflict between us.

Despite Rugg's oft-repeated goal of presenting "both sides" of "important questions," then, the real question concerned *which* side to present. At stake was nothing less than the nation's definition of itself. "What is Americanism?" another observer wrote, summarizing the furor over the Rugg books. "Is Americanism synonymous with free enterprise?"[38]

Harold Rugg's foes never wavered in their answer: "free enterprise" *was* America, the country's defining characteristic since its conception. "I am proud to be a soldier in the battle for the retention of the private enterprise economy in the United States," wrote the anti-Rugg warrior George E. Sokolsky in a compilation fittingly entitled

The American Way of Life (1939). "Upon this economy, often called the capitalist system, depends the continuation of democracy in our country." A longtime columnist for the Hearst press, Sokolsky also assisted the National Association of Manufacturers in its various efforts to advertise capitalism's virtues. In 1938 the NAM launched a major billboard and radio campaign to "sell" free enterprise "as continuously as the people are told that Ivory Soap floats." By 1940 it had also enlisted over six thousand local "sentinels" to persuade communities that capitalism was "*The* American Way." All that was missing, one NAM spokesman remarked in 1940, was "a fuller understanding of private enterprise among educators." At the end of that year the organization released summaries of nearly six hundred books in history, civics, economics, and social studies. According to the project's principal author, the business professor Ralph W. Robey, a "substantial proportion" of the texts displayed an overly "critical attitude" toward private enterprise. Hardly the sole offenders in their coolness toward capitalism, the Rugg texts were merely the tip of a massive "collectivist" iceberg.[39]

To Robey and other critics, the best evidence of this bias was the excessive—indeed, almost obsessive—focus on destitution and inequality in many textbooks. One text decried the "harrowing spectacle" of starvation in contemporary America; another bemoaned "poverty in the midst of plenty"; and a third worried that "the doors are closing on the American Dream." In Harold Rugg's *Introduction to the Problems of American Culture,* meanwhile, a set of illustrations contrasted Chicago's wealthy "Gold Coast" neighborhood with a nearby slum. "No one doubts such extremes exist," wrote Merwin K. Hart. "But why these sharp contrasts in words and photographs . . . if not to arouse social unrest in the people?" Moreover, critics added, texts typically attributed inequality to "the economic system"—that is, to capitalism—rather than to individual wisdom, talent, or initiative. Such analyses would "blunt the ambition of an American boy or girl," an anti-Rugg newspaper warned, spawning "a defeatist attitude" of "what's-the-use-of-trying-if-you-can't-get anywhere." If left unchallenged, the Rugg series threatened to trap students in a self-fulfilling prophecy. The more it emphasized the problems of capitalism, the more it encouraged children to capitulate to them.[40]

Worst of all, critics complained, textbooks frequently applied this "class appeal" to "the methods and work of the founders of this nation"—the Framers of the Constitution. Here text opponents took aim at Charles A. Beard's controversial interpretation, which held that well-to-do Americans devised and supported the Constitution to protect the value of their securities—and, more generally, to check the democratic impulses unleashed by the Revolution. In fact, Beard's own textbooks remained mostly devoid of this claim. But the Beardian viewpoint found its way into a number of social studies and history texts in the 1930s, including Harold Rugg's *America's March toward Democracy*. "The fathers of the Constitution feared 'too much democracy,'" Rugg declared in perhaps his most-quoted passage. "They were afraid of what the mass of people, who did not possess property, would do to the few who did." Another textbook stated outright that the Constitution "was drawn up by the wealthy element," while a third claimed it "supported the interests of the class which had the most to gain"—namely, merchants and large landholders.[41]

No other historical issue engaged text critics during the 1930s like the Constitution. In the 1920s, when ethnic issues predominated, text controversies centered on the Revolution and the different "races" that contributed to it; in the 1930s, as economic questions came to the fore, debate shifted to the class interests of the Framers. Ironically, the same activists who touted private enterprise as the essence of America denounced texts that imputed pecuniary interests to its founders. "Children can be taught that life is hard-boiled, materialistic, selfish," George Sokolsky wrote, attacking Rugg's conception of the Constitution. "Children can be made to believe that nothing moves men but money . . . But is that what you want your children taught?" Elsewhere, Sokolsky celebrated the modern American drive for property and personal gain; in fact, he indicted the Rugg texts for *impugning* these goals. Only too eager to embrace the profit motive in the present, Sokolsky objected when schoolbooks applied it to the past.[42]

Across the country, meanwhile, other tribunes of capitalism blasted the texts for depicting the Framers as capitalists. In New Jersey Bertie Forbes complained that the Rugg books turned the Constitution's authors into "a bunch of selfish mercenaries"; in Missouri O. K. Armstrong condemned Rugg for portraying them as "economic royalists"; and in the state of Washington the newly formed Patriotic Laymen's Education Association skewered him for attributing "selfish motives" to "the founders of the country." Among Rugg's attackers, in fact, only the Hearst-owned *New York Sun* acknowledged the Constitution's economic origins. Yes, the *Sun's* editors wrote, American merchants refused to accept worthless paper money under the old Articles of Confederation; yes, their wish to secure their fortunes constituted an important motive for the Constitution. Rather than censuring them for their "selfishness," however, textbooks should praise them for their prescience. "Get out the tumbrils for the wicked merchants of old Rhode Island!" the *Sun* editorialized, mocking Rugg's moralistic denunciations. "Give them no credit for foreseeing the demoralization and rioting which followed the issuance of fiat money. But before doing so ask Dr. Rugg whether he would accept at face value promissory notes unsupported by collateral." The Framers had behaved like good capitalists, and all future capitalists—indeed, all future Americans—were therefore in their debt.[43]

Similarly, Rugg's foes attacked his critique of the Constitution's primary watchdog: the Supreme Court. In another much-quoted passage, Rugg emphasized that judicial review—the right to interpret and strike down laws—*"had not been given to the Supreme Court by the Constitution."* Instead, under John Marshall, the Court "simply took this power upon itself," and thereafter, "the Court could even defeat the will of the people themselves." True, Merwin Hart responded, the Constitution did not mention judicial review "in so many words." But the Framers' debates amply demonstrated that they foresaw such a procedure, Hart argued, while Rugg's affront to the Court strongly revealed his affinity for its modern-day *bête noire,* Franklin D. Roosevelt. Just as the Rugg passage appeared, critics noted, Roosevelt embarked on his notorious plan to "pack" the Supreme Court. Even Rugg's majoritarian rhetoric—"the will of the people"—echoed FDR, who frequently condemned the Court for impeding the electorate's wishes.[44]

For antagonists on every side, the battle over Harold Rugg and his textbooks often boiled down to a debate over Franklin Roosevelt and his New Deal. No one seriously questioned whether the books were "New Dealish in tone," as *Time* magazine asserted in 1941. The only issue was what, if anything, to do about it. For the books' critics, the answer was simple: replace texts' "New Deal propaganda" with material that explained—and celebrated—America's heritage. To be sure, critics admitted, textbooks were not the only culprit; teachers shared the blame. In December 1940, for example, parents in Tuckahoe, New York, castigated a history instructor for requiring students to prepare biographical reports on Franklin D. Roosevelt. "American History did not begin with the birth of Mr. Roosevelt," an angry parent wrote to the teacher in a letter he also sent to school officials, "nor were all the noteworthy accomplishments of our presidents confined to his administration." The only possible rationale for the assignment, the parent claimed, lay in the teacher's "personal preference" for FDR. Textbooks and teachers conspired to impress a New Deal bias upon public schools, where students now learned to value "the WPA and the NYA" more than "the Supreme Court and the Constitution," as Sokolsky glumly concluded.[45]

To their defenders, meanwhile, textbooks' New Deal themes—especially the regulation of private enterprise and the expansion of government services—were justified by History itself. The 1930s demonstrated not just the popularity but also the inevitability of "new controls" upon the economy, as Harold Rugg argued in 1941. But critics like Sokolsky and Merwin Hart refused to admit this simple truth, providing a case study in "cultural lag." Hart, especially, was "a capitalist Don Quixote," according to the Rugg ally and civil libertarian Roger

Baldwin: even as new social conditions demanded state planning and regulation, Hart continued "tilting at the windmills of Communism in a crusade for free private enterprise." But "free private enterprise" was fast becoming a "has-been," Baldwin added, and nothing Hart did or said could bring it back. To Harold Rugg, in fact, the whole concept of "freedom" in America was undergoing an almost Copernican shift. Formerly defined in a private, negative fashion—as "absence of restraint" upon the individual—the term increasingly signified positive measures in the public interest.[46]

The fate of Rugg's textbooks told a very different story. Like the Roosevelt administration, Americans were abandoning the strong critique of capitalism and private enterprise that had marked the early 1930s. Less and less did FDR and his aides censure "plutocrats" or "economic royalists"; instead of slapping new regulations on business, meanwhile, they crafted new fiscal policies to influence overall levels of production, employment, and especially consumption. Given their continued emphasis on the "social control" of "private interests," then, Rugg's books—not their critics—suffered most conspicuously from "cultural lag." In a perceptive letter, the Iowa publishing executive E. T. Meredith noted that Rugg's critique of advertising contradicted the White House's own evolving economic philosophy. "Mr. Rugg points out that advertising constantly encourages people to buy. This, he apparently assumes, is a bad thing," Meredith wrote to the president of Columbia University in 1939. "I wonder if Professor Rugg has ever heard that the theme song of the most renowned economists for recovery is *'more consumption and more production.'*" Rather than echoing the New Deal, as foes often charged, Rugg had actually fallen behind it.[47]

Indeed, Rugg's critics more accurately captured the country's changing mood. In his own letter to Columbia officials, Rugg insisted that Meredith's remarks did not even merit a reply: clearly drafted in response to an appeal from the Advertising Federation of America, Meredith's attack was "professionally inspired" and hardly reflective of a popular campaign. The following year, Rugg boasted, orders for

his textbooks increased. In 1941, however, even his publisher's cata-
log acknowledged that "certain communities" objected to the books'
"liberal point of view." By August 1943 the American Legion estimated that some 1,500 schools had dropped the Rugg texts; across
the country, a Legion spokesman reported, the books were "going out
like a light." A year after that they were almost extinguished. From a
peak of 289,000 in 1938, sales plummeted 90 percent to 21,000 in
1944. In a span of just three years, their author descended from afflu-
ence to relative destitution. Embittered as well as impoverished, Rugg
soon renounced the textbook field in favor of more traditional academic pursuits. His texts held on in a few districts for several more
years, then disappeared from American schools altogether.[48]

The removal of Rugg's books did not herald a general "reign of terror" against left-leaning texts, as the columnist Max Lerner predicted
in 1941. Except for the Rugg series, nearly every leading textbook
emerged from the era unscathed. Shortly after it condemned Rugg,
the American Legion quietly retracted its attacks on Carl Becker,
Charles Beard, and several other authors. Amid a spate of negative
publicity, likewise, the NAM abandoned its textbook survey. With
more diplomacy than accuracy, NAM officials stressed that the text
summaries aimed simply to "illustrate" rather than to "appraise" the
books; when the abstracts' principal author openly condemned the
books in a newspaper interview, the NAM moved immediately to distance itself from him. Worried members cited the electric utilities
scandal of the 1920s, when power companies had been excoriated for
pressuring text publishers and teachers. "The net effect . . . is likely to
be unfavorable," warned a NAM official in 1941. "The NAM will long
be stigmatized as having attempted to establish a censorship of public
education."[49]

Even at this late date, in short, enough anti-business feeling remained to squelch any overall attack on liberal textbooks. Max
Lerner's imagined "reign of terror" would not materialize until after
World War II, when new fears of communist subversion fueled a
much stronger drive against so-called Red texts. "The Rugg type of

thinking is not completely eliminated in this country, but it is much less prevalent today," boasted the Burlington, Vermont, *Free Press* in 1950, a decade after it led the fight to remove Harold Rugg's books from local schools. As new texts were produced, the *Free Press* editorial writer hoped, students would be "indoctrinated with the American ideas of individual freedom, as opposed to those espoused by foreign countries." But Americans needed to keep on constant watch, the paper cautioned: once more, "foreign" influences were threatening to invade the body politic. Merging the nativism of the 1920s with "Red Scares" of the 1930s, the Cold War would spark the most furious textbook controversies that America had ever seen.[50]

The Cold War Assault
on Textbooks

In 1952 William F. Buckley Jr. asked American businesses to help fight "collectivism" in textbooks. Three years earlier his father had provided seed money for the *Educational Reviewer,* a small journal devoted to exposing texts' bias toward "centralized political power" over the "private enterprise system." The journal echoed many of the themes in Buckley's surprise 1951 bestseller, *God and Man at Yale,* in which he argued that Yale economists were undermining the capitalist system that had enriched the university's benefactors. But "subversive doctrine" in high school books was a far more serious matter, Buckley argued, and his family should not have to battle it single-handedly. Private entrepreneurs must not sit idly by while private enterprise was sabotaged.[1]

To Buckley's chagrin, American business largely ignored his appeal. "It has always struck me as remarkable . . . how unintelligently [businessmen] dispose of their money," he wrote. "Millions upon millions are poured into political campaigns . . . and so few nickels and dimes are aimed at mending the heart of this nation's trouble—the collectivist influence in education." The *Educational Reviewer* would soon expire for lack of donations, while "anti-capitalist" textbooks continued to dominate the classroom. Most astonishingly, some capitalists defended them. In one Long Island town an executive from the brokerage giant Merrill Lynch led the drive to retain the textbooks. Even the firm's top managers, Buckley complained, backed the books, unwittingly digging a grave for the free enterprise system that sustained them. "How little those in the business world know of what is happening to their country," one Buckley ally lamented.[2]

Throughout the Cold War, right-wing activists aimed to strip textbooks of "statism, New Dealism, and socialism," as an Illinois firebrand put it.[3] But their reach exceeded their grasp, reflecting the overall frustration of American conservatives in the 1950s. As many historians have shown, a powerful and wide-ranging anticommunist consensus dominated national life in the wake of World War II. Scholars have taught us a great deal about Americans who transgressed this consensus from the left—about their ideologies, their sufferings, and (in rare instances) their espionage.[4] We know much less about dissidents on the right, who argued that America's entire culture and politics—not just specific individuals or institutions—were veering toward socialism or even communism. To these critics, the question of personal loyalty was often moot. However many actual "Reds" it harbored, conservatives claimed, America increasingly shared the "collectivist" ethos of its communist foe. Only when the nation threw off its statist shackles would it rediscover the radical individualism it had lost.[5]

The Cold War attack on textbooks represented the right's effort to inscribe this view upon American schools. Hardly the exclusive province of members of the elite like William F. Buckley Jr., the struggle engaged thousands of parents, military veterans, and other grassroots activists. Converging on local school boards and classrooms, they protested textbooks' allegedly "socialistic" bias toward public housing, progressive taxation, and other hallmarks of the modern welfare state. To be sure, previous text critics had crafted similar arguments: during the "little Red Scare" of 1939–1941, for example, conservatives charged that Harold Rugg's emphasis on state controls subverted "the American Way of Life." In the 1950s, though, the right drew a much more explicit link between what a California woman called "Communism, Socialism, and New Dealism" in textbooks.[6] It also mounted fervid assaults on "world government," assailing texts' favorable accounts of the United Nations.

Most of the time, these salvos fell far short of their mark. Critics did succeed in removing certain books and in revising others to portray a somewhat less rosy view of Franklin D. Roosevelt and his legacy. Textbook publishers also altered their accounts of communism in general and of the Soviet Union in particular, maligning both as unalloyed evils—if they were mentioned at all. But no text discussed the American welfare state itself as communist or even as "collectivist," rightwing pleas notwithstanding. Instead, textbooks retained a tepid cast reminiscent of Dwight D. Eisenhower's "middle way," celebrating individual initiative and enterprise but also supporting many forms of state regulation and control. To those on the right, this rapprochement reeked of surrender. *"There is no compromise,"* an angry supporter wrote to the *Educational Reviewer,* excoriating "middle-of-the road" textbooks. "There is no in-between arrangement . . . whereby we can be a little socialist and a little free."[7]

Part of the failure of this effort to shape the Cold War curriculum stemmed from tensions between Protestants and Catholics, who were often unable to set aside their differences in the service of the conservative cause. Educational leaders also mounted a spirited defense of textbooks, enlisting parents and businessmen to rebut charges of "subversion." Indeed, the same Americans who backed laws barring communist teachers rejected the idea that textbooks transmitted "communistic" ideas. The concept of "subversive" textbooks took hold only in the South, where it was linked to a new threat: racial integration. Across the country, race would soon replace communism as the central issue in America's textbook wars.

Collectivism and Internationalism

In June 1949 the experienced text activist Amos A. Fries took aim at America's most popular civics book, Frank A. Magruder's *American Government.* "The United States is called a capitalistic country, but it does not have pure capitalism," Magruder declared in a passage Fries quoted. "The postal system, power projects, and progressive taxes are bits of socialism; and free public education and old age assistance are examples of communism." To Fries this statement exemplified the peril of postwar textbooks: by celebrating America's welfare state, they bolstered the communist enemy. So did the books' unabashed praise for the United Nations and "world government," a cliché of Soviet propaganda. Here Fries added a jab at the Rockefeller, Carnegie, and Rhodes Foundations, which lent their millions to "planned economy" efforts at home as well as to "one-world" movements abroad. Both developments had strong English roots; indeed, Fries quipped, "We know of no Rhodes scholar who has come back 100 percent American" following study in Great Britain.[8]

In many ways these comments echoed Fries's earlier complaints about textbooks. In the 1920s he had reviled the "pro-British" biases of history books that analyzed the American Revolution as an economic struggle. In the mid-1930s he had spearheaded the attack on Carl Becker's supposedly "pro-communist" discussion of Lenin and the Soviet Union. After World War II, however, critics like Fries began to argue that textbook accounts of *America* were themselves "socialistic" or even "communistic." Likewise, they denounced the United Nations and other internationalist organizations as Red rather than pro-British, in spite of Fries's lingering Anglophobia. Finally—and most ironically—Cold War critics attributed books' "anticapitalist" tone to capitalists themselves, who too often touted the same texts that subverted them.

The first major target of postwar textbook activists was Building America, a three-volume social studies series issued by the curricular arm of the National Education Association in 1947. Initial protests surrounded the series's "Russia" chapter, which allegedly exaggerated the achievements of the Soviet Union and underplayed its misdeeds. "If the book that I read was used in our schools throughout the nation . . . this country would be fully communized in 20 years," warned a citizen in California, where Building America came up for adoption. State officials hurried to point out that Russian diplomats had faulted the series for its *unflattering* portrait of their country. But American critics were unmoved, still insisting that the texts "favored" the Soviet Union. "I would suggest . . . you all go to Russia for at least five years," a second Californian told state officials. "When you return you can tell us truly if their way is better."[9]

Opponents also charged that Building America glorified Social Security and FDR's "court-packing" plan, both standard targets of Depression-era text attacks. To the new generation of text activists, however, such biases did not simply undermine "the American form of government," as one protester proclaimed. Instead, such "New Dealish" prejudices gave aid and comfort to America's Red foes. Critics alleged that the original material for the textbook series had been collected by "a group of Communists on the New York Works Progress Administration," demonstrating a personal as well as an ideological link between "Welfareism and Stalinism." But the strongest evidence lay in the texts themselves, which echoed socialist and communist demands for full employment, public housing, and other reforms. In the white-hot politics of the Cold War, the suggestion that America needed *any* reform was "subversive," several California legislators resolved. "There should be a constructive, positive approach," they insisted, "and emphasis should be placed upon the 'good things' of American life."[10]

Buckling under this barrage from the right, California rejected the Building America series in 1948. The following year the *Educational Reviewer* provided a new voice for similar attacks on other history and social studies books. Its first issue featured a scathing critique of Magruder's *American Government,* the same text that had caught Amos Fries's eye. For over a quarter-century "Magruder's" (as the book was known) had dominated high school civics instruction. But the text had recently embraced "Statist propaganda," the *Reviewer* charged, including a "Communist party line" on American inequality: depicting poor people as "under-privileged" rather than unmotivated, it invoked the federal government as their savior. Critics also bridled at the book's "Problems for Discussion," which set forth collectivist solutions in the guise of "critical" questions. "Why has unemployment been called 'America's Public Enemy No. 1'?" Magruder's asked in an oft-cited passage. "Do you believe that private industry alone can prevent it?"[11]

Other foes took issue with the text's chapters on foreign policy. In 1950 Georgia's state board of education barred Magruder's because, according to the board member May Talmadge, it "too strongly advocated World Government." "Too much emphasis is placed on Internationalism instead of Nationalism," added Talmadge, a cousin of Georgia's governor. "Instead of playing UP the 'questionable' advantages to be derived from loving and advocating every other country in the world, why is not a comparison made showing the great advantages of our free country over all others?" Talmadge especially objected to the book's praise for the United Nations, a "Godless" organization devoted to "the advancement of socialistic schemes." Georgia's school board would draw nationwide ridicule in 1951 for attempting to sell its remaining 30,000 copies of Magruder's to other states. Yet even if taxpayers had to absorb the cost of every old text, Talmadge insisted, Georgia should not hesitate to purchase new ones: "What goes into the minds of the children is much more important than having fine new play grounds and school rooms."[12]

By late 1951 the attack on "world government" had spread west—to Texas and California—and had found a new bogeyman: the United Nations Educational, Scientific, and Cultural Organization (UNESCO). In October Idaho Representative John T. Wood took to the floor of Congress to denounce UNESCO's nine-volume booklet series, Toward World Understanding. No state or school district seems to have used the series—or any UNESCO materials, for that matter—to instruct children. In Houston, however, conservative "Minute Women" sent copies of Wood's speech to all teachers and school officials, who promptly canceled the city's student essay competition on the United Nations. In Los Angeles, meanwhile, controversy erupted over a locally designed curriculum unit on UNESCO and its teachers' manual, which supposedly promoted "faceless citizenship in a monstrous world government." Joined by Hollywood luminaries like Bing Crosby and Cecil B. DeMille, an array of patriotic groups forced the school board to remove the manual as well as to reject a $335,000 teacher-training grant from the Ford Foundation. "The patriotism of the Los Angeles school board was so intense that it [could] see Henry Ford II . . . and the other men who dominate the Ford Foundation as Communist agents," quipped Robert Hutchins, an associate director of the foundation.[13]

Other critics skewered UNESCO for promoting birth control, an insult to Catholics and an insidious threat to American family life. Such charges became staples of attacks on textbooks during the Cold War, when any discussion of sexual practices—like any demand for social reform—seemed to play into communist hands. During the dispute over the Building America series, for example, Californians lambasted the books for discussing Margaret Mead's research on sexual codes in Samoa: such ideas could only make students question their own social mores, which in turn would soften them to Red appeals. In Salpulpa, Oklahoma, critics actually burned several high school books for their subversive messages about "socialism and sex." The most hostile attacks came from Texas, where segregationists charged that textbooks promoted racial intermarriage. Under the United Nations charter, critics noted, couples were guaranteed the right to marry regardless of race, nationality, or religion. Hence any "Communist" text that commended the UN gave at least an implicit imprimatur to miscegenation, a sign of "moral depravity" in "its lowest and vilest forms," as one Lone Star hate-sheet editorialized.[14]

That editorial united three themes of right-wing assaults on textbooks—communism, internationalism, and sexual depravity—and linked them to a fourth one: race. Across the country, critics pressed publishers and school boards to omit any mention of the Ku Klux Klan, lynching, or segregation; such passages would inevitably foment what one New Yorker called "racial agitation," a key component of communist propaganda. In Georgia the mere mention of black poverty in Magruder's *American Government* sparked threats of white retribution. Magruder "should be shot as a traitor to our Country," one citizen proclaimed in 1950. "This type of stuff might be expected in the Harlem district of New York, but that it should be taught in the Public Schools of Georgia is unthinkable." Two years later Alabamians discovered that one of their textbooks included a chapter on the Fair Employment Practices Committee and other efforts to fight racial injustice. Almost immediately the publisher agreed to delete the entire chapter. To guard against further "subversion," Alabama's legislature passed a law requiring all subsequent textbooks to carry a statement confirming that neither the author nor the people quoted had been members of a communist or "Communist-front" organization.[15]

The law was clearly aimed at the National Association for the Advancement of Colored People, long reviled by white southerners as a "Red" organization. In an impassioned letter to Alabama governor Gordon Persons, however, NAACP regional secretary Ruby Hurley charged that segregationist textbooks represented the truly "subversive" threat to the body politic. Segregation "may be a Southern tradition," Hurley allowed, "but it is not American, it is not democratic, it is not christian." Here she was joined by several national business organizations, which worried that Alabama's "pure text" law undermined a different American tradition: free enterprise. Even as conservatives rallied to save capitalism from doom, it appeared that capitalists were standing in their way.[16]

Long Divisions

The conservative economist Lewis H. Haney was known for his feverish denunciations of "collectivism" in social studies texts. In 1951 Haney himself became a target of attack. Leading this charge was the National Commission for the Defense of Democracy Through Education, which had been forged by the National Education Association during the Harold Rugg controversy a decade earlier. In newsletters, pamphlets, films, and even phonograph records, the Defense

Commission warned that Haney and other textbook critics were destroying public confidence in public education. Many of the leading attackers had ties to fascist groups in America, the commission claimed; like fascists in Europe, moreover, they used innuendo and outright fakery to sway gullible citizens. Even a congressional investigatory committee had concluded that the *Educational Reviewer*—for which Haney served as an adviser—"smacks too much of the book-burning orgies of Nuremberg," the commission noted. A similarly authoritarian spirit marked most other textbook assailants, who conspired—often in secret—to sabotage American schools.[17]

Haney's response to these charges was simple: attacks on textbooks reflected "hundreds of spontaneous outbursts," not a plot hatched by a handful of reactionary schemers. Publications like the *Educational Reviewer* merely gave voice to "the honest indignation of local citizens," who resented the inroads of "statism" upon "free initiative and thought." The only real threats to the public schools were the "goon squads" of the NEA's Defense Commission, Haney told a radio audience in 1951. Squelching popular protest wherever it arose, the commission used many of the same "Gestapo-like" smear tactics—especially "guilt by association"—that it imputed to text critics. Other conservatives likened the Defense Commission to a latter-day monarchy, based not on divine right but on supposedly "expert" knowledge. "The educators appear to deny that the majority of the people have the right to rule," wrote Amos Fries in 1951. So the people had to seize this power back, Fries added, restoring the American tradition of "free government" even as they rid the nation of its un-American texts.[18]

In the struggle over Cold War textbooks, then, each side portrayed the other as an evil cabal that manipulated or muzzled an innocent public. The truth lay somewhere between these extremes, reflecting a much more subtle politics than either set of antagonists acknowledged. While a small circle of national spokesmen led the assault on so-called collectivist texts, as educators correctly charged, the movement also attracted large numbers of grassroots activists. Likewise, the NEA's Defense Commission and other educational agencies hardly represented the tiny, conspiratorial "front" that foes imagined. Even as they insisted that experts should select textbooks, these schoolmen recruited thousands of parents—and especially businessmen—in the texts' defense. The result was a popular movement for professional control, backed by the same tribunes of free enterprise that the books allegedly undermined.

The anti-text campaign resembled three concentric circles, with a small core of full-time ringleaders at the center, publicists surrounding them, and local agitators on the perimeter. Like Amos Fries, many of the leaders were already well known from previous textbook disputes. Some of their innocuously named organizations were also connected to fascist groups that flowered during the Great Depression, although the exact extent of these links was often obscure. For example, Fries's Friends of the Public Schools had been founded in the 1930s by the notorious nativist Greta S. Deffenbaugh, with the single goal of checking "the rising tide of Roman political power" in America. Deffenbaugh was also a well-known anti-Semite, dating her text activism to an encounter with Jewish students in a Chicago night school many years earlier. Deffenbaugh claimed that the students had used penknives to slice the word "Christ" out of their textbooks, revealing their "deep hatred toward the Founder of a faith whose benefits the haters were enjoying."[19]

During the "little Red Scare" of 1939, however, the Friends of the Public Schools discovered a new enemy. Joining forces with Deffenbaugh, Fries persuaded her that communism was "a greater menace than Roman Catholicism," as she acknowledged in 1943. For the next decade the organization would debate the comparative perils of these twin foes. Even at the height of the Cold War, some members continued to insist that "the threat of Romanism" outweighed the threat of communism. But others argued that communism was the more dangerous enemy, especially given the Soviet Union's growing status as a world power. Updating Deffenbaugh's anti-Semitism for a nuclear age, one activist warned that "Kike leaders" and "Zionist agents" had transported the Soviet peril to the United States. Others stressed Catholics' leading role in stemming this Red tide, whatever their prior misdeeds. "If it came down to a showdown between the Catholics and the Communists," one associate told Fries, "you would find me standing with the Catholics, who, as a group, are doing more to oppose communism than are the Protestants."[20]

The *Educational Reviewer* was a distinctly Catholic combatant in the struggle against "collectivist" books. Funded by the devout Catholic William F. Buckley Sr., the *Reviewer* was edited by the Quebec-born writer and activist Lucille Cardin Crain. The product of a French convent school in Minnesota, Crain admitted privately that she was no longer a practicing Catholic. But she retained her public image as one, refusing to appease religious bigots in the interest of anticommunist unity. In 1949, for example, Lewis Haney urged her to omit Catholic sources and commentary from the *Reviewer*. "I have nothing against the Catholics," Haney emphasized, "but a lot of people do." Crain's reply was quick and curt: no. The journal's "primary criteria" should be "substance and competence," she insisted; indeed, sectarian prejudice could only hamper the larger textbook struggle. In a letter to the right-wing writer Rose Wilder Lane, Crain praised Fries for his yeoman's work against "radical trends." Yet Fries was also "violently anti-Catholic," she added, precluding the formation of a broad, cross-religious coalition against the common enemy.[21]

Ironically, other critics leveled similar charges against Lane. The daughter of Laura Ingalls Wilder, author of the Little House in the Big Woods children's series, Lane worked tirelessly to promote these novels in schools: as she told Crain, her mother's theme of self-reliance on the western frontier would "counter-act the predominant socialist influences" of American classrooms. But Lane also reviewed social studies textbooks for the National Economic Council, the brainchild of the anti-Semitic Merwin K. Hart. Hart had been flaying "collectivist" texts since the Harold Rugg controversy of 1940, when critics first exposed his connections to the Christian Front and other fascist groups. But his anti-Semitism did not become openly manifest until the postwar period, when Hart likened Jews to Nazis even as he denied that the Nazis had exterminated Jews. Most textbook assailants sought to distance themselves from Hart after that, fearful that his prejudice would taint their entire project. Lane seems to have stood by him, however, editing Hart's *Economic Council Review of Books* for at least four years.[22]

Charges of anti-Semitism also surrounded Allen A. Zoll, the most controversial figure of the right-wing network. Founded in 1948, Zoll's National Council for American Education issued some of the Cold War's most bitter invective against textbooks. Not only were texts filled with "Communist propaganda," Zoll maintained, but the educators who defended them were "stupid-intendents"—and Red ones at that. Schoolmen fought back, publicizing Zoll's longtime links to Elizabeth Dilling, Gerald L. K. Smith, and other anti-Semitic activists. News reports of these connections caused several notables to quit Zoll's group, including the boxer Gene Tunney and the World War II hero Jonathan Wainwright. But other text critics supported Zoll, dismissing the charges against him as either irrelevant or fraudulent. "I believe Allan [sic] Zoll's outfit is doing a splendid job," declared William F. Buckley Jr. in 1951. "As for Zoll's past, I am utterly uninterested in it . . . None of the leftist smear organizations has yet convinced me that they have stopped lying when they deal with Allan Zoll."[23]

Each of these leaders—Fries, Crain, Hart, and Zoll—distributed reams of literature and corresponded avidly with supporters in the field. As they readily acknowledged, however, their efforts were too limited in scope to alter school policy by themselves: at its height, for example, the *Educational Reviewer* sold a mere 2,000 subscriptions. To reach a wider audience, text critics resolved to find new avenues of "publicity." Indeed, the term became something of a talisman within the Cold War textbook movement. Crain was married to an editor at *Advertising Age* and had once worked at the Madison Avenue giant J. Walter Thompson, so she appreciated the importance of good promotion. So did Zoll's text reviewer Verne Kaub, a former public relations executive for a Wisconsin power company.[24]

In America the most powerful publicity agent was the daily newspaper. The text movement received its first boost from the Hearst-owned *Chicago Tribune*, which published a long series on "subversive" books in the autumn of 1947. The series was written by a little-known reporter named Frank Hughes, who would quickly become the most famous media voice in the Cold War text struggle. Borrowing heavily from reports by Lucille Crain and other activists, Hughes also shared his own research with them. Hughes warned Fries in 1949 that a Chicago suburb had removed one of Harold Rugg's "collectivist" textbooks only to replace it with a book praising state welfare services in Uruguay. "By God, sir," Hughes wrote to Fries, "this gang of social bandits is a tough one to whip, isn't it?" When Crain worried that Hughes's close connection to the text critics might be considered "unethical," the journalist scoffed. Sending Crain a list of financiers who might contribute to the *Educational Reviewer*, he also interceded with the *Tribune*'s publisher, Robert McCormick, to plant favorable editorials and news stories about Crain's efforts. "Maybe, all of us put together, we can make a dent on these guilty, defensive, pro-Communist bastards—who knows?" Hughes wrote to Crain.[25]

Hughes joined several other prominent right-wing journalists to forge a small but powerful publicity battalion. Its influence was best illustrated during the struggle over Magruder's *American Government*, which started with a brief attack on the text in the first edition of the *Educational Reviewer*. The radio hosts Fulton Lewis Jr. and John T. Flynn read excerpts from the *Reviewer*'s attack on their syndicated shows, while Flynn vilified the book in his weekly newspaper column. The author of the bestselling 1949 diatribe *The Road Ahead*, which compared the American welfare state to Soviet tyranny, Flynn also alleged that textbook publishing houses were saturated with communists. But the latter claim drew little attention until Flynn's attack on Magruder's in 1950, which was lifted almost verbatim from the *Reviewer.* His two broadcasts about the book, Flynn told Crain, generated the largest audience response he had ever received. In Texas several schools even replaced Magruder's with Flynn's own book. Frank Hughes skewered Magruder's in yet another *Chicago Tribune* series, meanwhile, working closely with Crain on both its content and its timing. The most concentrated attacks appeared in the *Indianapolis Star,* which ran seventeen anti-Magruder articles in less than a month. Like Hughes and Flynn, the *Star's* publisher, Edgar C. Pulliam, quoted extensively from Crain and other conservative text activists.[26]

Thanks to these efforts, millions of Americans became aware of the war against high school textbooks. Flynn's weekly column alone reached roughly 20 million people, while untold others heard his radio commentaries. But simple knowledge of the battle would not inspire citizens to enter it, as Flynn himself told Lucille Crain. A successful attack required not just "propaganda" but also "pressure," Flynn explained, "to get the people thus propagandized to use the material at the point where it is most needed." Actually, small local groups were already doing so. In Little Rock, Arkansas, citizens seeking to remove Magruder's textbook sent copies of the *Educational Reviewer* to school officials and teachers; in Beaufort, South Carolina, a group of mothers cited Amos Fries's *Bulletin of the Friends of the Public Schools* in their own demand for "patriotic" textbooks. Yet in a nation of thirty thousand school districts, Flynn pointed out, sporadic efforts of this sort would never eliminate "subversive" texts: witness the continuing success of Magruder's, which was still used in over 70 percent of American civics classrooms in 1951. A national problem, textbooks demanded a national solution.[27]

In search of this remedy, Flynn looked to two obvious sources: veterans and businesses. The Rugg textbook battle of 1940 and 1941 had demonstrated the patriotic potential of the nation's largest veterans' group, the American Legion, which had deployed both its national magazine and its local posts against Rugg's books. During World War II alone, moreover, Legion membership had skyrocketed from a million to 3.5 million; by the end of the decade it would top 4 million. Through its *Counter-Subversive Manual* and other publications, the Legion was already championing the postwar hunt for communists in government, labor unions, and especially schools. Together with other patriotic organizations like the Sons of the American Revolution, Flynn wrote, the Legion had the capacity to fight subversive textbooks "in practically every city and county in the United States." Crain agreed, predicting that a friendly word or two from national Legion leaders would "stimulate their local members" to take up the text struggle.[28]

In an exact echo of the Rugg dispute, however, many veterans *supported* the allegedly subversive texts that their leaders censured. After the California Legion's executive board blasted the Building America series in 1947, several local posts wrote vehement letters in the textbooks' defense. One Legionnaire even suggested that the attack on Building America was a communist plot to undermine public schools—and eventually democracy. Likewise, Legionnaires in Washington, D.C., mocked the "ridiculous statements" against textbooks by "crackpots" like Amos Fries. In Michigan a joint committee of Legionnaires and school officials condemned the "black-listing of instructional materials" via "hasty, ill-advised, or snap judgment." The committee further decreed that textbooks should examine "accomplishments *and* failures" in American history, so that students would develop the analytical abilities that democratic citizenship demanded. Adopting this report in 1949, Michigan's state Legion convention asked national officials to do the same.[29]

The Legion's top brass failed to take action on the Michigan resolution, underscoring a sharp but largely subterranean split within the organization over school textbooks. The issue would not erupt to the surface until June 1952, when the Legion's national magazine published a vituperative attack on "socialistic" texts. Written by Irene C. Kuhn, a regular contributor to various right-wing publications, the article mostly repeated old charges from Crain and other sources. But it placed them under an incendiary headline, "Your Child Is Their

Target," which sent shock waves through the American Legion. Critics condemned Kuhn's "untruths and misrepresentations," which would foster a general distrust of schools and foil the Legion's battle against the *real* foe: communist teachers. Thus far, a New Jersey veteran cautioned, school officials "had been extremely helpful" in rooting out "Reds" from the classroom. But if the Legion continued to cry wolf about textbooks, slinging baseless charges of "subversion," educators would eventually dismiss their warnings about teachers as well.[30]

Across the country, state and local Legion posts heaped similar abuse upon the Kuhn article. Already on record as opposing "malicious" attacks on textbooks, Michigan's state convention asked the *American Legion Magazine* to reject all future articles that insulted "the splendid work of the schools." In Dearborn, meanwhile, Ford Motor Post No. 173 charged that many "patriotic" text assailants were really just fascists in disguise. *"Hands Off Our Schools!"* screamed the post's newsletter. "Let's investigate and look behind names as we have in fighting the Commies. Remember, just like the Commie fronts, these outfits bode no good for democracy." To calm the tempest, the Legion's national convention passed a tepid resolution reaffirming its support for "the American teaching profession." But stormy divisions continued to plague the Legion, especially as attention shifted from "Commie texts" to UNESCO. While top officials reviled the agency for eroding American patriotism, a special Legion committee found that UNESCO's educational materials were "no more subversive than the fairy tales of Hans Christian Andersen." The Soviets had condemned UNESCO as a tool of *American* propaganda, the panel noted, while many leading business organizations gave it their firm support. But Legion leaders held fast to their anti-UNESCO position, insisting that communists were using the agency "to corrupt the minds of our children." The capitalist approval of UNESCO merely indicated that capitalists did not understand their own interests.[31]

Throughout the Cold War, indeed, text critics focused some of their harshest scorn on American businesses. From the start, activists presumed that the nation's corporate leaders would join veterans' groups in blocking so-called collectivist textbooks. Just like veterans, however, businesses frequently defended these texts against "irresponsible" attacks. A handful of small business groups and wealthy individuals did endorse the campaign against subversive texts. But most larger corporations and foundations refused to do so, sparking a mixture of outrage and confusion among American conservatives. Some critics argued that businesses were simply ignorant, blind to the mortal threat that textbooks posed. Others charged that corporations had actually conspired with communists to sabotage America. Whatever the reason, businessmen were clearly undermining their own cause. "The private corporations of America, tagged to be 'expropriated' and liquidated under the dictatorship of the proletariat, soften the coming generation for the Communist onslaught," surmised several California critics in 1947 on the eve of the battle over the Building America series.[32]

Building America had begun with a grant from the Rockefeller Foundation, which quickly became a *bête noire* of the right-wing textbook campaign. So did the Carnegie Corporation, especially after it joined hands with the Rockefellers in 1949 to underwrite the National Citizens Commission for the Public Schools. Chaired by the president of Time, Inc., Roy E. Larsen, the NCCPS distributed leaflets, films, and advertisements to rebut "attacks upon the schools"—particularly upon textbooks. Thereafter, text critics saw a Rockefeller or Carnegie hand behind every defense of "collectivist" texts. Some assailants charged that "radicals" like the accused spy Alger Hiss—a Carnegie Corporation official—had "infiltrated" the foundations, diverting them from science and medical research into "Marxist philosophy." To other observers, however, the problem lay less in the subterfuge of a few evil plotters than in the overall ethos of American business. Obsessed with the future, American capitalists could not understand the lasting significance of the past. "It wasn't by a slip of the tongue that Henry Ford said history is bunk," one critic wrote in an attack on the Rockefeller and Carnegie foundations. "If you don't understand the role of tradition, you're most likely to be concerned only with changing it, or destroying it, getting it out of the way . . . History can't possibly be anything else but bunk to people who have this as their object in life."[33]

After the foundations, text critics reserved their greatest disapproval for the National Association of Manufacturers. Typically regarded as America's foremost tribune of business conservatism, the NAM had helped fuel the attacks on Rugg in 1940 by sponsoring a lengthy survey of social science textbooks. But the move had backfired, eliciting angry charges of censorship against the organization. When new text attacks surfaced in the early 1950s, then, the NAM moved quickly to distance itself from them. Appointing an "advisory committee" composed of leading educators, the NAM denounced "unjustified and damaging attacks on schools" by critics "who labor under the impression that education . . . means socialism and communism." It added a plea for textbooks that examined "all systems of government" in an "objective" fashion, earning praise from the NEA's Defense Commission but protest from America's conservative text campaign. A Los Angeles radio host charged that the NAM had adopted "much the same line" as John Dewey, perhaps the most vilified symbol of subversion in the schools. In New York another text critic headlined an attack on the NAM with a rhetorical question: "Who Is Looking Out for Capital?" Not the NAM, apparently. Abandoning its former role as a zealot for free enterprise, critics claimed, the NAM had capitulated to the creeping collectivism of postwar America.[34]

Just a year after she founded the *Educational Reviewer,* indeed, a bitter Lucille Crain admitted that American capitalists had proven largely uninterested in her efforts. Business contributions to the *Reviewer* were sluggish; even worse, she told her friend Rose Wilder Lane, businesses too often backed "collectivist" texts and curricula. "Why does yours seem such a comfortable shoulder on which to weep?" Crain wrote to Lane. "Here I am again, complaining about businessmen digging their own graves." Lane's response was philosophical, arguing that American corporations paid too much attention to profits and not enough to ideas. Here, Lane claimed, capitalists actually mirrored their communist foes: "The trouble is their belief that money is power. It's Marxian, of course." In an earlier note to Crain Lane had used even harsher language—and a different communist authority—to lambaste American businessmen:

> I agree with Lenin that there is nothing to do with them but kill them. And of course I do not contemplate killing them. They will accomplish this end, themselves. Seriously, as a matter of tactics, my opinion is that these men cannot think and that therefore it is a waste of time and energy to try to induce them to. Generally speaking, this group is the most dangerous one in this country because they have their thinking done for them; their money subsidizes the destructive socialists (who hate them for that reason).

Only the most blunt, unadorned arguments would ever penetrate such thick and stubborn skulls, Lane added. She quoted her own recent letter to the brokerage kingpin E. F. Hutton, who—like executives at Merrill Lynch—had refused to aid Crain's *Educational Reviewer:* "If you Big Business Men had the sense that God gives little green apples, you would act to protect your own property, your own liberty, your own lives, and that action would save this country. It is not the masses that need educating; it is the Mr. Huttons. And in my opinion you are not educable."[35]

Several businesses and small foundations did join William Buckley Sr. in financing the *Reviewer*. But even these allies hesitated to publicize their position: after donating a small sum to the *Reviewer,* for example, the Chrysler corporation balked at Crain's request to condemn several "subversive" texts in the Detroit schools. Moreover, this little corps of contributors could not possibly keep the *Reviewer* afloat once Buckley's three-year $23,000 donation had expired. The *Educational Reviewer* suspended publication in 1953; Amos Fries's *Bulletin of the Friends of the Public Schools* also died that year, another victim of business parsimony. "If you were supporting the Communists," an enraged Buckley wrote to Crain, "I am sure that they would have gotten you substantial help from Wall Street and the Carnegie and Rockefeller Foundations." Ignorant of their own interests, American capitalists were traitors to their country as well.[36]

As other correspondents admitted, however, the problem could not be blamed solely on American businesses. Fault lay with *Americans,* writ large, who simply did not heed activists' warnings in sufficient numbers. "When will the American people waken—Too late?" an Indiana ally wrote to Amos Fries in 1948. *"So many just don't know, and do not seem to care."* Three years later a Washington, D.C., supporter underscored the same problem. "If more people would express themselves strongly I am sure that we could get prompt results," wrote Adelbert W. Lee, vice president of the D.C. school board and a friend of Lucille Crain's, "but I am distressed at the apathy . . . I only hope that more people will wake up before it is too late." Shortly thereafter, Lee's school board colleagues would dismiss his charges of "subversion" against Magruder's *American Government.* They would cite not just the opinion of "trained educators"—who readily vouched for the text—but also that of "average" Washingtonians, who gave solid electoral victories to the board's pro-Magruder majority. However much they feared "Communism in the schools," it seemed, most Americans did not find it lurking in their children's textbooks.[37]

Turning South

As the Sons of the American Revolution heaped abuse upon the Building America series, California's board of education asked its attorneys to analyze the SAR's central accusation: that the series illegally "indoctrinated" children. The attorneys quickly dismissed the charge. Far from barring indoctrination, they argued, California law seemed to *require* it. After all, a statute enjoined schools to teach "morality, truth, justice, and patriotism" to every student. "It should be evident that there is nothing inherently wrong with indoctrination," the attorneys explained. "The problem is [the] selection of principles to be indoctrinated." The SAR sought to inculcate one form of "patriotism," while Building America aimed to instill another. Now Californians would have to decide which version they wanted their children to learn.[38]

For the next decade citizens throughout America would face the same decision. As the California attorneys correctly assumed, the vast majority of Americans agreed that schools—and especially text-books—should teach "patriotism." They also agreed that schools should eschew communism, the moral and political antithesis of patriotic Americanism. Within this broad anticommunist accord, however, sharp differences arose. To the SAR and its allies, the battle against communism demanded a full-scale assault on "collectivist" texts. Yet theirs was a minority voice, even during the heyday of the Cold War. By 1954, if not earlier, both the critics and the defenders of American textbooks declared that the campaign against the books had failed.

True, the movement had achieved some important victories. But even these triumphs were often temporary, revealing the overall weak-ness of the right-wing text campaign. A few weeks after Chicago's school board rejected Magruder's, public protests forced it to return the book to the city's "auxiliary" list. In Georgia, likewise, the state board of education restored the text two years after it was removed. As a sop to critics the board agreed to delete Magruder's brief section about the United Nations charter. But the Texas education board re-jected a similar demand, refusing to appease the state's "UN-haters," as one official boasted.[39]

Moreover, almost every legislature that considered bills to regulate textbook content rejected such measures. Even as they refused an appropriation for Building America, for example, California lawmak-ers also voted down a law to bar "propaganda" and "controver-sial books and teaching" from state classrooms. Illinois legislators defeated a bill that would have allowed any citizen to call for an eval-uation of "un-American material" in texts. After President Eisen-hower condemned "book-burning" in a commencement speech at

Dartmouth College in 1953, nearby Vermont rejected a measure to establish a "state censorship board" for school texts. Only Texas and Alabama passed "pure-text" laws, as opponents called them. Requiring authors to take an oath of loyalty—and publishers to swear that deceased authors *would* take the oath, if they were alive—the Texas measure was never enforced; in Alabama a court struck down the state's text law before it could go into effect.[40]

Likewise, state legislatures' antisubversive committees balked at the prospect of investigating or censoring school textbooks. Convened in dozens of states, these "little HUAC's" devoted a huge fraction of their efforts to identifying—and removing—allegedly "un-American" teachers and college professors. But textbooks were a different matter altogether. After a Maryland citizen complained about texts in his district, including Building America, the state's special prosecutor for subversive activities found "nothing subversive" in them; later he would reject several demands to examine and censor other books. When Washington State's un-American activities committee asked for permission to investigate textbooks, lawmakers simply refused to grant it. Only Illinois, with its notorious Broyles Commission on Seditious Activities, seems to have created an official "textbook censorship committee." During the single meeting it held, however, this panel could not agree on a definition of "subversion" or a mechanism for detecting it in Illinois texts. Discussion quickly shifted to the far less controversial subject of "Red" teachers, echoing the nation's larger pattern. By 1950 twenty-six states required teachers to take loyalty oaths; four years later more than 90 percent of Americans agreed that communist instructors should be fired. But lawmakers drew the line at textbooks, marking a critical division within the nation's anti-communist consensus.[41]

Like state legislators, Congress refused to regulate—or even to review—school textbooks. Indeed, its lone foray into the text question provided a rare instance in which lawmakers on both sides of the aisle acknowledged that they had overstepped their bounds. After their victory in California's battle over Building America, the Sons of the American Revolution petitioned Congress for a national investigation of "subversive propaganda" in textbooks. The House Un-American Activities Committee started to comply, asking a random sample of schools to provide lists of the texts they used. But this sole request caused such an outcry among educators that HUAC's chairman, John S. Wood, abruptly canceled the survey. Normally the most fervent anticommunists in Congress, Republicans took the lead in opposing any further text investigation; in fact, they blamed the entire episode on overzealous Democrats. Thereafter, both parties skirted the issue. A second SAR textbook complaint was diverted from HUAC to the Senate Committee on Labor and Public Welfare, where Chairman Elbert Thomas promptly buried it. Predictably, text critics responded by accusing Thomas of "communistic" sympathies. Like critics' local and state defeats, however, the congressional episode actually confirmed that the critics themselves had breached the far boundaries of America's anticommunist consensus. Even at the height of its frenzied search for subversion, Congress refused to extend the quest into textbooks.[42]

Taken together, all these failures—in school boards, state legislatures, and Congress—undermined the text attackers' claim that they spoke for "the people." Throughout the Cold War, thousands of veterans and other citizens rallied against textbooks. But this popular movement generated an even more popular "countermovement," as one observer remarked in 1954. The following year no less an authority than Harold Rugg pronounced the campaign against textbooks "dead or dormant," strangled by an outpouring of public sentiment in the books' defense. Applauding the large numbers of Americans who had backed the books—businessmen, journalists, and even a sprinkling of veterans—another educator declared hopefully that "the tide in textbook attacks has turned." From now on, he predicted, "extremist" voices would find smaller and smaller audiences for their complaints against the books.[43]

The tide did turn, but not quite in the direction that educators expected. Rather than evaporating altogether, right-wing text criticism drifted south of the Mason-Dixon Line.[44] The regional difference came into sharp relief with the publication in 1958 of *Brainwashing in the High Schools* by E. Merrill Root, a former English professor and a longtime contributor to right-wing journals. Providing a fairly standard critique of "Marxian collectivism" in high school history texts, Root added a more original—and incendiary—charge: that reading these texts had caused American prisoners to succumb to communist indoctrination during the Korean War. The claim won widespread ridicule in the North, where critics quickly retorted that eighteen of the twenty-one "turncoat" prisoners had not completed high school. Indeed, Root's book generated far more opposition than the history texts he had flayed. After Root testified on behalf of an Illinois textbook censorship bill in 1959, lawmakers and other witnesses trained their fire upon *him*. The future U.S. senator Paul Simon mocked Root's effort to "measure subversion by the inch"; on the other side of the chamber, a Republican legislator lambasted Root for impugning the patriotism of text authors; and in the sharpest attack, the historian Ray Allen Billington charged that Root had simply imagined a "Moscow-inspired force" in American textbooks. The text bill went down to a resounding defeat, as much a referendum upon Root as upon the books he had hoped to remove.[45]

In the South, though, Root received a far friendlier welcome. Just before his Illinois debacle, lawmakers in Mississippi enlisted Root to analyze twenty-seven supposedly subversive texts in their high schools. A Quaker from New England, Root was no segregationist: in his report to Mississippi legislators he openly acknowledged his own support for voluntary mixing of races in schools. But Root's rabid anticommunism could nevertheless buttress the segregationist cause, as southerners came to realize. After all, his list of "Reds" who were cited—or worse, celebrated—in "collectivist" texts included William O. Douglas, Eleanor Roosevelt, and many other prominent voices for racial justice. After Root condemned twelve Mississippi texts for their "pink political fog," lawmakers immediately demanded that schools remove them.[46]

During these same years, text attacks by national patriotic societies also revealed a decidedly southern shift. Apparently inspired by Root's *Brainwashing in the High Schools,* the Daughters of the American Revolution released a list of 170 objectionable texts in 1959. Unlike Root, whose work focused only on history, the DAR included literature, biology, music, and even arithmetic books on its roster of condemned texts. Like Root's book, however, the DAR list mainly influenced schools south of the Mason-Dixon Line. Northern members of the organization seem to have ignored or even condemned the text effort: in Connecticut one DAR leader charged that *attacks* on subversive books "have done more to subvert a free society" than the texts themselves. But in the South women seized eagerly upon the DAR campaign. Examining local text lists alongside the DAR roster, activists unearthed forty-four "subversive" books in Mississippi; in Georgia the total swelled to sixty-nine. Alabama's DAR, rather than simply comparing book titles, established its own textbook study committee. The panel found subversion lurking in every corner of the curriculum, especially in literature anthologies. For example, one story chronicled a lazy squirrel who raided a birdhouse for nuts. "Have you ever heard or read about a more subtle way of undermining the American system of work and profit and replacing it with a collectivist welfare system?" the DAR panel asked. "Can you recall a socialistic idea more seductively presented to an innocent child?"[47]

As the 1960s dawned, the new trend of "Teaching about Communism" exposed sharp regional differences in the battle against it. By 1962 six states had passed laws mandating special instruction about communism; in thirty-four others education departments included such teaching in the state curriculum. The trend began in the North, where advocates argued that an "objective" approach to communism would best prepare students for detecting and resisting it. "It is not necessary to maintain the position that everything about communism is a failure," warned a booklet issued jointly by the American Legion and the NEA. "Instruction about communism should not resort to the use of totalitarian propaganda techniques." In the

South, however, a singularly hostile view still held sway. Florida's law specified that schools "lay particular emphasis" on "the dangers of Communism, the ways to fight Communism, the evils of Communism, the fallacies of Communism, and the false doctrines of Communism." In Louisiana a teachers' guide for the course flatly declared that "socialism and the welfare state are waystations on the road to communism."[48]

Both states used films produced by Harding College, a small Arkansas school that was fast becoming the intellectual center of Southern anticommunism. But Harding was also increasingly marginalized by the rest of the nation. Even as southern schoolchildren watched Harding's film *Communism on the Map*, which warned of a Soviet plot to conquer the globe, the U.S. Department of Defense banned the movie from its own training facilities. In neighboring Mississippi, meanwhile, the arch-segregationist governor, Ross Barnett, mocked northerners for ignoring the communist menace in school textbooks. Seizing control of his state's text-selection system, Barnett vowed that all future books would defend "the Southern and true American way of life."[49] Barnett's equation of "Southern" with "true American" neatly captured the key shift in Cold War textbook attacks. Born as a largely northern campaign to defend America's "free enterprise system" from "creeping collectivism," the war on textbooks had become a southern fight to protect the country from a much more imminent threat: racial integration.

Black Activism, White Resistance, and Multiculturalism

In 1966 the prominent black historian John Hope Franklin and two colleagues published a new junior high school history textbook and submitted it for adoption in California. The previous year the state had passed a law requiring history texts to "correctly portray the role and contribution of the American Negro and members of other ethnic groups." Entitled *Land of the Free: A History of the United States,* the new textbook was crafted to satisfy the recent California measure— and, the authors hoped, to capture the rich California market. "American practice has not always measured up to the ideal of 'government by the people,'" Franklin and his co-authors declared in the introduction, noting the nation's historical discrimination against blacks, Indians, and women. Thanks to these groups' latter-day campaigns for civil rights, however, "actual rule by the people has become more and more of a reality," they added. "Most Americans agree that this trend should continue."[1]

But the book's reception suggested otherwise. Letters to California state officials ran almost two to one against adoption of the text, which critics accused of fomenting "agitation" among black students and "self-loathing" among whites. "We do not believe that you can improve race relations by continued emphasis on injustices of the past," wrote two angry correspondents, citing the textbook's lengthy analyses of slavery, segregation, and the struggles against each. "Neither do we believe that a generation of white students should be made to feel guilty." Some critics recommended that the text add "balance" to its allegedly "pro-Negro" accounts: many slaves were "happy," one asserted, while the battle against Jim Crow had brought with it "Black Power, the Watts riots, and the high Negro crime rate." To other white conservatives, however, *any* discussion of racial conflict would corrode patriotism—and promote cynicism—among children of *every* color. "This is no place to 'debunk' our heroes," another Californian wrote, clearly referring to white "heroes" rather than to black ones. "It should be the place to teach respect and admiration for them."[2]

After several rounds of revisions, *Land of the Free* won adoption in California as well as in a handful of urban school districts across the country. Yet this so-called integrated textbook continued to draw fire from white conservatives, who were soon joined by some unlikely allies: black nationalists. Shortly after Philadelphia adopted *Land of the Free,* thirty-five hundred African-American students rallied outside the school board office for separate courses and textbooks on black history. Although *Land of the Free* was a vast improvement over earlier "lily-white" texts, the students acknowledged, they asked for a history curriculum tailored to their specific problems and perspectives. "We've been taught to hate ourselves, our features, our hair," explained a sixteen-year-old student at Benjamin Franklin High School. "The movement is attempting to get blacks to *think* black." At Franklin two hundred students staged an all-night sit-in to demand courses on black history and "Afro languages," as well as black teachers to instruct these new classes. They also asked that the city made famous by Ben Franklin rename their school after *their* hero: Malcolm X.[3]

Together, these dual attacks on *Land of the Free*—and, more generally, on integrated history—suggest a revision of scholars' own narrative about the fate of history instruction over the past four decades. Most accounts of the subject follow a fairly linear model, in which the "liberal" history reforms of the 1960s are arrested or even reversed by a "conservative" reaction in the 1980s and 1990s.[4] By contrast, I argue that these changes were contested—and, most significantly, *constrained*—from the very start. Reformers did win important victories, forcing text publishers to add minority achievements and to delete egregiously racist passages. Thanks to the strange tandem of white racial conservatives and black racial militants, however, the traditional themes of American high school history—freedom, progress, and prosperity—remained mostly undisturbed. White watchdog groups blocked any material that might undermine the grand national narrative: George Washington Carver and Jackie Robinson were acceptable, as one *Land of the Free* critic wrote, but Nat Turner and Denmark Vesey were not.[5] Out in the schools, meanwhile, black students increasingly insisted that *any* national narrative would neglect or erase their distinctive experience. Abandoning the longtime quest for "inclusion" in the "regular" curriculum, these young militants demanded a curriculum of their own—not just in history, but in literature and the arts as well.

More than historians have appreciated, the militants succeeded. Less than two years after the citywide student demonstration in Philadelphia, nearly half of the city's junior high and secondary schools offered electives on black topics. The most commonly listed course was black history; others included African history, black art, Swahili, and "Chinjanja, the language of Mali." But this sharp growth came at a cost. At least 90 percent of the students enrolled in the new courses were black, raising the specter of two "race curricula" in schools—separate, antagonistic, and irreconcilable. As one African-American historian pointed out, many students could now select between a "white" history course—the standard U.S. survey class—and a "black" one. Even worse, the new black classes provided white school officials with a handy excuse for "doing little or nothing" to alter the so-called regular curriculum, as another scholar warned. Once the clamor for separate black courses died down, he predicted, American schools could expect "a full-scale return to segregated courses"—in other words, to an all-white version of the past.[6]

He was only half right. The push for black history classes subsided in the late 1970s, causing one embittered observer to dismiss the entire movement as a "fad."[7] But the campaign left a strong imprint on the general history curriculum, which opened its doors to a new set of multicultural heroes. Ballooning to seven hundred or even eight hundred pages, textbooks increasingly revered Frederick Douglass, César Chávez, and Sitting Bull as well as George Washington, Thomas Jefferson, and Abraham Lincoln. Even Turner and Vesey were now depicted as noble martyrs, in sharp contrast to the murderous fanatics that earlier texts had described. But nowhere did history books suggest that the new set of heroes required readers to reevaluate the old ones—for instance, that Douglass's critique of slavery might tarnish the image of Washington or Jefferson. Diversity and banality went hand in hand, the twin legacies of America's tortured encounter with race in the twentieth century.

Pricking the American Conscience

"When I were a child in Virginia, came Negro History time and Abraham Lincoln's birthday, every blackboard had pictures up of famous colored peoples, and every teacher would tell us about the great mens and womens of the colored race," declared the poet Langston Hughes's fictional character "Simple" in an article Hughes published in 1960. "We had some good colored teachers down South, and they had race pride, and they cared about our history." Following the Supreme Court's *Brown v. Board of Education* decision in 1954, Hughes complained, blacks had lost their passion for the subject. Here he echoed spokesmen for the Association for the Study of Negro Life and History, which dwindled after the death in 1950 of its founder Carter G. Woodson. "With the beginnings in public school integration . . . some people may presume that emphasis upon Negro history should be unnecessary," an ASNLH pamphlet worried in 1958. "Nothing could be farther from the truth!"[8]

Both Hughes and the ASNLH exaggerated the decline of black interest in black history. Throughout the 1940s and 1950s, blacks attacked racist slurs and misrepresentations in high school history texts. In New York they blasted a book that repeated the shibboleth of ignorant blacks looting the South during Reconstruction; in Chicago they protested a text that praised the Ku Klux Klan for protecting defenseless whites; and across the country they petitioned the well-known race liberals Samuel Eliot Morison and Henry Steele Commager to revise a popular textbook that described the typical American slave as a cheerful, contented "Sambo." For the most part, however, these attacks had little effect. A miffed Morison refused to change his book, noting that "Sambo" had been his own childhood nickname—and that his daughter was married to Joel Spingarn, president of the NAACP.[9] Even champions of so-called intergroup education in the 1950s turned a blind eye—or a disdainful frown—on black text protests.[10] Promoting special school assemblies to enhance racial tolerance and sensitivity, they dismissed black textbook critics as being *too* sensitive—and insufficiently tolerant. "To insist that Negroes be given equal rights with other citizens is one thing; to insist that their particular sensibilities entitle them to exercise a kind of censorship is quite another," opined the *Washington Post,* denouncing blacks' "humorless touchiness" about the term "Sambo" in textbooks.[11]

The civil rights revolution of the 1960s would alter American textbooks forever. Joining hands with a new and more sympathetic generation of white liberals, black activists forced the removal of numerous racial slurs. In 1962, most notably, a fresh edition of Morison and Commager's text dropped its infamous "Sambo" passage. And blacks managed to insert a wealth of new—and overwhelmingly positive—information about African-American history and culture. In the Morison and Commager book, for example, a description of slave runaways and rebellions replaced the earlier material about joyful and passive bondsmen.[12] Simultaneously, though, a resurgent white conservative movement blocked any larger revision of American history that the black experience might have implied. Racially plural but ideologically static, the integrated texts would set the stage for yet another African-American attack on history instruction in the late 1960s.

As early as 1959 a publishers' journal reported that "the drive to desegregate schools" had sparked black demands for integrated schoolbooks. Within the next few years nearly every leading civil rights organization entered the textbook arena. In 1961 a NAACP resolution demanded texts that "properly present the contribution of the Negro to American culture"; in 1963 Urban League officials called for a "nationwide struggle" against "all-white" textbooks; and in 1965 the Congress of Racial Equality deplored the books' "stereotypes and distortions of the role of Negroes." That same year the Urban League convened a tense conference between black leaders and representatives of the publishing industry. Most of the publishers endorsed the blacks' aims but cautioned against "moving too fast," fearing that white school boards would eschew integrated texts. Outraged black leaders retorted that publishers should produce "what people ought to know, not just what will sell," as Urban League director Whitney Young proclaimed. "Don't approach integration like castor oil," Young urged. "For once, look at something not as a problem but as an opportunity . . . Your job as human beings is to do what is right. Take a position."[13]

At the same time, black leaders recognized that they could not rely solely on publishers' altruism. Like all educational struggles, an NAACP official noted, the text battle would be won or lost "on the local level"—district by district, school by school. Rather than simply condemning racist books, then, the NAACP also asked black communities to organize against them. Across the country, thousands of African-Americans heeded the call. In Brooklyn, New York, activists produced a report decrying "racist poison" and "white supremacist propaganda" in local textbooks; as far away as Chicago, blacks used the same report to demand new texts in their respective school districts. The loudest dispute occurred in Detroit, where blacks asked school officials to remove the city's eighth-grade history text, *Our United States.* The book included a fictional account of a southern plantation overrun by "Yankees" during the Civil War. After a northern soldier reads the Emancipation Proclamation, an elderly slave, "Uncle Josephus," steps forward and asks, "Please sir, may we please go back to our work now?" Under heavy fire, the Detroit school board agreed to issue a "supplementary booklet" in 1963 that addressed blacks' "struggle for freedom and rights," including slave uprisings. But the board refused to drop *Our United States,* deeming it the "best book available."[14]

In protest, the black activist Richard B. Henry—probably the leading voice in Detroit's textbook war—withdrew his son from the schools. He also demanded a "Purification Commission" of citizens and school personnel, to "review *all* books now in the system" and "weed out those which are white supremacist." As Henry's language underlined, blacks' concerns about textbooks cut across the curriculum. Activists attacked books not only in history but also in English, geography, civics, science, and even home economics. As early as 1957 blacks in New York denounced Mark Twain's *Huckleberry Finn* for its use of the term "nigger" and for its portrait of the slave character Jim. Three years later a Connecticut NAACP chapter condemned a local high school literature anthology for reprinting Edgar Allan Poe's "The Gold-Bug," which also used "nigger." Yet in most instances, blacks complained, books used in English classes simply ignored them. The worst offenders were primary-school "readers," which retained their lily-white cast of characters well into the mid-1960s. A 1962 cartoon showed a black mother reading a first-grade primer to her daughter, who asks plaintively, "Where Am I?" The caption gave the sad answer: "Still Missing."[15]

Demanding a place in American textbooks, black activists used three basic arguments in the 1960s. Not surprisingly, all three were strongly connected to the era's civil rights movement. First, blacks claimed that accurate history texts might help persuade stubborn whites to revise their views on present-day quests for racial justice. "If *white* Americans knew the true facts about the Negro and his place *in* American history as contrasted with the diabolical myths of the 'stereotype' Negro," asserted one Philadelphia advocate on the eve of the 1964 Civil Rights Act, "the American conscience would be stirred and awakened by this powerful moral imperative." Especially after the Act passed, meanwhile, text activists claimed that new books were needed to translate its goals into practice. Regardless of what the law said about "equal rights," they noted, most whites would not *regard* blacks as equal until schoolbooks depicted them as such. The third argument concerned black psyches, not white ones. If texts continued to ignore or denigrate African-Americans, black children would develop "feelings of separateness and inferiority," as several Philadelphia activists wrote in 1964. Here they echoed the theories of Kenneth B. Clark and other "damage" theorists, whose work undergirded *Brown v. Board of Education* and many other arguments against Jim Crow. If physical segregation was harmful to blacks, "segregated" textbooks were just as dangerous—if not more so.[16]

Distinct but compatible, these claims often appeared side by side. In the final book he wrote before his death, for example, Martin Luther King Jr. argued that biased school curricula had augmented both "white supremacy" and "the Negroes' sense of worthlessness." Two years earlier, King recounted, his children's integrated school had staged a program of "music that has made America great." The event featured songs from various immigrant groups, but none from black America's rich musical tradition. At the end of the evening, to make matters worse, all of the children—including King's—sang "Dixie." King wept that night, he recalled, both for white children who learned that "the Negro is an irrelevant entity" and for blacks who were denied "a knowledge of their heritage." Indeed, he insisted, the latter problem amounted to the "cultural homicide" of black Americans. "The Negro must boldly throw off the manacles of self-abnegation and say to himself and the world, 'I am somebody . . . I have a rich and noble history, however painful and exploited that history has been,'" King wrote. No "Johnsonian civil rights bill" could help African-Americans attain this type of freedom, he cautioned. Statutes and laws might guard black rights, but only study and learning could free black minds.[17]

Nevertheless, the same "Johnsonian" liberals who designed civil rights protections in Washington also sought to enlist federal power on behalf of integrated history texts. Sometimes this effort was simply a matter of using the bully pulpit, as when Hubert Humphrey—Lyndon B. Johnson's vice president—condemned the "Negro history gap" in American schools. Under the Elementary and Secondary Education Act of 1965, meanwhile, Congress earmarked about $400 million for schools and libraries to purchase "multi-racial" and "multi-ethnic" books. Yet many districts continued to adopt "lily-white" ones, sparking a bitter set of hearings on Capitol Hill the following year. Convened by the Harlem legislator Adam Clayton Powell, the hearings featured pleas by several black spokesmen to withhold federal funds from schools that used all-white books. After all, the spokesmen reasoned, Congress could already deny funds to districts that segregated students. Why not assign the same penalty to schools that purchased "segregated" texts?[18]

The answer, replied U.S. Commissioner of Education Harold Howe II, lay in America's venerable tradition of local control in education. Although he strongly supported black legislators' goal of integrated textbooks, Howe explained, he could not countenance any measure that allowed federal officials to "dictate" or "censor" content. Other critics seemed less worried by the principle of federal control than by its likely outcome: mixed-race books. "If they want to integrate, fine. If they don't, fine," North Carolina's school superintendent told the Powell hearings in a brief in favor of "local selection" of texts. "The events of the past week have been to force people to integrate [textbooks] beyond what they want to."[19]

As the last remark illustrated, the drive for integrated texts—like the battle for integrated schools—met with white resistance and recrimination. Hostility to the text campaign cut across America's regions, but it also differed from place to place. Southerners were the most likely to invoke an explicit racial doctrine: blacks and whites simply should not mix, whether in classrooms or in text illustrations. "When a publisher goes before an adoption committee in a southern state," one textbook company executive noted in 1965, "the first question he is asked is, 'Are there any pictures of Negroes in these books of yours?'" If the publisher's answer was yes, educators usually said no to the texts in question. Beyond the issue of illustrations, southerners often rejected books that mentioned "problems" or "difficulties" surrounding race. As late as 1969 whites in Birmingham, Alabama, blocked a textbook for alluding to the church bombing that killed four black girls in the city in May 1963. In truth, the text's authors bent over backward to appease local sensibilities: attributing the tragedy to lower-class "white extremists," they absolved Birmingham's political and economic elites. Into the early 1970s, however, *any* reference to racial violence, hostility, or prejudice often spelled the removal of a textbook.[20]

The slow trickle of black notables into the books also brought white protest in the South. In Florida a teacher who used a text showing black Union soldiers during the Civil War found the tires of her car slashed and its windows covered with warnings. Other critics objected to newly included "black heroes" like Frederick Douglass and Ralph Bunche, whose stories tended to place whites in a negative light. "For God's sake," pleaded a white Virginian in 1970, "give us some history to be proud of." Even as they condemned the inclusion of famous blacks in the texts, however, the same critics often alleged that these individuals were not black at all. "That man Bunche [is] around 75% white and COMES FROM GERMAN JEW STOCK, and has never used the Jungle brains of his Negro ancestors," wrote a particularly rabid white critic in Maryland. As illogical as they were hateful, his dual claims—that the textbook shouldn't include blacks, and that they weren't black anyhow—resembled the "broken-pot defense" of courthouse lore: my client did not steal the pot, and besides, it was already cracked.[21]

In the North, by contrast, whites tended to phrase their objections to textbooks in class terms rather than racial ones. Rarely did a northern white critic of integrated textbooks—or, for that matter, of integrated classrooms—invoke inherent differences between blacks and whites.[22] Instead, northerners complained that well-to-do elites had imposed a pinched, negative conception of America on hard-working, patriotic Americans. This view was particularly apparent in the hostile reaction that greeted the 1968 Kerner Commission Report on urban riots, which suggested that "racism" caused these disorders—and that textbooks were an important vehicle for its transmission. Nonsense, replied many working-class whites. "These were not wise men who descended from the mountain, tablet in hand, that were chosen to perpetuate the myth that the white race is racist," a New Yorker wrote after school officials cited the Kerner Report in a plea for more "realistic" discussions of racism in state textbooks. "The only people who accept the findings of that Report are the guilt-ridden liberal intellectual community who accuse themselves of being 'Reformed Racists' from 9 to 5 and repair to their exclusive country clubs after hours." The satirist Jules Feiffer captured this working-class white jeremiad in a cartoon depicting a worker in a hard hat who complained:

> When I went to school I learned that George Washington never told a lie, slaves were happy on the plantation, the men who opened the West were giants, and we won every war because God was on our side. But where my kid goes to school he learns that Washington was a slaveowner, slaves hated slavery, the men who opened the West committed genocide, and the wars we won were victories for U.S. imperialism. No wonder my kid's not an American. They're teaching him some other country's history.[23]

Most of all, white conservatives claimed, textbooks' new emphasis on race would bias children of all colors against their country. "Of course, we do have much of which we are not proud," admitted one California parent, "but why play up our mistakes, downgrade our heroes, and please our enemies?" She took aim at John Hope Franklin's *Land of the Free,* which harped on America's long history of prejudice—and thereby played into "unpatriotic" and "Communistic" hands. In fact, critics complained, *Land of the Free* mimicked the Soviet tendency to "re-write" history in accord with present-day concerns. Whereas Russian books inevitably brightened their nation's image, however, *Land of the Free* steadfastly darkened America's. "It is like a beautiful red apple, but inside this red apple we find a worm," wrote another Californian. "This book is written on negativism to give the child a feeling of guilt of the injustices imposed upon the Indians, the immigrant, and, particularly, the Negro, by his forefathers." The struggle over *Land of the Free* was part of a much larger fight "for the minds of our youth," the critic continued. "It is becoming very unpopular to stand up for America."[24]

After a long battle, *Land of the Free* won adoption in the state. But first the book was revised to temper its emphasis on "national shortcomings," mirroring America's larger pattern of textbook development in the 1960s. To be sure, hundreds of textbooks that had ignored or denigrated minorities now included accurate and sympathetic material about them. Texts also devoted increased attention to formerly tabooed subjects like Nat Turner's revolt and the World War II internment of Japanese-Americans. As a Michigan survey revealed, however, such episodes were rarely presented as "an integral part of the narrative." In other words, the new information about minorities was not allowed to alter the old story about peace, justice, and freedom. The price that white America exacted for diversity in the textbooks was triumphalism in their tone.[25]

Whenever new textbooks threatened to tarnish white America's image, indeed, white Americans mobilized quickly against them. In Michigan parents who happily countenanced Jackie Robinson and Louis Armstrong in their textbooks bridled at one book's description of Chicago's 1919 race riot. Quoting a Polish youngster who urged violence against "niggers," the passage outraged Michigan's large Polish-American population. "Education is getting a positive image about oneself," one parent explained. "No child, white or black, will get a positive image by reading about stabbings, war, the problems. For me, our history is still made up of heroes and heroines, but when you look at these books, there are no heroes and heroines."[26]

The last remark pointed to a final legacy of 1960s textbooks: the flowering of "ethnicity." From Poles and Puerto Ricans to Italians and Indians, dozens of ethnic groups won recognition in the texts. By 1966, in fact, a single primary school reader in Chicago depicted no fewer than fourteen different ethnicities. Copying black activists, ethnic spokesmen sometimes clashed with them as well: in California, for example, Native Americans and Hispanics both denounced *Land of the Free* for devoting too much attention to African-Americans and not enough to other groups. *All* Americans deserved a place in the texts, one Chicano activist wrote, which would ensure "greater pride in their ethnic group" as well as a "greater sense of personal worth and dignity." Congress enshrined this view in law with the Ethnic Heritages Act of 1972, providing federal funds to stimulate "greater awareness of cultural variety" in the curriculum.[27] By this late date, however, many black Americans were doubting whether "regular" school courses could do justice to *their* culture. Although they had been the key architects of America's new multi-ethnic textbooks, blacks increasingly abandoned this project in favor of a separate history: their own.

Black Resistance to Integrated History

The Black Action Movement of Kalamazoo, Michigan, typified this militant trend. Composed mainly of high school students, the group sent a letter to its local school board in 1967 deploring several "violent incidents" between black and white pupils. Then the group listed two major demands: black representation on the cheerleading squad and black history courses in the curriculum. As one observer noted, the first request echoed the integrationist impulse of Kalamazoo's NAACP, an "older and less militant" organization. But the call for separate classes reflected a growing sense of nationalism among young blacks—and an impatience with the NAACP's "integrationist" approach. In the gymnasium, to be sure, blacks still aimed to "make history" by breaking racial barriers. But in the classroom, increasingly, they wished to *study* that history on their own.[28]

Within the next four years dozens of school districts reported similar demands by black students. In Plainfield, New Jersey, three hundred students boycotted classes for a day, gathering at a local youth center to hold their own history "teach-in"; eighty-two blacks walked out of school in Erie, Pennsylvania, earning a two-week suspension from their incensed principal. Even Evanston, Illinois—"one of the Midwest's wealthiest, most conservative, most self-satisfied suburbs," in the words of one journalist—witnessed a "history strike" by two hundred African-American students. The largest demonstration for black history courses occurred in Philadelphia, where thirty-five hundred students rallied outside the Board of Education headquarters. School officials later admitted that they had been caught unaware by the protest, which culminated in a violent melee with local police. "The voices of students were heard loud and clear on college campuses at least four years ago [but] most of us in basic education failed to read the signals clearly," said the city's school superintendent, Mark Shedd, "and bang, the student rebellion has crept downward in age group." Like black university students, it seemed, black high schoolers wanted courses that were "relevant" to their "needs"— especially in history.[29]

Many of the protests occurred in cities that had already adopted integrated history textbooks. Yet as one Detroit school official explained, students wanted "their *own* history" rather than a "revised edition of American history." By 1969, indeed, young black militants already rivaled white conservatives as the leading critics of the integrated approach. Of course, blacks and whites had sharply different reasons for their opposition. Whereas whites worried that new texts overemphasized the black experience, African-Americans argued that the texts underestimated it. "I think if they intermingle black history with regular U.S. history, they'll miss a lot," argued a member of the Black Peacestone Rangers at a Milwaukee high school. "They won't put as much as they would if there was a separate course." Even where textbooks and course syllabi included substantial material about blacks, moreover, this information received short shrift in the classroom. The problem was captured by a cartoon in a New York underground student newspaper, showing a white teacher at a blackboard. "Today we're going to talk about Negroes in America," the teacher announces. "We have just talked about Negroes in America, now on to the principal battles of . . ."[30]

Second, students complained, teachers who *did* discuss black history presented it from a "white" rather than from a "black" perspective. Black achievements and struggles were used to demonstrate the overall strength and justice of "America," obscuring the nation's continued oppression of African-Americans. "When you study America they say, America—land of the free," complained a black student in Peoria, Illinois. "I see blacks asking for freedom, but they don't get it . . . And the teachers refuse to admit this." Here, too, blacks reversed the white conservative critique: whereas whites thought integrated history belittled the grand national story, blacks claimed that it bolstered that same story. Although Frederick Douglass and even Nat Turner might receive respectful hearings in integrated textbooks, the texts more often lionized a Crispus Attucks or a Jackie Robinson. Like the books' white heroes, Attucks and Robinson seemed to confirm the essential virtue of America; Douglass and Turner did not. "When I said write a report about a great American, I meant someone like George Washington or Benjamin Franklin," declared a teacher in a 1968 cartoon, scolding black students in her class. "I've never even heard of Denmark Vesey!"[31]

To many young blacks in the late 1960s, the solution to this problem was obvious: they needed separate history classes, in which *they* chose the heroes. For all of their eloquent attacks upon "white" teaching, blacks rarely questioned one of its central tenets: that history required the selection and celebration of "great" individuals (almost always men). Instead, blacks demanded new ones. "Crispus Attucks laid down his life for America, but would he have laid down his life to stop the white man in America from enslaving black people?" asked Malcolm X in a much-quoted 1964 address. "So when you select heroes . . . let them be black heroes who have died fighting for the benefit of black people." Like Martin Luther King Jr., Malcolm X frequently argued that blacks needed to study their history in order to surmount their sense of inferiority. To Malcolm and his young black admirers, however, the destructive effects of physical segregation could only be overcome by an equally segregated curriculum. Especially where black students had been scarred by Jim Crow, schools needed separate courses stressing "the positive elements" of blacks' "racial and cultural heritage," as one sympathetic white scholar wrote.[32]

It followed that these classes should be taught by blacks, students argued, not by "Negroes" or whites. "Negroes" referred to black teachers who had been "debased, demoralized, and brainwashed" by "white" history, a black student newspaper in New York put it. Nor could white instructors successfully oversee "the *true* instillment of *self-image*" into young blacks, the paper added. If whites were hired to teach black history courses, they would "teach the lessons from a *white* point of view, thereby *whitening* the images of our already little known heroes." In Los Angeles, similarly, blacks scoffed when a white teacher was assigned to a black history course. "He couldn't be relevant if he wanted to," one student jeered. True, other blacks admitted, well-meaning white teachers had amassed impressive knowledge of the black past. Try as they might, however, these instructors could never offer the direction and inspiration that black students needed. "If you want to learn how to be a carpenter, you get apprenticed to a carpenter, not a bricklayer," one activist explained. To learn "true" black history, a black child must "apprentice" with a black teacher.[33]

Many black students applied the same argument to the rest of the curriculum. From the arts and foreign languages to science and even math, blacks' distinct culture mandated different classes. "They don't have any black oriented courses in this school," complained one student. "In home economics they don't teach the black girls to cook for the black men they will eventually marry; in sewing class they don't teach them how to make any Afro or Afro-American clothing."[34] The problem was especially acute in English literature, where white citizens and school boards often blocked works by James Baldwin, Claude Brown, Eldridge Cleaver, and Langston Hughes. As in the battle over history, some blacks joined with like-minded whites to demand the study of these authors in the regular curriculum.[35] More commonly, however, black students demanded their own "Black Literature" courses alongside black history.[36]

Especially in large cities, they succeeded dramatically. In less than five years, black students effected one of the most remarkable transformations of the public school curriculum in the twentieth century. By 1970 Los Angeles offered four separate electives in black history, black literature, African studies, and Swahili; a single high school in Berkeley created eight different "black-oriented" courses, including African dance, economics of African-Americans, and history of jazz. In theory, such courses were open to students of every race. In practice, though, white students avoided them. Chicago initially provided black history electives at all of its forty-seven high schools, but soon removed the courses from predominantly white schools for lack of enrollment. Only in Cleveland did a majority-white school garner sufficient registration for a black history course; significantly, most *blacks* in that school eschewed the course because it lacked an "adequately militant viewpoint." Everywhere else, it seemed, black students dominated black history. In Madison, Wisconsin, pupils in the course even created their own study lounge. "Knock Before Entering or Suffer Consequences," warned a sign on its door. "This is a Black Concentrated Study Area. All Blacks Welcome."[37]

Likewise, most African-American adults probably welcomed the new black-studies courses. According to polls, only a small fraction of black Americans supported the separatist political agenda of militant groups like the Black Panthers. But blacks demonstrated much more sympathy for the Panthers' cultural goals, which included separate black history courses in the schools. Without such courses, warned the Michigan congressman John Conyers, "our nation's traditional white education will continue . . . turning black students into whitened sepulchers to assure the stability of the status quo." Out in the schools, most black teachers and administrators still backed the long-range goal of integrated history. But in the short term, they said, schools must provide separate black history classes "to help older students make up for years of neglect." A truly integrated American history *required* a segregated curriculum, at least for the time being.[38]

To be sure, several prominent black educators refused to board the black-studies bandwagon. In Philadelphia, for example, the black minister and school board vice president Henry N. Nichols complained that new black courses threatened to establish a "South African Bantu system" in the city. The NAACP's executive director, Roy Wilkins, warned against replacing "white history" with "black history," George Washington with George Washington Carver; in fact, Wilkins suggested, schools that divided courses in this fashion might be in violation of the 1964 Civil Rights Act. Even among the NAACP's militant critics, blacks often questioned the separatist tendencies of black studies. "I happen to be one black power advocate that does not go along with the idea that we can do it all by ourselves," declared the Washington, D.C., educator and activist Julius Hobson. Instead, Hobson told a congressional hearing, blacks should "integrate our history into American history and do it on an honest basis." Another black skeptic cautioned that separate courses were more likely to reinforce—not to revise—the myths of "white" history. After all, black history courses allowed white school officials to appease black "agitators" while ignoring the biases of the regular curriculum. Radical in its rhetoric, "black history" would be deeply conservative in its consequences.[39]

From Black History to Multiculturalism

The movement for a separate black history in American schools fizzled almost as quickly as it flared, leaving a vapor trail of frustration and recrimination. One basic cause of the decline was the lack of qualified teachers. Eager to hire blacks to teach "black-oriented" courses, too many schools, one critic wrote, appointed instructors "whose only credentials are 1. an Afro hair style and 2. a dashiki and beads." In the classroom, hastily prepared black-studies textbooks and curricula often transmitted their own historical inaccuracies: one text informed students that Columbus had received permission "to exploit the underdeveloped lands" from "the King of Europe." Most of all, black history courses were simply boring. Like regular history classes, they quickly devolved into lists of names and dates that were memorized—and forgotten—each year. "Who's this Crispus Attucks that keeps getting killed off every semester?" black students in California quipped.[40]

Created to spark pride among African-American youth, black history seemed to have the opposite effect. By 1978 NAACP director Benjamin Hooks complained that young blacks' interest in their past had never been lower. The black columnist Jim Cleaver reported visiting East Berlin, where "little white children" told him "the life story of Paul Robeson"; back in Los Angeles, however, black children had never even heard of him. "It is about time that we stopped sitting on our butts, crying the blues about what the system does or does not do, and make some changes in the minds and the education of our children," Cleaver wrote. He even looked back wistfully on the "Negro History" of his own childhood in the segregated South, where teachers "understood that Black children needed to know about their forebears." To black militants in the late 1960s, "Negro" signified racial treason, a bootlicking capitulation to white authority. But as Cleaver sadly noted, the self-proclaimed "Negro" children at his Kentucky elementary school—a school named, appropriately, after the black poet Phillis Wheatley—had known far more black history than most present-day African-Americans did.[41]

Still, blacks could point to several clear and indisputable victories that emerged from the turmoil over race and history in the 1960s. Dozens of states passed laws or resolutions requiring the study of American minorities, including Hispanics, Asians, and Native Americans as well as African-Americans. States and school districts also made new efforts to celebrate Negro History Week, which was renamed African-American History Week and then Black History Week in the early 1970s. By 1973 even George C. Wallace proclaimed it in Alabama. Probably America's preeminent symbol of white racism and recalcitrance, Wallace urged Alabamians "to pay special attention . . . to the many contributions that African-Americans have made to our state and nation." In 1976 Congress designated the entire month of February Black History Month; by 1980 every state had adopted it for their schools. Long barred or simply ignored in American classrooms, the study of African-Americans had actually become a requirement in them.[42]

Also, textbooks devoted far greater attention—and more accurate information—to blacks and other minorities. As recently as 1966 southern school districts had balked at the mere appearance of blacks in textbook illustrations. By the early 1980s, however, students across the country read about Sojourner Truth and Frederick Douglass, Booker T. Washington and W. E. B. Du Bois, Martin Luther King Jr. and Malcolm X. Textbooks also admitted an assortment of other ethnic luminaries, ranging from Pocahontas and Sacajawea to Roberto Clemente and Cesar Chavez. Given white America's longtime resistance to diversity in history, this development was no less astonishing—and no less momentous—than George C. Wallace's proclamation of African-American History Week.

Several demographic and political changes accounted for the sharp rise of integrated textbooks in the late 1960s and 1970s. The first, ironically, was the decline of integrated *schools* in the urban North. The era witnessed an enormous exodus of whites into private schools or the suburbs, turning formerly biracial city school districts into heavily black ones. By 1976 twenty-one of America's twenty-nine largest school districts had black majorities. In Detroit, where blacks accounted for 44 percent of residents in 1970, 64 percent of students in the schools were African-American. Just ten years later blacks made up 63 percent of the city's population—and 86 percent of its school-children.[43]

Publishers quickly identified these newly segregated school systems as huge potential markets for "integrated" textbooks. As early as 1963 the publisher of *Our United States*—the text that had sparked black protest in Detroit—began to remove offending passages. "If we win an adoption in Detroit, we don't care about Mississippi," the publisher explained. "We sell more books in Detroit." The following year Detroit did readopt the revised version of *Our United States*. Four years after that the city school board released one of the nation's first district-wide standards for "multi-ethnic publishing." Warning against too many illustrations of "slum environments," the Detroit guidelines instructed publishers to show minorities "in positions of leadership." Most significantly, the guidelines specified that 25 percent of pictures in each text should include a member of a minority group. Although nonwhites made up just 14 percent of the nation's population, one publishing official noted, they were a majority in Detroit. "Twenty-five percent representation is a compromise which is acceptable in Detroit," he concluded, "and should be equally acceptable in other areas of the nation."[44]

By the early 1970s even the South began to adopt integrated texts. Lest they lose customers south of the Mason-Dixon Line, publishers initially released all-white "mint julep" editions along with their integrated ones. Thanks to strong federal oversight and intervention, however, southern school systems became *more* integrated during the same years when urban districts in the North became less so. On the eve of the Civil Rights Act of 1964, only 2 percent of southern black children attended majority-white schools; just six years later one-third of them did. With more blacks going to the polls as well as to integrated schools, officials risked their political careers if they continued to adopt mint julep texts. "There were few public attacks [on] history textbooks so long as the ideals they represented remained dominant," wrote a Virginia observer in 1970, noting black protests against a history text that described "cheerful" slaves. "What used to be good politics has become bad politics." Virginia's state board of education dropped the offending text two years later. The board also directed that new texts include more illustrations and information about racial minorities, especially African-Americans and Hispanics.[45]

Nevertheless, two other factors continued to constrain what textbooks could say—and what students could learn—about America. First, texts retained an emphasis on "positive images" in history: every ethnic group could have its place in the textbook sun, so long as no textbook ever said a dark or critical word about its members. "The principle that lies behind textbook history," Frances Fitzgerald would observe in 1979, "is that the inclusion of nasty information constitutes bias even if the information is true." Hence texts that formerly had described Spanish conquistadors' attacks on Indians now made no mention of this violence, lest Hispanic readers take offense. Native Americans might object, as well, arguing that these passages reinforced the stereotype of Indian-as-weakling or Indian-as-victim. Best, then, to downplay or omit the entire episode. Likewise, passages about present-day minorities omitted anything about their problems; even illustrations invariably showed them with smiles, Fitzgerald noticed, as if "all non-white people in the United States took happy pills."[46] The more America widened its ethnic scope, the more it seemed to narrow its critical lens.

Second, textbooks never revised—or even examined—the larger narrative that supposedly bound these "happy" groups together. To be sure, the fulsome praise of America in its history books was as old as America itself. Thanks to the dual efforts of white and black activists, though, this tradition emerged essentially unscathed from the turmoil of the 1960s. Whites allowed new actors into the national story so long as the story stayed the same; blacks often abandoned this narrative altogether in a quest to create their own. The result was a history of many parts but no whole, other than a bland affirmation of "freedom" and "democracy." Just as Black History Month was added to the school calendar, black history was tacked on to American textbooks. Presented in this detached and disjointed manner, it allowed citizens of every color to avoid the crucial question: What does the black experience tell us about America?

In March 1968 the author James Baldwin testified before Congress on behalf of a proposed National Commission on Negro History and Culture. Baldwin heartily endorsed the commission's goal of promoting greater study and awareness of black history. But he also insisted that this study occur as part of *American* history, lest whites and blacks alike miss its real meaning. "It is our common history. My history is also yours," he told lawmakers. "My history, though, contains the truth about America. It is going to be hard to teach it." By presenting black history as a separate story, American schools undoubtedly made it easier to teach. But they also evaded its difficult implications, adding a special poignancy to Baldwin's final plea: "I am the flesh of your flesh and bone of your bone; I have been here as long as you have been here—longer—I paid for it as much as you have. It is my country, too. Do recognize that that is the whole question. My history and culture has got to be taught. *It is yours.*"[47]

GOD IN THE SCHOOLS

On July 21, 1925, a jury in Dayton, Tennessee, convicted John T. Scopes of violating a state law that prohibited the teaching of evolution in public schools. Immediately, both parties to the conflict claimed victory. To the anti-evolution stalwart William Jennings Bryan, who assisted the prosecution, the *Scopes* verdict upheld the "moral" truths of the Bible over the "material" explanations of science. Despite their defeat in Dayton, meanwhile, Scopes's attorneys insisted that they had triumphed in a much more important venue: the court of public opinion. "I think this case will be remembered because it is the first case of this sort since we stopped trying people in America for witchcraft," declared the leading defense lawyer, Clarence Darrow. Another Scopes attorney called the trial a "victorious defeat," because "future generations will know the truth" about human evolution.[1]

Both sides were wrong. Wary of causing further controversy, publishers quietly pared most material about evolution from high school biology textbooks. Anti-evolutionists remained fairly quiet, too, withdrawing from public view to build their own fundamentalist ministries, schools, and colleges.[2] But they returned to the fray in the 1940s and 1950s, when a new battle about religion shook American public schools. Contrary to the shared presumptions of Bryan and

Darrow, the conflict did not concern *whether* to teach religion but rather *what* religion to teach. Mainline Protestants asked schools to transmit an expansive, "social" brand of Christianity, stressing the Bible's proclamation of peace in this world rather than its promise of salvation in the next one. Here they clashed not just with Jews and Catholics but also with a resurgent fundamentalist movement, which sought only to convert each student to Christ.

Mainline Christians abandoned public school religious training in the early 1960s, when the Supreme Court banned teacher-led prayers and Bible reading. But religious worship continued, promoted by African-Americans as well as by white conservatives. Advocates of prayer in the schools initially aimed to restore a "Christian America," returning a wayward nation to the word of God. By the 1980s, however, they phrased their appeal in terms of minority rights rather than scriptural authority. On the question of sex education as well as on prayer, Christian conservatives argued, schools should award *their* culture the same respect and recognition that racial and ethnic minorities received.

Here conservatives echoed the renewed drive against evolution, which followed a similar path from moralism to pluralism. After the Supreme Court's 1968 decision in *Epperson v. Arkansas,* which struck down state bans on the teaching of evolution, Christian activists started to demand measures requiring "equal time" for biblical and Darwinian viewpoints. The Court's 1987 ruling in *Edwards v. Aguillard* dealt this movement a temporary setback, rejecting a Louisiana law that would have required schools to present "creationism" alongside evolution in the classroom. But anti-evolutionists simply shifted their focus from legislatures to school boards, where they won a host of equal-time provisions. Like prayer supporters, they were careful to request the inclusion of their beliefs rather than the exclusion of others. Even Moral Majority founder Jerry Falwell conceded that John T. Scopes should not have been convicted at Dayton, because Scopes was "teaching both points of view—evolution and creation."[3]

To skeptics, conservatives' embrace of pluralism was simply a ploy to reinstitute religious instruction. From a different standpoint, though, the new pluralist consensus represents a momentous opportunity to improve *all* instruction in our schools. In history classes, especially, a wide variety of perspectives on America's checkered past would encourage students to develop their own interpretations of it. A healthy democracy requires citizens who have the skills and desire to make up their own minds—about evolution, history, and everything else.

Religious Education
in Public Schools

In January 1946 Erwin L. Shaver, America's leading religious educator, sent a triumphant bulletin to newspapers across the country. A court in Champaign, Illinois, had upheld the city's system of "released time," Shaver announced, whereby students moved to different classrooms once a week to receive religious instruction from their respective churches. As director of Weekday Religious Education (WRE) for the International Council of Religious Education, a multi-faith umbrella group, Shaver had watched nationwide WRE enrollments skyrocket from 250,000 in 1935 to about 1.5 million by the end of World War II. In New York City alone, more than 170,000 pupils participated in the program. "The world situation . . . has stirred us as never before," Shaver wrote, alluding to the "human depravity" of the war. "People in all walks of life are turning to moral and religious education . . . It is essentially a grass roots expression of spiritual need."[1]

Privately, however, Shaver worried that some of the roots might sprout into poisonous weeds. Even as judges upheld WRE, he warned, "fundamentalist" groups were mounting "a vigorous bid for control" of it. Whereas mainline churches stressed Jesus' message of peace and social justice, Shaver noted, fundamentalist WRE classes attended only to his pledge of individual redemption. Hence they also drew upon "'hill billy' singing" and the other "emotional" techniques of revival, hoping to shepherd young flocks into Christ's kingdom. "There are many people in these movements who cannot be assimilated," Shaver cautioned in a confidential report on "conservative Christians" and the public schools. "Their stock in trade is criticism of the established churches and opposition to liberal social outlook and interpretation of the gospel." Especially in rural areas, he added, fundamentalists were poised to displace the "modernistic" churches that had started WRE. Although the courts had affirmed the concept of weekday religious education, in short, its content remained very much in dispute.[2]

Two years later the U.S. Supreme Court would overturn the Illinois rulings and invalidate Champaign's WRE plan. Writing for the majority in *McCollum v. Board of Education*, Justice Hugo Black famously ruled that Champaign's released-time system breached the First Amendment's "wall between Church and state." But WRE continued, fueled as much by competition between Christians as by their shared contempt for the Court's decision. In one California community students could select from four released-time options during the 1949–1950 school year: Mainline Protestant, Evangelical, Roman Catholic, and Christian Science. The mainline class would emphasize "Living as World Christians," according to its advertisement in the local *Released Time Weekly Herald*. By contrast, the evangelicals' announcement stressed "belief in the Bible as God's Word" and "knowledge of Christ as personal savior." Catholics celebrated the sacraments as well as "the establishment of the Church by Christ," while Christian Scientists taught children to interpret the Bible in light of Mary Baker Eddy's *Science and Health*. Only Jews declined to participate in the program, complaining that it underscored "religious differences"—and thereby undermined harmony across them.[3]

Where released time was suspended or eliminated, finally, ministers sought to infuse the *regular* curriculum with new religious content. Nothing in the *McCollum* decision forbade Bible reading in the schools, clergymen emphasized. Nor did the Supreme Court bar prayers, religious pageants, church music, and other devotionals that might "fill part of the gap" left by vanishing WRE programs, as Shaver wrote in 1949. Shaver especially welcomed the new ecumenical movement to teach "moral and spiritual values" in public schools, reminding children of different faiths about the "divine authority" that bound them together. Even at this high level of abstraction, however, interfaith unity was often elusive. Jews opposed almost all school-based religious exercises, which would either bootleg Christianity into the schools or distill every theology into a bland, colorless brew. The latter concern was echoed by fundamentalist Protestants, who flinched at the idea of "compromise" with other faiths. "Religion taught on the basis of common elements reached by striking out all differences in creeds might satisfy more liberal religionists," declared one fundamentalist leader in 1951, "but to the evangelical Christian it would be not only inadequate but also repugnant." Better to strip the schools of all traces of religion than to teach children a religion that was not true.[4]

Together these examples illustrate the sharp antagonisms surrounding religion in postwar public education. Most historians of the subject adopt a legalistic "church/state" perspective, stressing the courts' efforts to delimit *when* and *how* religion might be taught or practiced in the schools.[5] By contrast, I trace the bitter struggles between religious groups over *what* the curriculum would contain. Working sometimes within and often beyond the shifting boundaries of court doctrine, liberal Protestants promoted courses and exercises to stress "Christian social relationships" and "the real meaning of brotherhood," as a Virginia minister wrote.[6] In this they were challenged not just by Jewish groups—a central theme of the church/state literature—but also by Christian fundamentalists, who sought to inject their own values and perspectives into the schools. Even Jews occasionally tried to influence the curriculum, despite their leaders' demands for a "strict separation" between religion and government.[7] Defending released-time programs as well as joint Hanukkah-Christmas celebrations, some Jews argued that "the people of the

Book" should support, not suppress, religious instruction. Echoing liberal Protestant fears of fundamentalists, other Jews warned that sects like the Lubavitchers would move into the schools if the mainstream rabbinate refused to do so.

In the late 1940s and 1950s a powerful consensus about religion—a "faith in faith"—seized American culture and politics. Congress added "under God" to the Pledge of Allegiance, made "In God We Trust" the slogan for currency, and set aside funds for its own prayer room; in the White House, Dwight D. Eisenhower famously remarked that Americans required "a deeply felt religious faith—and I don't care what it is." Songs like "The Man Upstairs" and "Big Fellow in the Sky" climbed to the top of the charts; Hollywood blockbusters included *The Ten Commandments* and *A Man Called Peter;* and a doll that could kneel in a praying position was marketed by the Ideal Toy Company, which hailed "the resurgence of religious feeling and practice in America today."[8] Yet this apparent agreement on the importance of "faith" masked crucial debates about its actual content, as the struggle for WRE demonstrates. Throughout the early postwar period, released-time classes would expose the bitter rivalries and antagonisms beneath America's façade of religious consensus.

Weekday Religious Instruction

As America emerged from the Great Depression, religious leaders in New York and North Carolina launched ambitious new efforts to shore up religious instruction in their respective states. In 1940 a special White House conference on "Children in a Democracy" had reported that half of American youngsters never attended church or Sunday school. Stepping into this breach, New York churchmen won a bill allowing public schools to release students so that they could obtain religious training. In North Carolina, meanwhile, ministers persuaded the state board of education to let them offer "Bible" as a regular, accredited course during normal school hours. In both states, churches would set curricula and provide classroom supplies for the weekday program. They would also bear all of its expenses, including publicity costs and teacher salaries.[9]

Almost immediately each project registered impressive gains. In New York City alone, student released-time enrollment soared from 4,500 in February 1941 to over 100,000 in January 1942. By 1943 more than 20,000 pupils in 75 North Carolina communities elected to take Bible courses at school. In both states religious education assumed a distinctly ecumenical flavor. Although New York City released its Protestant, Catholic, and Jewish students to separate off-school "WRE Centers," the program was administered by a citywide "Interfaith Committee" representing all three religious groups. In the heavily Protestant schools of North Carolina, Methodists and Baptists shared Bible classes with Presbyterians and Episcopalians; in a few towns, handfuls of Catholic, Quaker, and even Jewish children joined them. Hence teachers took pains to avoid narrow, "denominational" viewpoints, as one instructor wrote, instead stressing the broad message of justice, tolerance, and love. "If we are to have an era of peace and brotherhood," another North Carolina teacher explained, "the rising generation must have a deepened understanding and appreciation of God's word."[10]

Elsewhere, too, weekday religious education surged in the 1940s. Northern school districts tended to follow some version of the "Gary Plan," named after the released-time system pioneered in 1913 in Gary, Indiana, by Superintendent William Wirt. As in New York, larger districts typically released pupils to off-school locations; in rural areas students were more likely to remain inside the schools for their weekly "church" lessons. South of the Mason-Dixon Line schools usually adopted the "Chattanooga Plan" of the Tennessean J. P. McCallie, a private academy principal who persuaded his city's public schools to offer elective Bible courses in 1922. Both types of WRE declined during the Great Depression, when church coffers tightened considerably. But religious instruction rebounded during World War II, sparked not just by apocalyptic news from abroad but by a healthier economy at home. In Fremont, Ohio, all but 8 of 1,278 elementary pupils in 1945 received weekly lessons from two church-sponsored teachers, who "rode circuit" between the town's various primary schools; in Morgantown, West Virginia, 94 percent of the entire student body enrolled in Bible class; and in Chattanooga itself more than 15,000 children in 55 schools took the course. Across America, at least 2,000 communities—including 21 of the nation's 38 largest cities—provided some form of WRE to their public school students by 1946.[11]

To boost enrollment in these classes, churches advertised WRE in newspapers, radio spots, and store windows as well as in sermons and Sunday schools. In Pittsburgh the cover of a WRE promotional pamphlet featured an attractive teenage couple holding hands. "AN ALL AROUND PERSONALITY means you at your best—mentally, physically, socially, and spiritually!" the pamphlet exulted. In North Carolina churches distributed scripts for a play, set outside a high school registrar's office, that encouraged students to sign up for Bible class. Seeking an "easy" elective to fill his schedule, a student asks his friends whether Bible fits the bill. Another scoffs at the course, declaring that "only sissies go in for that religious stuff." Both students are quickly corrected by their peers. "What do you mean, sissies?" one boy replies. "You don't call our football squad sissies do you? And half of them were in there this year." Another student warns that Bible is hardly a "krip" course: it demands as much work as other electives, if not more. But it is also "lots of fun," a third pupil attests. In the end, of course, the two skeptical students register for Bible. "I'm not convinced," one of them cautions, "but I guess it can't hurt me. If I don't like it, I can get out."[12]

Many students, it seems, did just that. "When they find out how much work is involved they drop out," reported a churchman in North Dakota, one of the few northern states to offer high school Bible courses. Religious instruction was more popular among younger children, thanks to the "project method" that elementary-level teachers often employed. In this they merely emulated the Master Teacher, one WRE instructor noted, since Jesus "sent His disciples on missions, that they might 'learn by doing.'" In North Carolina Bible classrooms, for example, students built soap carvings of Rachel's Tomb, produced puppet shows based on the life of Joseph, and reported on Joshua's conquest of Jericho for an imaginary "Radio Station Israel." When they reached the New Testament, they even created newspapers announcing the Crucifixion and the Ascension. The smallest children were often content simply to listen to Bible stories, which one boy deemed "as good as the comic strips." ("That was a new comparison for me," his teacher wrote, "but high praise from his standpoint.") Older students watched movies depicting the Creation, Cain and Abel, and Noah's Ark, plus a special film about "the life of George Washington Carver."[13]

As the juxtaposition of Carver and the Bible suggests, religious educators often used WRE to preach racial equality and justice. "Upon us rests the responsibility of presenting the Prince of Peace," wrote the Spindale, North Carolina, Bible teacher Louise Bashford in 1943. "If we fail we leave [students] surrounded by the hardness and the cruelty of war that breeds hate; lost in the inequalities of an economic system that begets servants of mammon; slaves within the mental stockades of racial injustice. We cannot fail. We must not fail. Ours is a Holy task." Other Tar Heel Bible teachers circulated "The Prayer of a Modern Pharisee," which used the Pharisee's plea in Luke 18:11— "God, I thank thee, that I am not as other men are"—to mock contemporary prejudice. "Especially, Lord," the parody began,

> I thank thee that I am a Southerner and not a Yankee. Thankful, too, am I, to be an occidental and not an oriental—one of those "lesser breeds without the law." True that Confucius and Gautama Buddha and Abraham and Moses and Kagawa and Gandhi were, or are, great men, but I never liked slanting eyes or the wrong shape of nose . . . I thank thee that I am white, not yellow or red or brown or black. The Bible does teach that "While man looketh on the outward appearance, God looketh on the heart," but the outward appearance counts for a lot below the Mason and Dixon line.[14]

During "Brotherhood Week" in February 1941, New York WRE teachers brought black and white students together to deliver an "interracial radio program" over the air. More typically, however, northern WRE instructors focused on bridging religious differences rather than racial ones. One Massachusetts minister argued that the simple act of uniting diverse Protestant denominations in a single released-time class reminded children how much heritage and faith they shared. Other WRE programs studied non-Christian religions, underscoring common impulses and attributes in the entire human family. "Now we know Jews are just like everybody else," wrote a sixth-grade WRE student in Ann Arbor, Michigan, after a class visit to the local synagogue. "We are *all* God's children." Jewish students received a similarly ecumenical lesson, an Ohio WRE teacher added. As she led a class of third-graders in a lesson on biblical geography, the lone Jewish member experienced a shock of recognition. "Why, Jerusalem and Jordan River!" the boy exclaimed, rushing toward the three-dimensional "Holy Land Map" at the front of the room. "Why, we Jews also study about them."[15]

In the same breath, though, the instructor admitted that this child was "not permitted to study with us" during released-time periods. Hence the episode also seemed to confirm the worst fears of WRE's critics: however "separated" from the rest of the school curriculum, religious instruction would inevitably seep into it. In one Illinois community an eighth-grade newspaper published features about released-time classes; in another Prairie State town the religion teacher visited English and history classes to probe spiritual themes in these subjects; and in an Ohio grade school art teachers helped children construct covers for their WRE notebooks about the "Life of Jesus." Such obvious admixtures of religious and secular instruction would eventually cause the Supreme Court to strike down released-time plans, at least the ones that operated on public school property. In the meantime, Americans would struggle over the question of WRE in schools—and especially over the answers WRE was designed to give.[16]

Debating WRE

Louis Hurwitch was changing his mind. As dean of the Hebrew Teachers College in Boston, he had opposed released-time education when it came before the Massachusetts legislature in 1941. Like other Jewish spokesmen across the country, Hurwitch had worried that WRE would stigmatize Jewish children by separating them from other students. After the legislature authorized released time, however, he put his fears aside. Under Hurwitch's supervision nearly four hundred Jewish public school students went to local synagogues for WRE in 1945; two years later, more than two thousand would do so. Enlisting many youngsters who did not otherwise attend temple, released-time classes also provided new opportunities for young graduates of Hurwitch's teaching college. "It is true we were handed a lemon," he quipped, "but instead of throwing away the lemon, we should make good lemonade with it." Although national Jewish organizations had soured on WRE, as Hurwitch acknowledged, Boston's Jews were squeezing every possible advantage from it.[17]

Hurwitch's remarks reflected the complex politics of released time, which often sparked furious debate within religious groups as well as between them. Like Jewish leaders, Baptist organizations consistently opposed "any type of relation of the church to the state," one Illinois Baptist asserted in a 1948 attack on released time. But many local Baptist churches in the same state sponsored WRE, complaining that national spokesmen had "exceeded their authority" in condemning it. For most of the decade, other mainline denominations maintained a consensus on the need for weekday religious education. Yet they fought bitterly over its content, as fundamentalists within the denominations tried to push WRE curricula in a more conservative, "evangelical" direction. Other challenges came from the expanding number of independent churches, which not only muffled WRE's liberal message but also diverted funds "that might otherwise support denominational work," as a worried committee of mainline ministers noted in 1942.[18]

Ironically, only Catholics seemed united behind weekday religious education. For most of the century, dioceses had condemned WRE as a threat to Catholic education: if children could receive religious training in public school systems, the argument went, they would have little reason to attend parochial ones. Amid the boom of WRE during the 1940s, however, Catholics became its strongest champions. In New York and Chicago, where Catholic children were released to separate classrooms, they made up over three-quarters of the cities' total WRE enrollment; in smaller districts, they sometimes joined other children in so-called nondenominational classes. No simple pattern governed these arrangements. In the majority-Catholic town of Shelburne, Vermont, every WRE pupil studied with an Episcopal priest. "I have all the Roman Catholic or Jewish children," the priest wrote privately, "therefore teaching can not be quite of the same type as if I had only my own young people." In nearby Fairfax, by contrast, Catholics formed their own class after the local Catholic priest denounced mixed-faith instruction. Whatever their views on the specific procedure for released time, though, Catholics remained firm supporters of the overall concept. Indeed, Protestants frequently attributed WRE's 1940s explosion to the new Catholic consensus in its favor.[19]

Especially after 1945, meanwhile, any setbacks for WRE were routinely blamed on "the Jews." As the Champaign, Illinois, case wound its way to the Supreme Court, observers remarked that the nation's "big three" Jewish organizations—the American Jewish Congress, the American Jewish Committee, and the Anti-Defamation League—had each condemned released time as "unconstitutional." But this apparent Jewish unity masked profound differences in strategy and philosophy. Both the Committee and the ADL initially denounced the court challenge to released time, preferring to fight WRE through "suasionist" channels: publicity campaigns, meetings with school officials, and so on. Out in the field, members feared that *any* opposition to released time—legal, suasionist, or otherwise—would trigger a backlash against Jews. In the rough, day-to-day world of the average American community, one rabbi argued, Jews who condemned WRE would be attacked by their neighbors as "selfish" and "secularist." However baseless in fact, both charges had a wide popular appeal. "Can Jews assume an absolute isolationist or separatist position," the rabbi asked, "especially when the overwhelming proportion of the population clamors for public school cooperation in the solution of this problem?"[20]

Across the country, more and more Jews gave a clear answer: no. "It is one thing for a national body in some far distant place to pass a resolution on this subject," a WRE defender mused in 1944, "and [another] for local leaders to apply it." Anti-Semitism had declined since its 1930s heyday, he added, but Jews were wary of reawakening it. Rather than opposing WRE outright, then, most Jews simply kept their children out of so-called nondenominational programs. To the chagrin of national spokesmen, others formed their own released-time classes. By 1946 more than 2,500 Jewish children in New York City received WRE; the following year nearly 2,300 Jews in the Boston area did the same. Nor were such programs restricted to America's largest cities. After the New York legislature authorized released time, Jews in Rochester quickly formed 9 WRE classes with 228 students. Convening once a week for religious instruction, the classes also met frequently as a group for debates, dances, and "glee club" performances of Hebrew and Yiddish songs. "The Released Time Plan [should] no longer be considered as a necessary evil," Rochester's Jewish WRE director declared, "but as a partial contribution to the Jewish education of our youth." If properly taught, he added, WRE could reinforce—but never replace—Jews' regular after-school "Talmud Torah" classes.[21]

Indeed, teachers of "Talmud Torah" often became the most zealous Jewish advocates of released time. During the first two years of WRE in New York, Talmud Torah registration rose by 1,500; by 1947, educators estimated, roughly a third of Jewish released-time pupils had been "inspired" by WRE to attend after-school or Sunday religious class. WRE also provided at least an introduction to Judaism for thousands of children who never studied it. Since few girls in New York City attended Talmud Torah, one observer explained, released time was their only opportunity for formal religious training. In Jewish homes, a Boston rabbi lamented, parents had been "sadly remiss" in teaching both sexes about their religious heritage. Released time could never substitute for this "home training," but it was better than no training at all.[22]

Jewish educators also hailed WRE for fostering greater understanding and tolerance among children of different faiths. Here, too, they reversed their prior concern. When released time began, many Jews charged that it would harm interfaith relations by "segregating" students according to religion. But children kept to their own kind anyhow, Jewish educators now argued; rather than ignoring religious differences, schools should use WRE to erase the stigmas associated with them. "Whereas a Jewish child is regarded by many of his Christian schoolmates as an infidel, Released-Time would show the Christian child that the Jew too has a religion," one advocate of WRE predicted in 1944. "It is a more positive kind of labeling." To be sure, Jewish children who did not participate in WRE still suffered frequent bouts of prejudice and embarrassment. In Illinois one school confined Jewish students to a cloakroom during the released-time period; in Massachusetts a teacher told them flatly that they would "go to hell" unless they embraced Christ. To Jewish WRE supporters, such episodes demonstrated why Jews should embrace—not resist—the released-time option. "We cannot refuse to take care of the children . . . who are forced to remain at school," wrote a Boston Jewish educator in 1947, explaining his own conversion to WRE. "I felt that just as we were doing our best for the *displaced* children in Europe, we should also do our best for our *misplaced* children in this country."[23]

Finally, the same educator warned, "charlatans and quacks" would take advantage of WRE if mainstream Jews declined to do so. Here he alluded to the Brooklyn-based Lubavitcher sect, which founded its own Committee for the Furtherance of Jewish Education in 1942. By 1948 the group had extended its operations to New York's other boroughs as well as to Boston, Chicago, and several other locations. Traditional rabbinical councils in all these cities had opposed released time, a Jewish WRE proponent argued, thereby allowing "obscure groups" to influence it. But even where rabbis were friendlier to WRE, they often disagreed about what it should teach. "Among Jews more than any other group, there is the problem of intra-group relation-ships of Orthodox and Reform," a Baltimore rabbi pointed out in 1942, "leaving us unable to establish a unified system of teaching as do the Catholics or the Protestant Federation of Churches."[24]

Just as Christians exaggerated intra-Jewish harmony, however, so did Jews overestimate the consensus among Christians. Throughout the 1940s, Protestants probably suffered the sharpest internal strife over WRE. Some of this conflict reflected simple competition between mainline denominations, each seeking to sway released-time classes closer to its own theology. But the most vehement attacks came from self-described "fundamentalists," who rejected the authority of *any* mainline church over WRE. They announced this challenge in 1943 in an editorial in *United Evangelical Action,* the era's leading tribune of fundamentalist thought. "Do not be deceived," the editorial thundered:

Religious education on released time from public schools may be one of the greatest means of evangelism for the coming generation or it may be the most destructive to faith that could be imagined. If there is religious education on released time the questions of the origin of the race, the deity of Christ, the infallibility, authenticity and authority of the Bible cannot be avoided. If the teaching of Protestant children is left to leader-ship selected by the average federation or council of churches the effect will be disastrous to faith . . . The evangelicals of the nation have a responsibility to impress the boards of education with the fact that so-called Protestantism is divided into two entirely and irrevocably di-verse groups. These boards must and will recognize the right of united evangelicals to establish in these communities their own system of Chris-tian instruction for the benefit of their constituencies. The time for action is NOW.[25]

For the next fifteen years a loose coalition of ministries, publishing houses, radio programs, and private educational agencies would flood American schools with this critique. Lacking any type of cen-tralized management or control, they were bound instead by a single idea: redemption through faith. "Any given child is already lost, or soon will be, if he is not brought to Christ," surmised J. Irvin Over-holtzer, director of a small organization called the Child Evangelism Fellowship. "Since this is true, the only reasonable and safe thing to do is to lead each child to Christ as early as possible." In teacher guides and other literature the CEF provided detailed suggestions for effecting such conversions. It also denounced "modernist" mainline churches, which allegedly diverted WRE from God's word. Whereas the Bible proved that Christ was the one true God, many WRE classes acknowledged the so-called truths of other religions; whereas the Bible demanded faith in Christ as a condition for salvation, WRE pro-moted the fallacy of "good works"; and whereas the Bible described salvation as a matter of individual conscience, WRE increasingly discussed it in terms of social justice. To save the children, then, fundamentalists would have to seize control of weekday religious education.[26]

By the end of World War II they could boast several impressive vic-tories. In Buffalo a "Fundamentalist Ministers Committee on Week-day Christian Education" wrested nearly half of the city's WRE classes from the mainline church council. A fundamentalist group in Duluth, Minnesota, captured more than 90 percent of the program, marking the largest municipality to leave the official mainline fold. "Ours is a work based upon convictions—not compromise," intoned the program's director; "we took our stand for the fundamentals of our faith." In one fifth-grade class, he exulted, "not a single child had failed to definitely accept Jesus Christ as a personal Savior"; in another school, second- and third-graders had held a "spontaneous prayer meeting" to plead for "the salvation of the father of one of these children." Other cities were sure to follow Duluth's example, a Denver minister wrote, rescuing WRE from the clutches of "mod-ernist" mainline denominations.[27]

For their own part, most mainline churches reacted to the funda-mentalist challenge with a patronizing mix of sympathy and disdain. At best, fundamentalists were backward waifs, lost in a wilderness of fear and superstition; at worst, they were vicious barbarians, pounding at the gates of the denominations' tranquil Eden. Regardless of their motives, fundamentalists' single-minded focus on personal salvation ignored the social complexities and inequalities that surrounded it. "An educated leadership . . . thinks of salvation in large terms," explained a mainline minister in 1942. "It concerns itself with the causes that underlie attitudes and behavior. It realizes that economic conditions, unsatisfied physical needs and undernourished bodies, require change in environment as well as better educational methods." Whereas mainline WRE reflected new research in human development, he added, fundamentalist methods contradicted it: "emotional" conversion tactics upset students, while rote memorization of the Bible prevented them from appreciating its nuances. Only a renewed effort among mainline churches would halt this invasion of ignorance, bringing WRE into accord with recent trends in child psychology.[28]

But in at least one respect, critics acknowledged, fundamentalists understood child psychology all too well. Their loud rituals of conversion provided passion and drama, stirring students' hearts as well as their minds. Ironically, the same mainline ministers who blasted fundamentalists for neglecting "child nature" often complained that children were naturally drawn to fundamentalism. "The stereotyped program of the Bible Clubs has an emotional appeal and exciting style of presentation," admitted a liberal minister in upstate New York, "but we don't have material to put into a teacher's hands which will do the job." To be sure, the International Council of Religious Education—an umbrella group of mainline WRE churches—distributed course outlines, textbooks, and teachers' guides. But these resources were no match for the simple, stark excitement of fundamentalist classrooms, as a frustrated Nebraska clergyman wrote in 1948. Writing a few weeks after the Supreme Court's *McCollum* decision, which seemed to strike down in-school WRE, the Nebraskan threatened that if "emotional, evangelistic, and fundamentalist" WRE classes continued in the state he would report them to local school authorities. Hardly a "resolution" of the conflict over released time, *McCollum* would trigger new battles over religious education in America's public schools.[29]

Religious Education after *McCollum*

"It is safe to say that no decision by the highest court in the land has ever caused greater consternation than this one," pronounced the Rev. W. T. Smith, of Peoria, Illinois, in March 1948. "It is equally safe to say that the issue is not closed." Here Smith joined the rising chorus of American outrage at the Supreme Court's decision in *McCollum v. Board of Education*. Hundreds of churches and school districts had quickly announced that they would continue their released-time operations no matter what the Court said. In other schools the decision rejuvenated efforts to infuse the regular curriculum with religious instruction. Some communities were looking anew at their long-defunct laws allowing Bible reading in the classroom, for example. Actually, Smith concluded, *McCollum* "may be a blessing in disguise": even if it suppressed released-time classes, it would spark a new spirituality within "regular" ones.[30]

Smith's comments neatly encapsulated the central themes of public school religious instruction after *McCollum*. Despite the dire predictions of the ruling's critics, released-time programs continued to flourish well into the 1950s. Some schools brazenly defied the Supreme Court, while others adjusted their WRE systems to comply with its decision. In the end, as Smith foresaw, *McCollum* would have a greater impact on religious practices in "regular" classes than it would on released time itself. Anticipating the eventual demise of WRE, states and school districts established in-school religious exercises that all of their students—at least in theory—could accept. But controversy would soon surround these so-called common-core practices, too, setting the stage for America's next great religious upheaval in the early 1960s.

Initial reactions to *McCollum* often assumed an apocalyptic tone, summoning imagery of hellfire and damnation. Critics also drew on the new red-hot rhetoric of the Cold War, condemning the decision as a victory for "Godless Communism" over American freedom. "If the Supreme Court are free to say what liberties we have every Monday morning, we are like the peasants of Russia, under their Politburo," screamed an angry resident of Illinois. Under the Court's ruling, an Oklahoma newspaper complained, schools could teach the Communist Manifesto but not the Sermon on the Mount. Others compared *McCollum*'s attack on released time to the *Dred Scott* decision of 1857, which upheld slavery: in each case, they argued, Americans could justifiably flout the Court in the name of Christ's higher law. Still other critics invoked their rights as parents. "So the U.S. Supreme Court says I can't have my kid released from school an hour a week to study religion in my church?" asked a shopkeeper in Ohio. "The Supreme Court can go jump in the lake, so far as I'm concerned."[31]

Following this initial burst of indignation at *McCollum*, however, critics came to realize that they had vastly exaggerated both its scope and its effect. Since the decision's Illinois test case involved WRE classes inside public schools, state and local school officials quickly decided that it did not apply to off-site released-time instruction. But in-school classes also continued, because educators rarely took action against them. In a dance of mutual evasion, local school boards deemed the issue a state concern; thereafter, state superintendents declared it a local one.[32] Four months after *McCollum* only three states had ordered a halt to in-school WRE. And they found the ban unenforceable. "There is no possible way my office can control such a situation," Michigan's education commissioner told a local church council after his department ostensibly barred released time. "There are 15 large school districts and 300 smaller school districts who teach religious education in school buildings." Enforcing this lone order would require his office to hire at least a thousand extra employees, the commissioner concluded.[33]

To be sure, released-time enrollment declined—probably by 10 percent—in the wake of *McCollum*. Some in-school programs moved to churches and other off-site locations, creating new transportation problems; others disbanded altogether, fearful of legal challenges and increased expenses. But nationwide WRE registration soon returned to its pre-*McCollum* level, spurred by a second Supreme Court decision: *Zorach v. Clauson* (1952). Upholding New York's WRE system, *Zorach* made explicit what northern school officials had already presumed: if released time occurred outside schools and without public funds, it was constitutional. After struggling in the shadows of *McCollum* for four years, religious educators hailed *Zorach* as a ray of sunlight. "Weekday Religious Education Has a Future!" proclaimed the longtime WRE leader Erwin L. Shaver. Thanks to *Zorach*—the "Magna Carta" of WRE, as Shaver called it—released-time programs could at last operate in full confidence of their legality. A rise in registration was sure to follow, Shaver wrote, as more and more Americans raced through the Court's new "green light" on WRE.[34]

Just as Shaver predicted, WRE grew steadily for the rest of the decade. At least 4 million children received some type of weekday religious instruction by 1959, nearly doubling the nationwide total from 1953. Yet even after *Zorach* "cleared the air" about "what was permissible," as one observer noted, thousands of school districts continued to engage in practices that the Court did not permit. Across the South, in-school Bible classes boomed: in Charlotte, North Carolina, churchmen even complained that the Bible course was siphoning students away from their own Sunday schools. In the North an estimated 32 percent of released-time classes met on school property—only a slight decrease from the pre-*McCollum* rate of 40 percent. Defending the continued use of rural public schools for WRE, Vermont's lieutenant governor asserted that Supreme Court doctrine did not apply to the Green Mountain State—because its own constitution predated the federal one. In Ohio and Indiana several WRE programs actually returned to the public schools after a brief move away from them.[35]

Moreover, released time was still racked by the same battles between mainline denominations and fundamentalists that had raged since the 1940s. If anything, the continued growth of evangelical churches—and the ongoing erosion of traditional denominations—intensified this struggle. Vermont churches announced a new rural WRE project in 1954 to combat the New England Fellowship, a Boston-based fundamentalist group that sent teachers into remote areas to "win all of the young people in the community for Christ." But the NEF continued to flourish, both in Vermont and in Maine: by 1960 nearly a fifth of Maine school districts reported WRE instruction by a teacher from the fellowship. Other mainline critics focused their bile on the Rural Bible Mission, which masqueraded as a denominational movement in order to gain a foothold in the public schools. "School boards frequently thought these teachers represented the regular, organized, cooperating churches," wrote an angry mainline WRE worker in Michigan, "whereas they really represented only a segment of the fundamentalist group." All the more reason to infuse the regular school curriculum with "more religious teaching," a St. Louis church council urged, which would honor Americans' shared "theistic tradition" as well as enhance their "interfaith understanding."[36]

The final remark illustrates the most significant new development in religious education in the 1950s: the quest for a "common core" of values and practices that could bind the different faiths together. The effort began amid the initial after-shock of *McCollum,* when churchmen feared that released-time programs would crumble and die. "What we need for the public schools," proposed the WRE advocate D. Leigh Colvin in April 1948, "is to find a universal and nonsectarian moral code as a substitute for the religious instruction forbidden by the decision of the Supreme Court." Fortunately, Colvin added, America already had one: the Ten Commandments, "the recognized moral code of the nation irrespective of denominations." Back in 1916 Colvin had spearheaded an interfaith effort to print posters of the Commandments and distribute them to public schools. From Washington, D.C., to Wichita, boards of education had approved their display. Reviving this effort would provide "a successful non-sectarian substitute" for banned released-time programs, Colvin argued. So would daily readings of the Bible, which more than a dozen state courts had already deemed a "non-sectarian" book.[37]

Elsewhere, too, religious leaders demanded Bible reading to compensate for the expected loss of WRE. The loss never came, but daily scripture reading continued to grow. Reexamining statute books, ministers found that most states allowed Bible reading and that a dozen even required it. "The law provides that the Bible may be read in the public schools," reported North Dakota's Interchurch Council in 1949, "but it is not likely to be done unless someone promotes it." The council proceeded to print and distribute 15,000 leaflets, each containing 90 suggested scriptural passages plus a copy of North Dakota's Bible-reading statute. In Massachusetts church officials sought to reinvigorate the state's long-forgotten Bible law by publishing a "syllabus" of excerpts from the Old and New Testaments. By 1957, 175 Massachusetts school districts used the 40-page booklet; in Boston alone, 3,000 teachers did so. Although the state's 1866 law simply required daily readings of the Bible "without comment," teachers often used the booklet as a discussion tool in their regular instruction. Praising the booklet's "tie-in value," one teacher correlated its passages from Genesis with her science unit on the earth, moon, and stars; similarly, during a civics lesson about democracy she read Psalm 66 to illustrate "God's government of nations."[38]

Like released time, Bible reading received an extra boost from the Supreme Court. In 1952, the same year it upheld New York's WRE plan in *Zorach,* the Court let stand a New Jersey decision *(Doremus v. Board of Education)* that affirmed both Bible reading and the Lord's Prayer in schools. Significantly, the lower court had found that both practices were "non-sectarian." Across the country, then, church groups increasingly demanded so-called common or nondenominational prayers along with scripture reading in the public schools. The most frequent prayers were grace before meals and morning recitations of the Lord's Prayer. In 1959, for example, teachers in 82 of 89 primary schools in Indianapolis led children in the Lord's Prayer; in every one of the 65 schools with a lunch program, students recited some type of mealtime grace. Other states composed their own "common" devotionals, taking a cue from the prayer suggested in 1951 by the New York State Board of Regents: "Almighty God, we acknowledge our dependence upon Thee, and we beg Thy blessings upon us, our parents, our teachers, and our Country." Roughly one-fifth of New York's school districts adopted the Regents' prayer by 1955, although New York City chose to institute the fourth stanza of "America" instead:

> Our fathers' God to thee
> Author of liberty
> To Thee we sing;
> Long may our land be bright
> With freedom's holy Light
> Protect us by Thy might
> Great God, our King.[39]

Finally, dozens of school systems in the 1950s adopted programs to teach the "moral and spiritual values" that were supposedly shared by every American faith. In San Diego a special advisory panel distilled these common principles into three overarching themes: "Existence of God," "Reverence for God," and "Brotherhood." In Los Angeles teachers were enjoined to help children "become more loyal to the church of one's choice" as well as to respect other religions. "No, we are not teaching religion in any sectarian sense of the word," cautioned an instructors' guide, "but to vitalize for young people the great spiritual truths underlying man's search for God through the ages." Practically, however, most so-called Moral-and-Spiritual (M-S) programs assumed a distinctly contemporary cast. In Weymouth, Massachusetts, the local M-S committee sponsored a student letter-writing campaign to President Eisenhower, urging him to adopt "In God We Trust" as the motto of all American schools. After the launch of the Soviet Union's *Sputnik* satellite, the committee produced a school assembly to remind pupils of America's spiritual—if not always technological—preeminence. "Show us a hammer and sickle and we'll show you our flag," read the assembly program. "Show us the 'Communist Manifesto' and we'll show you our Bill of Rights . . . Show us Malenkov and Stalin and Lenin and we'll show you 33 presidents, chosen by vote—and we'll show you a Man on a Cross."[40]

Just like advocates of released time, supporters of religious instruction in the "regular" curriculum often championed it as a weapon against the Red menace. "In these days of world-wide conflict between the free world and the slave world of godless communism, it is more vital than ever before that our children grow up with a sense of reverence and dedication to Almighty God," proclaimed Governor Thomas E. Dewey of New York, praising his state's Regents' prayer. In Ohio a proponent of in-school Bible reading warned that American "subversives" typically lacked "religious conviction"; the more students learned about scripture, by implication, the less they would listen to radical appeals. "Why is there such a deep and renewed concern today about religion in the public schools?" asked an educator from Spokane, Washington, kicking off a discussion on the subject at a conference in 1955. The audience quickly agreed on an answer: "Fear of the materialistic philosophy of communism." To prevail in its global struggle, speakers argued, America would have to rediscover the "theistic tradition" that had formerly united it.[41]

At the same conference, however, other participants urged "that theism not be perverted into humanistic ritualism"—that is, into a set of superficial bromides, "uniting" all religions but satisfying none of them. Their worries pointed to deep divisions among Americans over so-called common religious practices in the schools, which sparked just as much controversy as WRE programs did. Fundamentalists expressed the sharpest concerns, welcoming schools' renewed emphasis on the Bible and prayer but blasting their effort to combine—or, worse, to equate—different faiths. "With the Jews, Roman Catholics, Mormons, and other religious interests . . . Jesus Christ as the Messiah and Saviour of men could not be taught," fumed a Philadelphia fundamentalist group, attacking a proposed program on "shared" beliefs in the city's public schools. "Any religion that is worthy of the name must present the way of everlasting life." Despite its nonsectarian pretense, the fundamentalists added, Philadelphia's "common-core" project was "nothing more than the 'sectarian' program of the ecumenical movement." [42]

In a classic case of strange bedfellows, Jews frequently joined fundamentalist Christians in rejecting the common-core approach. "If faith in God is to be inculcated in the schools in such a manner as to do no violence to the beliefs of Catholic, Protestant, and Jew, it will be so pallid and anemic as to be meaningless," cautioned New York's Board of Rabbis in a near-perfect echo of the fundamentalist position. Another New Yorker worried that schools were actually evolving "a strange new hybrid religion," as distasteful to Jews as it was to other faiths. More typically, Jews charged that this supposedly common religion was simply a subterfuge for smuggling Christianity into the classroom. Under the guise of "shared" beliefs, for example, Kansas kindergartners sang a hymn about Jesus' love; a Massachusetts junior high school showed the Nativity movie *Three Wise Men;* an Indiana principal donned clerical robes to lead a high school Good Friday service; and in an Easter assembly in Florida students reenacted the Crucifixion. However much school policies might stress America's "common" faith, a Pittsburgh Jewish leader told local educators, Christian teachers would inevitably twist religious instruction toward their own distinctive beliefs.[43]

As in the struggle over released time, though, many Jews dissented from this "separationist" position. The Weymouth, Massachusetts, rabbi welcomed his school district's aggressive program to promote "moral and spiritual values," despite its obvious Christian themes. "He feels that boys and girls today are not getting enough religious training," an acquaintance explained, "and that such a procedure compensates." In nearby Watertown an irate parent skewered her local Jewish Community Council for its steadfast opposition to "nonsectarian" prayer: "Many of us question the wisdom of a *Godless* school. Why, for the sake of our future generation (and plain common sense) can't there be *something* of a religious nature in our public schools?" The rising tide of juvenile delinquency demonstrated children's need for "spiritual guidance," she added, especially for training in the Ten Commandments. Shared by all three major faiths, the Commandments also covered "every crime punished in our courts."[44]

Other Jews objected to religious instruction in principle but acquiesced to it in practice, arguing that any resistance would harm "community relations" with their Christian neighbors. They had good reason to worry. Especially during the Christmas season, the pinnacle of religious instruction in most public schools, Jewish complaints provoked threats of boycotts and even violence. "If you Jews don't stop interfering with the Christian Gentile and mind your own business, word will be sent out by 'United Gentiles' to withhold all trade from the Jews," a Massachusetts newspaper editorialized in 1949, after a Jewish couple in Chelsea condemned Christmas hymns in the schools. The couple's personal mail was even more vitriolic:

> If you don't like our christian holidays why not go back to Palestine. It is the likes of you Jews that are ruining this beautiful country.
>
> This country was founded on the principles of Christianity by Christians. You Jews are in the minority . . . As long as you don't like it here, why don't you get out? Israel awaits you!
>
> Go back to Russia where you belong . . . No wonder you're persecuted wherever you go. No wonder you haven't a country.
>
> Why, my dear, should you try to enforce upon others the unhappiness which you say you feel . . . To be so selfish and narrow minded is a usual Russian Communistic plan.[45]

Eight years later the memory of the Chelsea episode was still so fresh that a rabbi in Hull, Massachusetts, warned a Jewish parent against complaining about Christmas celebrations in her schools. Elsewhere, too, Jewish leaders counseled extreme caution in handling the "sensitive and explosive" issue of Christmas exercises: while refusing to participate in the exercises, they advised, Jews should also refrain from publicly denouncing them. Increasingly, though, local Jewish communities selected a third option: joint Christmas-Hanukkah cele-brations. Unlike the standard Christmas program, according to a Cleveland spokesman, a "mixed" holiday would give Jewish children "a sense of status and belongingness." Even more important, per-haps, it would teach Christian children to tolerate—even to appre-ciate—the Jewish faith. "The holidays have so much in common—merrymaking, lights and candles, excellent stories and songs," pro-claimed a teachers' guide published and distributed to Cleveland pub-lic schools by the local Jewish Community Council. "Certainly here is a wonderful opportunity to help children to feel comfortable about cultural differences—the essence of intergroup understanding."[46]

Just four years into their experiment with joint holiday celebra-tions, however, Jews in Cleveland renounced them. "It was felt that it was unwise to attempt—and impossible to achieve—the separation of the religious and cultural elements of the holidays," explained one JCC leader. The city's mainline church federation also condemned the joint celebrations for presenting "a distorted and secularistic pic-ture of culture." Whereas the JCC went on to recommend the elimi-nation of all public school holiday celebrations, though, the church federation asked that schools reinfuse them with "theistic" elements.[47] As in the debates over released time and school prayer, it seemed, the search for "common" holidays simply underscored Americans' re-ligious differences. By the early 1960s a new set of Supreme Court decisions would shatter the dream of interfaith consensus once and for all.

School Prayer and the
Conservative Revolution

In the midst of Martin Luther King Jr.'s "kneel-in" protest in Albany, Georgia, in July 1962, a newspaper reporter asked King about a different type of worship: school prayer. King was in Albany to fight racial segregation; later that day, for the third time in eight months, local authorities would jail him. But he drew a sharp distinction between prayerful protests against discrimination and teacher-led devotionals in public schools, which the U.S. Supreme Court had struck down several weeks earlier. On his knees, awaiting arrest, King gave his full support to the Court. Its prayer decision was "sound and good," he declared, "reaffirming something that is basic in our Constitution, namely, separation of church and state."[1]

The following year Governor George C. Wallace of Alabama threatened to conduct his own type of "pray-in"—*against* the Supreme Court. Wallace was already famous for his defiance of court-ordered integration—for literally "standing in the school-house door" to block two black students from enrolling at the University of Alabama on June 11, 1963. Six days later the Supreme Court announced a second decision barring religious exercises—this time, Bible reading and the Lord's Prayer—from public schools. Wallace's reaction was swift: "If [the Court] says we cannot read the Bible in some school, I'm going to that school and read it myself." At stake were the "civil rights" of white teachers and students, who would go to prison before they abandoned school prayer. "I don't care what they say in Washington, we're going to keep right on praying and reading the Bible in the public schools of Alabama," Wallace asserted. "I wouldn't be surprised if they sent troops into the classrooms and arrested little boys and girls who read the Bible and pray."[2]

Wallace was exaggerating for effect, of course. At no time did federal troops mobilize to stop school prayer and Bible reading, which remained common practices throughout the 1960s. Coupled with King's defense of the Supreme Court, however, Wallace's comments heralded a critical shift in the politics of public school religious instruction. During the 1940s and 1950s a strong consensus undergirded the concept—if not the content—of school-based religious education. Liberals stressed the "social teachings" of the gospel and conservatives emphasized its message of personal salvation, but the two camps agreed about the overall need for religious instruction in public schools. The Supreme Court's prayer rulings brought a sudden and bitter end to this long-standing accord. Lest they jeopardize the Court's precarious authority on racial questions, most liberals backed its bans on prayer and Bible reading. Meanwhile, as a caustic Minnesotan noted, segregationist "Southern Gentlemen" such as Wallace led the battle to retain religious exercises. Gleefully defying the Court, they seized the prayer issue as part of what the Minnesotan called their broader "vendetta" against *Brown v. Board of Education* and the struggle for black freedom in general.[3]

When Wallace traveled north to campaign for the presidency in 1964, though, crowds applauded his attacks upon the "Godless" Supreme Court as loudly as they cheered his censure of civil-rights reforms. Popular rejection of the Court's prayer decisions—like "massive resistance" of its racial dicta—transcended regional as well as religious boundaries.[4] Concentrated largely in the urban North, Catholics vilified the prayer bans as "atheistic" or even "communistic"; at least one bishop directed that all masses ask God to forgive the Supreme Court. School prayer also awakened fundamentalist voters, who had traditionally eschewed politics in favor of converting each conscience to Christ: the prayer issue demanded social action *on behalf* of individual souls. Within mainline churches the issue became a bone of contention rather than a force for unity. Although denominational spokesmen stood firmly behind the Court, local ministers as well as laity rallied against it—and, increasingly, against their national leaders. In Indiana, for example, one supporter of school prayer scored the "hollow, hypocritical hallelujahs rising from certain doctors of divinity" in 1963—the "men of turncoat cloth" who had turned away from God in his moment of need. Six years later a resident of Maine linked this apostasy to a much wider array of ills: "The Lack of Prayers and Bible Readings in The Public Schools and the Flood of Lewd and Obscene Shows and Films, Photographs and Literature in The State of Maine and other States . . . is The Major Factor for The Rising Rate of Juvenile Delinquency, Crime and Violence, Demonstrations, Racial Riots and Disrespect for Law and Order and Common Decency. Almighty God must be restored to His proper place."[5]

To its foes, the ban on school prayer reflected an overall pattern of cultural decay in the 1960s. As a host of scholars have reminded us, "the Sixties" was a polarized era rather than a "radical" one.[6] From fashion and the arts to sexuality and race relations, many Americans celebrated a new spirit of openness and experimentation. Outside the universities and other cosmopolitan locales, however, a far larger number of citizens lamented these trends—and laid the groundwork for the conservative revolution that would ensue. The struggle over school prayer echoes as well as extends this interpretation, underscoring not just the general cultural divisions of "the Sixties" but also their specifically religious dimensions.[7] In fact, critics of the "Godless" Supreme Court often *attributed* pornography, crime, and racial unrest near the end of the era to the Court's decisions about school prayer at its inception.

Since school prayer remained a vibrant issue well into the 1980s, it also illuminates more recent changes in modern conservatism. At the start of their crusade, prayer advocates often cited America's divine mission: to correct for lax or irreligious parenting, schools needed to lead children (and, by extension, the nation) back to God. By the late 1970s supporters of school prayer increasingly invoked the "rights" of religious parents—and decried such parents' alleged "oppression" by secular public schools. Here, like other members of the so-called New Right, prayer activists copied much of the rhetoric of the civil rights movement and other social-justice efforts in the 1960s. Even as prayer advocates inveighed against the moral laxity of "the Sixties," they also embraced the decade's most indelible legacy: an expanding consciousness of "rights," both for individual Americans and for the ever-multiplying groups that they formed.[8]

Bootlegging Religion into the Schools

Leo Pfeffer had good reason to celebrate in June 1963. As counsel for the American Jewish Congress, he had already helped persuade the Supreme Court to strike down a state-composed school prayer in *Engel v. Vitale* (1962). Now the Court barred Bible reading and the Lord's Prayer in schools, ruling in *Abington v. Schempp* that both practices violated the establishment clause of the First Amendment. Whereas *Engel* had earned "almost universal condemnation," Pfeffer wrote, the public reaction to *Schempp* was much milder. "It is not too optimistic to suggest that this may well be the last major battle . . . in the area of religion in the public schools," Pfeffer predicted. "The controversy will begin to disappear as a major national issue." He contrasted *Engel* and *Schempp* to the Court's segregation rulings, which continued to arouse "tensions and conflicts" across America. Frosty race relations would plague America forever, he believed, but religious strife would melt away.[9]

A brilliant lawyer, Pfeffer was less successful as a soothsayer. Whatever their constitutional status, religious exercises were simply too ingrained to remove from many public schools. In 1962 roughly half of American states had laws allowing or requiring Bible reading in the schools, at least five states authorized the recitation of the Lord's Prayer, and about one-third of all districts conducted daily devotional services.[10] To be sure, some American communities quickly altered their policies in accord with *Engel* and *Schempp*. As in the case of school desegregation, however, just as many districts mounted various forms of resistance to the decisions. Outright defiance was most common in the South, where state officials openly denounced the Court and urged school boards to ignore it. In the North schools often sidestepped the new rulings through a subtle blend of quiet subterfuge and legalistic evasion. And millions of Americans across the country lent their support to campaigns for a school prayer amendment to the Constitution. Although none of these campaigns succeeded, both their size and their persistence demonstrated a deep popular demand for religious worship in the public schools.[11]

From Congress to statehouses and school districts, southerners took the lead in pressing for prayer—and in resisting the Supreme Court. By 1966 all but three of the senators from the former Confederate states backed some type of constitutional amendment to protect school prayer. Even in the absence of such a measure, southern governors and educational leaders expressly flouted the Court's prayer prohibitions. Testifying in Congress on behalf of a prayer amendment in 1964, George Wallace proclaimed that Alabama would ignore the Court—no matter what happened to the amendment. South Carolina's attorney general boasted that he was "not much concerned about what the Supreme Court has ruled"; in Georgia a gubernatorial candidate promised that he would "not only go to jail, but give up my life" for school prayer; in Mississippi the governor openly encouraged all teachers to lead their classes in worship. Across the South, it seems, thousands of instructors did exactly that. In 1965 nearly two-thirds of southern primary-level teachers reported that they still conducted morning devotionals at school.[12]

In the Midwest, by contrast, only a fifth of instructors led their classes in worship; in the Northeast, where eight of ten teachers had conducted prayers before *Engel*, just over one-tenth said they still did so. But these figures vastly underestimated the actual amount of religious instruction north of the Mason-Dixon Line. Unlike their southern counterparts, northern state officials often urged or even ordered districts to obey the Court's new dicta. In surveys about "compliance" with the Supreme Court, then, northern teachers and school officials had a clear incentive to conceal classroom prayers. Moreover, schools that did remove prayer often replaced it with other types of religious activity. After suing the small town of North Brookfield for its defiance of the Court's prayer ruling, for example, the attorney general of Massachusetts (and future senator) Edward Brooke assured the town that it could continue its Christmas and Easter services in the schools. Throughout the state, schools responded by stepping up their holiday celebrations. In Sudbury the local board announced that schools could celebrate both Christian and Jewish holidays, "in lieu of a vacuum" created by *Engel* and *Schempp*. In nearby Sharon the board decreed that schools could commemorate all "seasonal" holidays so long as "no theologically significant exercises" were included.[13]

Across the country, a "December frenzy" gripped American public schools after the Supreme Court's bans on prayer. Some districts honestly attempted to remove "religious" elements from holiday celebrations, stressing instead their "cultural" or "historical" dimensions. But other schools pointedly *increased* the theological content of these events, aiming "to 'compensate' in Christmas programs for what has been banned explicitly in the daily school routine," as a Jewish observer complained in 1963. Three years later a survey of Christmas practices at 170 schools in the Indianapolis area revealed that 136 schools taught "religious carols," 51 produced plays about "the Christ story," and 53 displayed Nativity scenes. Even in the heavily Jewish New York suburbs of Long Island and Westchester County, one annoyed resident reported, schools exacted "a kind of vengeance or resistance to the court decision" by organizing newly "religious" Christmas celebrations.[14]

Other communities invented fresh ways to "bootleg" religious exercises into their schools, as a Los Angeles prayer advocate acknowledged in 1966. The most popular mechanism was a "moment of silence," which twenty-three states authorized or mandated after the *Engel* and *Schempp* rulings. Since both the "Star-Spangled Banner" and "America" invoked God's blessing, other districts replaced their morning devotionals with stanzas from these songs. A third tactic involved prayer at athletic events, both for team members and for their audiences. "We have kicked the Bible out of schools, but coaches realize its importance in the locker rooms," explained a minister in St. Petersburg, Florida. On the other side of the state, football players at Miami Senior High School attributed their 1966 national championship to team prayers. "The Lord Jesus Christ . . . can make a great athlete out of a good one and a winner out of a loser," proclaimed the squad's all-city defensive end in a pamphlet distributed by a local youth group. "Wouldn't you rather be a winner than a loser?"[15]

States and school districts also smuggled prayer and Bible reading into classrooms via so-called teaching-about-religion courses. Here schools took their cue from Justice Tom Clark's majority opinion in *Schempp,* which stressed that the Bible and other religious writings could still be studied for their "literary and historic qualities"—so long as they were "presented objectively," as part of a "secular program of education." In practice, teachers often ignored or defied these distinctions; indeed, one critic wrote, "teaching about religion" quickly became the "opening wedge" for the teaching *of* religion in America. Especially in the South, where many churches had sponsored public school Bible classes in the 1940s and 1950s, they simply continued these courses under *Schempp*'s "literary and historic" rubric. As late as 1967 at least thirty-seven North Carolina districts still offered "Bible" in their schools. But now the courses were "objective" and "secular," advocates claimed, thereby meeting the constitutional strictures that Clark had laid down in *Schempp.*[16]

Privately, though, North Carolina church officials admitted that Clark's neutral approach was "not being used in our State." In fact, courses "about" religion often became *more* Christian—and more conservative—as the 1960s continued. In Florida a "Bible History" instructor boasted that his course had helped recruit more than a hundred new members into an after-school "Youth for Christ" club in 1967. "I never realized that God was such an approachable Person!" exclaimed a South Carolina student, praising her own school's "Bible survey" course. "I was always taught to respect God, but I just didn't know that you could have daily communion and fellowship with Him!" A few weeks later the same student announced her decision to attend a Bible college after high school. "I want everybody to have what I have!" she told her teacher. "And I'd like to spend my life sharing it with them." Gone was the old emphasis on the gospel's social message, which had done so much to "Christianize" the public's "attitudes on the race question," as a North Carolina man remembered. The sudden change was national in scope, he added, affecting southern and northern schools in equal measure. At its root lay the complex, often tortured relationship between religious education and "the race question" in the 1960s.[17]

When Should the Majority Rule?

A few days after the *Engel* decision, New York's leading black newspaper published a fiery column supporting the Supreme Court's ban on school prayer—and attacking its white critics. "Among the loudest complainants are Senators Talmadge of Georgia and Eastland of Mississippi," wrote James L. Hicks in the *Amsterdam News,* citing two of the most vehement segregationists in Congress. "Do I need to say any more?" Although the Court's 1954 antisegregation ruling "was moulded in the image of Jesus Christ," Hicks noted, men like Talmadge and Eastland had refused to abide by it; now these same racists insisted that the Court's decision was "preventing them from living like Christ." An accompanying cartoon depicted a pair of white "Church Bigots," carrying Bibles and a sign that read, "Supreme Court Unfair—We Need Prayer!" The protesters were trampling on two other demonstrators, one black and one white, whose sign demanded "Equal Rights for All." Like Hicks's column, the cartoon scored white hypocrites who demanded school prayer but denounced the black freedom struggle. The cartoon's caption, "Standing in the Way," carried a second implication: any black person who supported school prayer would also assist the racist foe.[18]

Several weeks later a black reader took sharp issue with these claims. If blacks' quest for justice truly embodied a Christian spirit, Fannie Ledbetter wrote to the *News,* their struggle would require *more* prayer—not less. "In these times of disquietude, we should all pray for guidance each day," Ledbetter argued, "and schools are no exception." She was echoed by a wide range of civil rights supporters, white as well as black. "In my mind I keep seeing a Public school with doors open wide and children and teens of all races, colors and creeds entering therein," a Michigan woman wrote to her congressman in 1963. "Over the door of the school is a big sign which says, 'ANYTOWN PUBLIC SCHOOL—ALL ARE WELCOME—JESUS KEEPOUT!' And I see Him read the sign, and slowly and sadly turn away." In Indiana newspapers published a cartoon of a Supreme Court judge "standing in the school-house door" like George Wallace. Jesus appears on the steps, seeking to enter the school, but the judge rebuffs him. "Sorry, This School's Segregated!" the caption blares.[19]

Together, these two cartoons reflected an important truth: whereas segregationists stood united behind school prayer, the issue divided America's civil rights community. Like James Hicks, civil rights supporters often backed the prayer ban on the simple principle of "My enemy's enemy is my friend": since so many segregationists attacked *Engel* and *Schempp,* integrationists needed to come to the Court's defense. Others went on the attack, savaging racists who violated Christ's teachings of love but who also tried to inscribe them in schools. To still other civil rights advocates, this very message of love made classroom prayer integral—not antithetical—to the freedom struggle. Since God's word inspired the campaign for racial equality, school prayer could only further this larger, sacred cause.

Nowhere were these divisions sharper than among African-Americans. From the start, most national black leaders and organizations backed the Supreme Court's prayer rulings. Across the country, however, many blacks proved reluctant to do so. In Philadelphia a June 1962 survey of six African-American pastors revealed that all but one opposed the ban on prayer. One minister said that religious exercises enhanced school discipline; another feared that the prayer ruling would undermine "moral and religious standards" in society at large; a third demanded a constitutional amendment to overturn it. Shortly thereafter, a council of Philadelphia-area black Baptist clergymen voiced "profound disagreement" with the Supreme Court. As a rule, the council's secretary maintained, courts should not "interfere" with "our greatest institutions"—namely, "homes, churches, and schools." Strong proponents of judicial intervention on questions of race and segregation, many African-Americans demanded judicial restraint when it came to school prayer.[20]

Similarly, black supporters of school prayer often seemed to discover a new solicitude for majoritarian rule. Most black civil rights claims were phrased in terms of timeless verities, not of vote totals: whatever the white majority might desire, activists argued, both the Constitution and the Bible mandated freedom and equality for African-Americans. During the school prayer debate, however, blacks frequently argued that the popular will should trump all other principles. "It is undemocratic to deny the majority influence of a country for the opinion of the minority," declared a group of African Methodist Episcopal Zion pastors, blasting the Court's *Engel* decision. Likewise, a black Virginian expressed surprise that "a supposedly Christian country" would bar public school devotionals. "As it is a 'free' country and the majority rule, I think that they should prevail," he argued. "But, in order to be equitable, they could let the minority place their fingers in their ears and keep silent." By putting the term "free" in quotation marks, he signaled that a majority-white American society had not yet granted racial justice to its black minority. In the same sentence, however, he insisted that schools should privilege the majority-*Christian* perspective—regardless of the sentiments of non-Christian minorities.[21]

Also, many blacks claimed that the special circumstances of African-American communities necessitated public school prayer. Traditionally, they asserted, black schools had placed a heavy emphasis on religious exercises. When the Supreme Court barred these rituals, it also attacked an important part of the African-American educational heritage. At North Carolina's all-black Caswell County Training School, for instance, "chapel" services anchored the weekly schedule. In the wake of *Engel* and *Schempp*, blacks from the Caswell area felt cast out to sea; by 1967 they were circulating petitions for a school prayer amendment. Elsewhere blacks cited the dire social problems afflicting their neighborhoods—especially crime, drugs, and unwanted pregnancy—and argued that prayer might help relieve them. "The schools have gone to the devil and the children have gone to hell under the present setup," intoned a legislator from New York's Harlem district, backing a state law for silent classroom meditation. Subtle church-and-state concerns paled next to the poverty and chaos of inner-city America, which needed the hope and discipline that school prayer provided.[22]

Like African-Americans, white civil rights supporters differed sharply on the prayer issue. Especially among Catholics, spokesmen who praised the Supreme Court on race often condemned its rulings on prayer. "New justices discovered the injustice toward the Negroes hidden behind the fair-sounding slogan of 'separate but equal,'" noted a diocesan newspaper in Indiana in an attack on *Engel*. "Someday soon, God willing, new justices will discover the injustice to religious people hidden behind the slogan of 'separation of Church and State.'" Among Protestants, by contrast, most race liberals seem to have endorsed—or at least accepted—the Court's bans on prayer and Bible reading. After the *Schempp* decision in 1963, the general board of the National Council of Churches—America's foremost theological tribune for racial equality—voted 65–1 to support the ruling. "Worship is a distinctive function of the church," the NCC proclaimed; if performed in school, it would lose its sacred quality and undermine "genuine Christian faith." Witness students' mockery of the Lord's Prayer, which they often profaned with lines like "Give us this day our jelly bread" and "Lead me not into Penn Station."[23]

The nation's leading liberal newspapers backed the Court on race as well as on prayer, often drawing an explicit link between them. In 1966 the *Washington Post* reproved the Senate minority leader, Everett Dirksen, for proposing twin constitutional amendments to override Court decisions on legislative apportionment *and* prayer. In his screeds against the Court's "one man, one vote" rulings, the *Post* pointed out, the Illinois senator championed the rights of rural—and typically white—minorities; but in pleading for school prayer, he suddenly became a staunch proponent of majority rule. Later that year Dirksen would lead a two-week filibuster to kill an "open housing" measure barring racial discrimination in the real estate industry. A cartoonist for the liberal *St. Louis Globe-Democrat* pictured Dirksen in prayer, hands clasped, standing atop a prostrate man who bore the label "Civil Rights Bill." Lest anyone miss the point, the caption proclaimed, "NEARER, MY GOD, TO THEE . . ." Even as he demanded Christianity in schools, critics alleged, Dirksen's recalcitrance on civil rights contradicted the most basic elements of that faith: charity, equality, and love.[24]

In both civil rights and school prayer, Dirksen's anti-Court leadership also symbolized the northward thrust—indeed, the *nationalizing* thrust—of "massive resistance." A close friend of Lyndon B. Johnson's, Dirksen had played an integral role in breaking the filibuster against the 1964 Civil Rights Act and in ensuring passage of the 1965 Voting Rights Act. Yet as Martin Luther King Jr. brought black protest north of the Mason-Dixon Line, especially into Dirksen's home state of Illinois, the senator's ardor for civil rights cooled. Invoking the sanctity of "property rights," Dirksen denounced the 1966 open housing bill; shortly thereafter, the measure died. Then he turned to the battle against school prayer, linking *Engel* and *Schempp* to the Supreme Court's race-related decisions. In all these cases, Dirksen argued, "judicial arrogance" had eroded individual freedom. "I'm not going to let nine men say to 190 million people, including children, when and where they can utter their prayers," Dirksen asserted in a much-quoted challenge to the Court.[25]

In local communities, meanwhile, praise for the so-called Dirksen Amendment—like hostility to civil rights—transcended regional boundaries. To be sure, school prayer still drew its strongest support from the South. As opposition to the black struggle spread across the country, however, it pulled pro-prayer sentiment with it. "The Supreme Court has usurped the powers of Congress and of the elec- torate . . . in the Civil Rights cases as well as the School Prayers Case," a California admirer wrote to Dirksen, "and have deprived the States of their rights." A second Californian congratulated Dirksen for "holding the line" on open housing and prayer, while a Kansan praised his "courage" on both counts. "I hope you will not be detered for a moment because of the opposition of some of the national church leaders," the Kansan wrote. "They simply do not represent the rank and file of people who occupy the pews." Here Dirksen's Kansas ally alluded to the National Council of Churches, whose "pseudo- liberals" or even "Super-Duper Liberals" demanded integration in the schools—but kept God's word out of them.[26]

Inside the NCC, officials typically attributed these critiques to "cultural lag." A large fraction of the laity had reacted "with emo- tional impulsiveness" to the Supreme Court's prayer bans, the NCC spokesman Dean Kelley noted in 1964. Once they obtained "factual and objective information," however, most critics would come to share the "calm judgment" of church leaders like him. Kelley was wrong. First, many devout Americans took offense at the very idea that reason should control religious passion. "We have been accused of being emotional, as if that were a cardinal sin," proclaimed a Mary- land prayer advocate. "It is true, we are emotional. Belief in God, and in everyone's right to acknowledge him in any and all environments, is emotional." Second, Kelley radically underestimated the link between school prayer and other cultural concerns—especially crime, pornography, and the war in Vietnam. Critics would soon fashion these issues into a powerful general assault on "liberalism," not just within America's churches but across American society. The country was already starting its rightward swing, in short, and men like Kelley—*not* his enemies—would soon be lagging behind.[27]

Creating a School Prayer Movement

New England newspapers published an unusual photograph in the spring of 1969: children praying at their local public school. The children hailed from Leyden, Massachusetts, where the school board had recently voted to resume morning devotionals. "It's the little people, the ones tired of smut, dope, and draft card burners, who are supporting us," one board member explained. To the state's education commissioner, however, the board's attack on lawlessness in American society contradicted its own illegal behavior. "If communities can arbitrarily pick and choose those laws which appeal to their taste or manners of living," Commissioner Neil Sullivan warned, "then the future of this country is in jeopardy." He also blasted national school prayer groups, which used the Leyden incident to fuel their campaign for a constitutional amendment. Self-proclaimed champions of "law and order," they nevertheless praised Leyden's "deliberate violation" of both.[28]

Widely reported in the national press, the Leyden episode illustrates three important aspects of the movement to retain school prayer in the 1960s. First, advocates of school prayer increasingly phrased their demands in the language of right-wing populism.[29] They were "the little people," as the Leyden board member said, the "silent majority" whose traditional values of work, family, and decency were being drowned by the permissiveness and decadence of "liberal" society. Second, these activists often borrowed tactics and even arguments from the "liberals" they detested: even as they condemned "draft card burners," prayer protesters in Leyden engaged in their own form of civil disobedience. Last, those in favor of school prayer also formed a loose national network, with a single national goal: a constitutional amendment. Drawing heavily upon women, Catholics, and evangelical Christians, dozens of different amendment groups would help launch a new conservative politics in the United States.

Although the activists never won a prayer amendment in the 1960s, a stream of proposals kept the issue alive. Just ten weeks after the Supreme Court's 1962 *Engel* decision, 49 amendment bills had been introduced in Congress; by 1964 the total would swell to 144. A single organization, Project America, collected more than a million signatures for the prayer amendment during a seven-month span in 1963 and 1964. Simultaneously, dozens of film stars lent their names—and often their dollars—to Project Prayer, which organized several huge petition drives of its own. "Not all of Hollywood's motion picture stars are aligned with liberals who are seeking to change the American way of life," a Louisiana newspaper gushed. "In these days when [stars] are being linked to civil rights demonstrations on the part of lawless trespassers, it is good to note that there are representatives of the film industry who seek to preserve our constitutional freedoms." A more skeptical columnist quipped that Project Prayer's roster of celebrities—including John Wayne, Ginger Rogers, and Ronald Reagan—seemed "more versed in marital infidelity than religious fundamentalism." Nevertheless, he acknowledged, the campaign had helped whip millions of citizens into a "letter-writing frenzy" on behalf of a prayer amendment.[30]

Out in the field, dozens of local groups collected donations and signatures for school prayer. Such campaigns were typically started by an aggrieved mother. In Holland, Michigan, Mrs. Howard W. Graves founded an organization called Restore School Voluntary Prayer (RSVP) after her eight-year-old daughter announced that her class could not pray for President Lyndon B. Johnson's speedy recovery from his 1965 appendectomy surgery. Several months later Graves presented 27,000 petition signatures to House Republican leader Gerald R. Ford, most of them collected in Ford's own Michigan district. Similarly, the Brockton, Massachusetts, activist Rita Warren started a prayer drive after her daughter came home one afternoon and asked, "Mom, do you know they won't let us pray in school?" Subsequently, Warren spearheaded a successful statewide referendum to allow school prayers; when state officials continued to bar them, she shifted her focus to the federal amendment campaign. The best-known housewife-activist was Louise Ruhlin of Cuyahoga, Ohio, who sold fruitcakes outside her son's school—and sold her own stock, at a loss—to help finance a prayer drive. Targeting congressmen who had rejected the prayer amendment, Ruhlin and her team of "middle-aged ladies in tennis shoes," as one annoyed legislator dubbed them, posted billboards urging voters to turn the lawmakers out of office.[31]

Like Rita Warren, an Italian immigrant, many of the women who joined these campaigns were Catholic. For most of their history, American Catholics were the country's foremost champions of the separation of church and state. After the courts ruled against school prayer, however, Catholics "made a complete reversal" and became "the most vigorous defender of religious practices in the public schools," as the school prayer opponent Leo Pfeffer reported. Nearly every leading Catholic cleric condemned the *Engel* and *Schempp* decisions, while several Catholic newspapers warned that "litigious minorities"—meaning Jews—would face violent retribution if they continued to resist school prayer. Long a persecuted minority themselves, Catholics, like African-Americans, discovered a new affinity for majoritarian politics during the struggle over school prayer. "Catholics do have short memories," wrote one Jewish spokesman in 1962. "They seem to have forgotten their own struggles against the Protestants . . . to prevent Bible reading and prayer recitation in the public schools—presumably because they were not Catholic enough."[32]

To Catholic spokesmen, by contrast, the Church's position had remained consistent throughout. During the vicious "Bible riots" that swept several northeastern cities in the 1840s, Catholics "DID NOT ASK THAT PRAYER IN THE SCHOOLS BE DISCONTINUED," a Philadelphia diocesan newspaper screamed in 1962. Instead, a New

Mexico paper asserted, Catholics had objected only to "forced participation in Protestant practices," especially study from the King James
Bible. Now the Supreme Court proposed to strip *all* religious practices
from the schools, thereby enshrining "secular humanism" as a "state-
sponsored religion," one bishop complained. Here Catholics began to
echo the rhetoric of fundamentalist Christians, who slowly entered
the political arena to fight for school prayer. "The Catholic Church
(properly led) could have great impact . . . if it would but 'ecumeni-
cize' with the *real* Protestants—the more fundamental types," a
Catholic litigator argued. "There are vast areas for common action
with these people."[33]

Writing in 1973, the litigator noted the steady growth of fundamentalist activism since *Engel* and *Schempp*. True, many fundamentalist Protestants still eschewed politics: in 1965 the future Moral
Majority founder Jerry Falwell contended that their only task was to
lead each American conscience to Christ. "Preachers are not called to
be politicians, but soul winners," Falwell declared, attacking clergymen who participated in civil rights protests. "We need to get off the
streets and back into the pulpits and into the prayer rooms." In
school prayer fundamentalist Christians discovered a social issue that
directly concerned individual souls, spanning the historical gap
between political action in this world and personal salvation in the
next one. Hence the prayer issue also brought thousands of fundamentalists into politics for the first time. "If we stand idly by and let
things like this go on, I fear that in generations to come when God is
mentioned to a child they will say, 'Who's that?'" a woman from
Ottumwa, Iowa, wrote in 1968, explaining her own "conversion" to
the politics of school prayer. "Christians of Ottumwa, stand up for
your religious convictions!"[34]

The prayer issue also bridged a growing rift within fundamentalism
itself. One branch of fundamentalism, most strongly associated with
Carl McIntire and the American Council of Christian Churches
(ACCC), insisted on biblical inerrancy as well as strict separation
from "apostate" or mainline churches. Another wing, calling itself

neo-evangelical or simply evangelical, shared many of McIntire's views on scripture but did not place as strong an emphasis on either doctrinal purity or separation from mainline denominations; in fact, the evangelicals recruited heavily from mainline congregations.[35] Significantly, the two camps came to agree that Christians should fight the Court bans on prayer and Bible reading. After the *Engel* decision, the National Association of Evangelicals (NAE) urged worshipers to attend PTA meetings and circulate petitions to retain prayer in their local schools; when schools started to comply with the ruling, the NAE threw its weight behind a constitutional amendment.[36] McIntire and the ACCC actually welcomed *Engel*, but only because it struck down a "common denominator" prayer that ignored Jesus Christ— "the only mediator between God and Man." Once the Court ruled out Bible reading, by contrast, McIntire and the ACCC zealously embraced the amendment cause. "It is time now for us to turn the tables and take up the crusade," McIntire wrote after the *Schempp* decision was announced. "The Christians have been too quiet, too placid, and have not recognized that it is a part of their responsibility also to work for decency and integrity in our schools."[37]

Tensions occasionally gripped this growing coalition of patriotic societies, women, Catholics, and fundamentalists. Whereas the evangelicals welcomed Catholics into the battle for school prayer, for instance, McIntire and his followers still eschewed any cooperation with the "Beast of Rome." Together, however, school prayer's disparate advocates began to enunciate a common argument—and a common ideology—for their cause:

> The Supreme Court has taken God out of our schools and freed many known criminals thru technicalities, our televisions and newspapers scream violance is the order of our day, our Attorney Geneal Clark writes that he can't touch Stokely Carmical and the various looters and burners in our cities . . . There were a few good things in the past, such as moral fiber, faith in one's fellow man and country, reward for work well done, and protection by police. I felt I had a great deal more civil liberties then than now.

Like Sodom and Gomorrah—like Rome—America is rotting from within. Immorality is flourishing and pre-marital sex is being condoned even from the pulpits; juvenile delinquency is on the rise . . . America is in an advanced state of moral decline.

I certainly approve of teachers . . . praying in the classroom. There certainly are enough teachers preaching atheism, distrust of the establishment, civil rights (with no civil responsibility). We certainly need SOMETHING to counter-balance all the harm that has been done.[38]

Of course, activists admitted, the ban on school prayer was not the sole reason for America's epidemic of pornography, crime, and civil unrest. Rather, the ban was the primary symbol of an evil, decadent elite that *did* cause such ills: "liberals." To some critics, especially fundamentalist Christians, these despised "liberals" were quite literally agents of Satan.[39] Others identified liberalism with "loose convictions," as a Californian wrote, noting an overall erosion of "courage and backbone"—that is, of moral standards—in the body politic. Although liberalism had infected only a fraction of Americans, critics warned, its wily proponents were attempting to inflict it on the rest of the population. "The liberals falsely claim to believe in democracy—the will of the people—the vote of the majority," wrote one prayer activist a few months after the *Schempp* decision, "but when they can, they will use every legal device to kill legislation, although it may be popular, that is contrary to their leftist philosophy."[40]

But prayer supporters also mimicked this "leftist" foe. Even as they skewered liberals for fomenting social agitation in God's name, prayer activists often invoked scripture to justify their own forms of civil disobedience. Citing Daniel's refusal to obey Darius's ban on prayer, a rural New York minister argued that the Bible actually *mandated* resistance to *Engel* and *Schempp*. "A Christian surely can not let her mouth be stopped by state directives," the minister asserted. "If opening her class with prayer were to cost her her job, it would not be the first time that a Christian suffered because of convictions." Other activists praised sporadic student protests against the prayer ban, which themselves echoed the rhythm and rhetoric of civil rights demonstrations. In Newport, Kentucky, students posted "Ban the Bible Ban" signs in their high school; when school officials removed the signs, ninety pupils affixed similar messages to their shirts and dresses. In Hicksville, Long Island, more than fifty students recited New York's banned "Regents' prayer" during their school's prescribed moment of silence. Following a plea from the school principal, student leaders ended the protest. But several pupils continued their "prayer rebellion," as a local newspaper called it, declaring that they would sooner receive suspensions from the school than suspend their own devotionals to God.[41]

Like left-wing activists, also, prayer activists developed a distinctive style of protest music. In the mid-1960s they helped popularize a special 45-rpm "school prayer record" by the Hal Webb Team, a gospel-style group. Lest anyone miss the point, one side of the record bore a song entitled "Let's Put Prayer and Bible Reading Back in School"; the other side was called, simply, "You Better Do It." Even as he railed against civil rights "agitators" in mainline churches, similarly, the fundamentalist leader Carl McIntire distributed protest songs against the prayer ban. One number, "Please Pray," was set to the tune of "My Bonnie Lies over the Ocean":

> Oh, Mommie, please give me a cookie
> To take for today's lunch at school
> But I'll have to thank God for it here, now
> For to pray there is now 'gainst the rule . . .
> Please pray! Please pray!
> Let's pray we may still pray each day, in school!
> Please, pray! Each day!
> That they'll soon change this very bad rule.[42]

For the prayer and civil rights movements alike, jokes provided a respite from injustice as well as a pithy critique of it. One favorite tale involved a teacher who comes upon a group of boys kneeling in a school hallway. "What are you doing on your knees?" she inquires. "Shooting craps," comes the quick reply. "Thank God," the teacher says. "I thought you were praying." Occasionally prayer supporters even engaged in forms of what leftists called "guerrilla theater"— abrupt, humorous acts designed to shock viewers' consciences. Anonymous activists in New Jersey papered school fences with a satirical notice: "IN CASE OF ATOMIC ATTACK, THE FEDERAL RULING AGAINST PRAYER IN SCHOOLS WILL BE TEMPORARILY SUSPENDED." The protest made the national news, to prayer defenders' delight. "Now *this* should give our more liberal friends something to ponder over," a Michigan woman exulted.[43]

Despite their jabs at "liberals," finally, prayer activists often shared their enemies' emphasis on "rights." In Michigan one activist claimed that "the Christian is being discriminated against"; in Maryland another argued that the Court had removed her "religious freedom"; in Indiana a third likened this oppression to the passion of Christ. "The same bigotry that persecuted Him and His followers then continues today," the Indianan averred. "It seems to me that this is no longer a democracy, where the majority rules, or where tolerance unites us. It is instead an era . . . that has upheld the so-called rights of the individual, but has ignored the rights of the majority."[44] The final comment highlighted a key difference that still separated prayer activists from their liberal counterparts: whereas the left often defended embattled minorities, prayer supporters claimed to speak for a plurality of Americans. By the early 1980s, however, the school prayer movement would fully embrace the status—and the politics— of a suffering minority. Even as a new conservative president endorsed their aims, supporters of school prayer veered ever closer to the "liberal" dogma they purportedly despised.

School Prayer and the New Christian Right

In August 1982 the so-called New Christian Right convened a three-day "Family Forum" in Buffalo, New York. Speakers included Jerry Falwell and Phyllis Schlafly, along with the nation's top-ranking educational official, Secretary of Education T. H. Bell. Reviewing several school-related issues—sex education, "obscene" textbooks, and prayer—Bell remarked that a single theme bound them together: parental control. "Education is a family matter," he proclaimed, praising the forum's efforts. "The parent is the foremost teacher, the home is the most influential classroom, and schools should exist to support the home." On controversial subjects like prayer, other speakers insisted, a parent's wishes should trump every other concern—including popular majorities. No matter how many Americans wanted to prohibit classroom prayer, schools would have to provide it to the families that still desired it.[45]

Bell's comments illuminate what was truly "new" about the New Christian Right and its battle for school prayer. First, media-savvy groups like Falwell's Moral Majority provided publicity and focus for a school prayer movement that had long lacked national direction or organization. Second, as Bell's praise showed, the movement finally won the approval and support of national political leaders—including the conservative president who appointed Bell, Ronald Reagan. Last, despite titles such as "Moral Majority," the New Right developed a refashioned gospel of *minority* rights in its campaign for school prayer. Less and less would activists invoke the virtues of "America," writ large, or the need to "correct" families that had forsaken those virtues. Instead, like the Israelites in Babylon, prayer supporters would sing a sacred song in a strange land.

Except for a few local flashes, the school prayer movement was quiet during the early 1970s. Many fundamentalist Christians placed their own children in private academies, rendering the question of prayer in public schools less directly relevant to their lives. After the Supreme Court's 1973 ruling in *Roe v. Wade,* abortion replaced prayer as fundamentalists' primary political concern. In 1976, however, the ascendance of a self-proclaimed evangelical Christian to the White House seemed to reenergize the school prayer movement. Jimmy Carter's avowal that he was "born again" brought many fundamentalists into his corner, confident that Carter would inscribe their beliefs in law. Carter disappointed them. Despite his personal opposition to abortion, he refused to support an anti-abortion amendment or to stack the courts with pro-life judges. On school-based worship, similarly, Carter declared that "government ought to stay out of the prayer business." The comment raised the ire of Jerry Falwell, already angered by Carter's apostasy on abortion. After all, Falwell wrote in 1980, Carter had prayed at the signing of the Arab-Israeli peace accord. Why shouldn't schoolchildren pray at the beginning of school?[46]

By then Falwell had discovered a new champion of school prayer in Carter's rival Ronald Reagan. The first president to back a prayer amendment, Reagan defended it with a typically dramatic—and probably fictional—wartime anecdote. "I like the America of the four Chaplains—Hebrew and Christian—who gave their life jackets and lives to save some American soldiers from drowning in World War Two," he noted in 1984, attacking "secularization" in the public schools. "I'm quite sure they didn't first ask the religion of the young men they saved." That same year Reagan told a convention of evangelicals that the reinstitution of school prayer "would do more than any other action" to "reassert the faith and values that made America great." Most of all, he argued, prayer would help bring alienated youth back into the national fold: "If we could get God and discipline back in our schools, maybe we could get drugs and violence out."[47]

Besides this unprecedented rhetorical support from the White House, school prayer received a huge boost from the Christian Right's famous direct-mail and television empires. In millions of letters and telegrams, activists linked the Court's ban on prayer to pornography, homosexuality, abortion, and the proposed Equal Rights Amendment. Falwell himself claimed a mailing list of 7 million families, generated mostly by his *Old Time Gospel Hour* television show. The show broadcast a special program about school prayer, and the televangelist Pat Robertson's *700 Club* devoted several segments to the issue. Meanwhile, a group called the Leadership Foundation distributed more than 42 million pieces of prayer-related material along with a one-hour television spot, *Let Our Children Pray,* which aired on over 100 different stations. All told, more than 60 organizations probably engaged in direct-mail, television, or radio efforts to promote prayer in the public schools.[48]

Like most social issues on the New Christian Right's agenda, however, school prayer failed to make much legislative headway. A prayer amendment passed in the Senate in 1979, only to stall in the House in 1980; reintroduced in different versions during each of the next three years, it never achieved the necessary two-thirds vote in either branch of Congress. Citing the barrage of mail in favor of the amendment, many supporters continued to proclaim the majoritarian basis of school prayer: since most Americans wanted it, schools should offer it. But other prayer activists discovered a new solicitude for minority rights. Following a prayer amendment defeat in 1984, Falwell compared prayer advocates to the Jews in Egypt; as an assistant explained, they were a "persecuted minority group" whose "rights" had been eroded by the public schools. Across America, prayer proponents fashioned similar appeals. In Pennsylvania activists argued that prayer bans robbed Christian pupils of their "cultural heritages"; Oklahomans claimed that the bans "could be psychologically damaging" to "students of the Christian faith"; in Massachusetts prayer advocates established a Christian Civil Liberties Union to fight for their own "freedom of religion."[49]

Especially in the South, this new language helped buttress the continued disobedience of Supreme Court doctrine on school prayer. Under the old majoritarian argument, supporters would have to relinquish prayer once enough voters turned against it. Using the new nomenclature of "rights," by contrast, activists could claim an *a priori*—and unassailable—"freedom" to worship in schools. "I'd rather be right with God than [with] the Supreme Court," gloated a self-described "bayou rebel" in Louisiana after his school district reinstituted prayer in 1982. Significantly, the same district had defied a court busing order to achieve racial balance the previous year; in that sense, one observer noted, the prayer issue was "just the latest chapter in a history of resistance" by the white South. In Birmingham,

Alabama, elementary school pupils began each day by bowing their heads and asking God to "help me . . . find new ways of just being kind"; in Greenville, Mississippi, they thanked God before lunch; and in China Grove, North Carolina, high school students selected Bible verses to read over the school intercom system.[50]

For their own part, African-Americans also continued to challenge the courts' prayer directives. In Raleigh, North Carolina, an African Methodist Episcopal Zion pastor argued that prayer would improve the "moral standards" of black communities; in Chicago a minister complained that schools could provide information on "dope traffic" and sex but not on "spiritual values"; and in Albany, New York, another black cleric averred that the Bible enjoined everyone—including schoolchildren—to pray. Despite their differences on busing and other issues, meanwhile, African-Americans increasingly allied with whites on behalf of school prayer. At a high school in Rockingham, North Carolina, for example, students of both races asked God to help them "love all people, no matter what their color or country is."[51]

By this late date, such expressions of liberal spirituality were rare. Instead, as a North Carolina critic wrote in 1983, nearly every prayer or religious practice in the public schools reflected a "fundamentalist version of Christianity." In Virginia, where Bible classes had once taught race liberalism, such courses were "tinged with threats of hell-fire" and "full of talk about . . . trying to convert a heathen world." North of the Mason-Dixon Line the same trend was evident: insofar as prayer or religious study continued in the public schools, it was dominated by conservatives or fundamentalists. In North Dakota self-described born-again Christians revived a 1927 law requiring the posting of the Ten Commandments in every classroom. According to one of its authors, the law originally aimed to encourage "less war and more peace" by emphasizing God's sixth injunction: Thou shalt not kill. By contrast, its new supporters stressed the commandment to worship God, and him alone. Opponents of the measure risked eternal doom. "What are you going to answer the Lord on Judgment

Day to the question he will ask, 'Why did you object to having my commandments hung on the wall of your school'?" wrote one supporter in March 1979. "Better give that some thought." The very question demonstrated the dramatic change in the scope and purpose of religious instruction in American public schools. Formerly a movement to promote peace and justice in this world, school prayer became a vehicle for insuring personal salvation in the next one.[52]

The Battle for Sex Education

The sex education controversy reached Kalamazoo, Michigan, in the early months of 1969. Its catalyst was a scheduled appearance by Gordon V. Drake, the author of a vitriolic pamphlet condemning the Sex Information and Education Council of the United States (SIECUS). Circulated across the country by right-wing groups like the John Birch Society, Drake's pamphlet charged that SIECUS—a small team of physicians and scientists—spread "raw sex" through America's schoolhouses, softening children's moral backbone and making them "easy targets for Marxism." For several years Kalamazoo schools had quietly taught sex education without any major criticism or disruption. When a local Birch Society chapter announced plans to host Drake for a speech, however, citizens quickly divided into hostile camps. As in countless other communities throughout America, sex education soon became Kalamazoo's most hotly contested school issue.[1]

On one side stood the town's educational and medical establishments, led by the Kalamazoo pediatrician and SIECUS board member Frederick J. Margolis. Properly taught, Margolis believed, sex education would improve rather than injure children's morality. "We want to convey attitudes and feelings so that people learn to associate sex, not with promiscuity, VD, something dirty, but with a positive good,

[an] essential part of human living," he told the *Kalamazoo Gazette*. True, he acknowledged, parents bore the primary responsibility for sex education. But "their fears and their own limited backgrounds too often stand in the way," forcing schools to take up the slack. The doctor reserved his greatest disdain for Drake and his supporters in the John Birch Society, who presumed to tell educators how to teach about sex. Since Drake lacked any "real training" in "medicine or psychiatry," Margolis argued, Kalamazoo would do well to listen to people who did. The *Gazette* agreed, praising Margolis as a "nationally recognized expert on sex education"—and blasting its critics as ignorant, far-right "Birchites."[2]

In letters to the newspaper, though, citizens who opposed sex education bristled at this automatic association with the Birch Society. Only a fraction of critics bore any link to the society; the rest were simply parents, as one put it, outraged at the intrusion of "sexperts" into their sacred domain. "Isn't it strange that God gave children to parents and not to the experts, since the experts think they only are qualified to teach our children?" a Kalamazoo mother wrote. "I am perfectly willing to let the experts teach my children reading, writing and arithmetic. When it comes to matters which will affect their moral character, I will handle the job." Youth were suffering from "degradation on all sides," another mother noted, citing drugs, promiscuity, and the elimination of school prayer. Rather than capitulating to the "perverts" in SIECUS, then, parents must seize control of American public schools—and "turn back the tide of degeneracy" in American public life.[3]

Like advocates of school prayer, opponents of sex education spoke the language of right-wing populism. They were the defenders of tradition—work, family, nation, God—in a society that seemed to mock these time-honored values. But several important differences marked the twin struggles for school prayer and against sex education, highlighting Americans' profound ambivalence on the issue that linked these controversies: parents' rights. In the prayer debate, conservatives tended to claim that *children's* rights should trump parental ones: since so many families neglected or ignored the religious instruction of their young, schools would have to provide it. On the question of sex education, conservatives made exactly the opposite argument: parental views must take precedence over "expert" pronouncements. Of course, a similar contradiction plagued the liberal camp. On prayer, liberals championed parents' rights: lest schools insult even a single family's creed, all forms of religious practice should be banished from the classroom. But when it came to instruction about sex, liberals were perfectly willing to violate these individual preferences. Indeed, the very fact that children did not receive sex education "at home"—at least not the brand of sex education that liberals thought best—became the central justification for instituting it at school.

The same tangled politics enmeshed sex education until the early 1980s, when several new patterns emerged. Rather than opposing all forms of sex education in schools, the so-called New Right started to demand its own version of the subject: "abstinence-only" education. Whereas an earlier generation had condemned liberals for stripping religion from the schools, meanwhile, the New Right indicted them on a much more serious charge: imposing their *own* religion, a "secular humanism" that supplanted God's authority. To challenge this ascendant faith—and especially to combat the loose sexual ethics it encouraged—Christians would need to promote their own sex education curriculum in the schools. Like the anti-drug programs that also proliferated during these years, New Right sex education bore a simple message: Just Say No. Abstinence outside marriage was right; masturbation, homosexuality, and all forms of premarital sex were wrong.

As in the prayer dispute, New Right spokesmen sometimes buttressed this argument with liberal rhetoric: since students came from a diversity of "cultures," some conservatives said, schools should transmit Christian as well as humanist views of sex. But to others the very goal of "presenting both sides" demonstrated humanism's evil influence. "Even the attempt to teach [sex education] without values attaches a value to it," warned one opponent. "The value is that all varieties of sexual and social behavior are of equal validity."[4] Such complaints reflected an exaggerated, almost fantastic view of so-called mainstream or liberal sex education, which still displayed a deep unease about premarital sexual relations. At least rhetorically, however, liberals favored "discussion" of sexuality in the classroom; conservatives, by contrast, demanded a single set of dicta. No simple compromise could "solve" the problem of sex education, which touched upon the deepest religious and philosophical rifts in post–World War II America.

Sex Education and the Sexual Revolution

Two empty envelopes were mailed to SIECUS director Mary Steichen Calderone on August 1, 1969. Playing on Calderone's M.D. and M.P.H. degrees, the first was addressed to "Mary Stinken Calderone, Mistress of the Devil, Misfit Prostitute of Hell." The second envelope was sent to "Sex-Maniacs In seducing Every Child, Under Satan's Directives," a parody of the "SIECUS" acronym. Across the bottom the sender had scrawled, "Steal a Bible and Read Matt. 23:15 and see Where God Himself Has Already Condemned You to Eternal Torture and Hell, and Remember this on your Deathbed." But the most vituperative remarks appeared on the back of the second envelope:

> God Said, about Seducers of Children: You will Wish You Had Never Been Born . . . You'd Be Better Off if a Millstone Were Tied Around Your Neck, and You Be Cast into the Depths of The Sea. He Meant that the Drowning Would Be Better Than Being Cast into the Depths of Hell, where You Will Have Mouten Steel Poured into You From Two Directions . . . and Where Your Diet Will Be Puss, Excretions, Roaches, Maggots, and Spiders. Think it Over in Bed Tonite, as Well as On Your Deathbed.[5]

Both missives were mailed anonymously from New Orleans, where an array of citizen groups had mobilized against a proposed sex education program. Although Calderone and SIECUS had no direct connection to the program, critics condemned them for fostering "immorality"—or worse, subversion—in the schools. Converging first on the city school board and then on the state legislature, opponents soon won a law barring any sex education in Louisiana below the ninth grade; by 1970 the state would prohibit the subject altogether. Across the country, a similar pattern obtained. In a narrow two-year span, hundreds of school districts and nineteen states considered measures to ban or limit sex education. Regardless of location, Mary Calderone served as the central lightning rod for this swift current of discontent. One Chicago minister accused her of plotting "to corrupt Christian America"; in Tennessee a columnist deemed her "head madam at SIECUS"; and in upstate New York parents charged that "sexual perverts and communists" permeated her organization. "Why don't you queers, pinkos and pimps crawl under some damp rock and have your own sex orgy until you die from exhaustion?" wrote a Michigan resident in a typically spiteful letter to Calderone. "Nothing would suit me better."[6]

At first glance, Calderone seemed an unlikely target for this condemnation. Hardly the brainchild of Calderone and SIECUS, sex education (or "sex instruction," as it was formerly called) dated to the outset of the twentieth century. It grew slowly in the early decades but gained speed in the 1940s and 1950s, well before Calderone entered the picture.[7] Also, SIECUS itself was a minuscule organization: publishing a single book and a handful of teachers' guides, it bore little resemblance to the "octopus" or "interlocking directorate" that its enemies imagined. And, like the sex educators who preceded them, Calderone and SIECUS sought to control—not to unleash—children's sexual impulses. Beneath its rhetoric of "choice" and "honesty," the "new" sex education conveyed an overwhelmingly conventional morality—indeed, some said, an *old-fashioned* morality—of monogamy and self-discipline.[8]

Why, in that case, the explosive reaction against SIECUS—and against sex education—in the late 1960s? The answer lay in the complex set of developments that contemporaries called the "sexual revolution." Defying simple definition, the term encompassed everything from cohabitation and homosexuality to pornography and the Pill. Its diverse and often contradictory strands were united by an impatience with the sexual status quo, a desire to free America from its repressive straitjacket.[9] Profoundly ambivalent about this "revolution," particularly its acceptance of sex outside marriage, sex educators nevertheless shared in its spirit of candor and experimentation. To critics, then, sex education became a symbol of everything that was promiscuous, permissive, and decadent in American life. Significantly, these attacks occurred at the height of the sexual revolution. Most accounts of the revolution place its enemies at the end of the story, when the supposedly libertine Sixties gave way to the conservative Seventies.[10] But the sex education controversy reminds us that the sexual revolution was contested at every turn, not just in its final laps. If millions of Americans—especially youth—celebrated new freedoms and frankness, just as many citizens sought to arrest these very trends. "Revolution" and "counterrevolution" occurred simultaneously, in other words, reflecting the overall polarization of the "radical" 1960s.

As early as 1964 both *Time* and *Newsweek* published cover stories describing a "sexual revolution" among young Americans. That same year Mary Steichen Calderone helped found the Sex Education and Information Council of the United States. The daughter of the photographer Edward Steichen and niece of the poet Carl Sandburg, Calderone grew up amid the artistic avant-garde of Progressive-era New York City. After a failed first marriage, she attended medical school and eventually became medical director of the Planned Parenthood Federation of America. But Calderone grew frustrated at Planned Parenthood, which emphasized birth control services to the neglect of "sexual problems" such as impotence and frigidity. Since these problems stemmed from Americans' muddled attitudes and outright misinformation about sex, Calderone reasoned, the nation needed a separate agency devoted solely to sex education. Thanks to bequests from John D. Rockefeller and other philanthropists, SIECUS soon boasted eight full-time staff members and an annual budget of $500,000. It also enlisted several prominent "sex experts" to serve on its board of directors, including the Oregon educator Lester A. Kirkendall and the St. Louis gynecologist William H. Masters, the coauthor (with Virginia Johnson) of the 1966 bestseller *Human Sexual Response*.[11]

To their foes, these "sexperts" represented the vanguard of the nascent sexual revolution. But SIECUS actually functioned as the revolution's rear echelon, restraining the more radical warriors at the forefront. On the one hand, Calderone welcomed the new public discussion and acceptance of "sexual energy," which she deemed a "vital life force" and a key to human happiness and fulfillment. On the other, Calderone and her colleagues aimed to channel this energy into its traditional venue: the marriage bed. "Let me assure you . . . that I stand squarely for monogamy," she wrote in 1968 in a typical response to a critic, "for the committed relationship in marriage that is life-long." Condemning "casual sex" between men and women, Calderone also denounced homosexual relations of every sort; "healthy" sex education, she argued, would help prevent both of these behaviors.[12]

Out in the schools, meanwhile, sex education courses proliferated: by 1968, according to one estimate, half of American school districts taught the subject. Few of these programs had any direct connection to SIECUS, which sent consultants to some thirty communities and literature to several hundred others. But the "new" sex education classes shared SIECUS's joint emphasis on expression and control, welcoming "discussion" of the sexual impulse but stressing the need to discipline it. As educators admitted, the very *goal* of "discussion" was to encourage such discipline. "We don't lecture or give sermons," a school superintendent explained in 1968. "The truth is, though, we *are* selling middle-class morality." When the topic of premarital sex came up for "debate," for example, teachers frequently distributed statistics on venereal disease, abortion, and divorce. Such techniques lent a scientific gloss to the "hell-fire warnings" of the past, a journalist observed, but their objective was exactly the same: to foster monogamy in marriage.[13]

Still, the journalist added, the "new" sex education signaled a much more frank, direct attitude toward sexuality. The subject "has changed its aura from that of a shady mistress to that of a prim matron," she quipped, "who can be taken everywhere in broad daylight." Formerly tabooed terms—"erection," "orgasm," "masturbation"—now found their way into American classrooms; however much sex educators stacked the deck in favor of traditional morality, their vocabulary diverged sharply from that of their forebears. Nowhere was this trend clearer than in the new crop of books, films, and slide shows that arose in the 1960s to supply the burgeoning sex education market. The most controversial item was a text called *How Babies Are Made,* which featured drawings of dogs and chickens copulating as well as a cartoon of a man and woman in bed together; although they were covered by a sheet, the man clearly lay atop the woman. In a popular movie called *The Game,* meanwhile, a teenage boy pressured a reluctant (and virginal) girl to have sex in the back of his father's car. To be sure, both the book and the film embodied a staunchly traditional, "Cellophane-wrapped" view of sex, as an amused British reporter noted: the modest cartoon identified its subjects as "mother and father," while the movie concluded with a stern warning against premarital intercourse. To underscore the point, the reporter's article was entitled "Unpermissive America." To millions of Americans, however, these same materials embodied the evils of a society that seemed to permit *everything*—at least when it came to sex.[14]

From Soviet Subversion to the Sick Sixties

Attacks on sex education were hardly unique to the 1960s. On the contrary, they had accompanied the subject since its inception. In the early 1900s, for example, Catholics charged that sex education—like Darwinism—denigrated religious interpretations of human life.

After World War II they also protested a popular new sex education film, *Human Growth,* which included diagrams of male and female genitals and even footage of a baby's birth. But the loudest condemnations of sex education came from right-wing patriotic and veterans' groups, who suspected that the entire subject was a diabolical Soviet plot. "Why all of a sudden this emphasis on SEX?" asked Amos A. Fries, who also led campaigns against allegedly "Red" history textbooks. "Is this departure—that is, teaching Sex Education—part of the efforts of Communism aimed at destroying morality among American youth?" In California the state Un-American Activities Committee even convened a hearing in 1947 to investigate "sex books" in the schools. After collecting testimony from parents, teachers, and physicians, the committee concluded that the sex education texts "follow or parallel the Communist Party line" for "the destruction of the moral fibre" of America.[15]

Such accusations seem to have declined in the early 1950s, possibly reflecting a decrease in sex education itself. But they reawakened near the end of the decade, when "the superabundance of sex" in the mass media—television, movies, and advertising—gave new life to theories of a "Red Sex" conspiracy. "Few contemporary authors dare mention Communism in connection with the so-called 'sex revolution,'" one critic noted in 1959. "Yet evidence exists that there is a connection." Specifically, he claimed, sex educators used Pavlovian "mind-conditioning" methods to promote "unrestrained sexual license," which Soviet theorists had long identified as a precondition for the worldwide triumph of their ideology.[16]

The conspiracy theory would be revived ten years later, courtesy of the John Birch Society. Founded in 1958 by the Massachusetts candy manufacturer Robert Welch, the society detected a Soviet plot in almost every aspect of American life. Most notoriously, Welch even condemned Dwight D. Eisenhower as a "conscious agent of the Communist conspiracy." The Birchites seem to have ignored sex education until January 1969, when Welch told a Houston audience that the subject was part of a "filthy Communist plot"; its "real purpose," he insisted, was "to keep our high school youth obsessed with sex." That same month Welch announced the formation of the Birch Society's Movement to Restore Decency (MOTOREDE). In the long run, MOTOREDE would aim to reclaim "the morals, manners, customs, traditions, and values that have preserved our civilization," as its first bulletin blared, highlighting America's alarming epidemics of crime, pornography, and drug abuse. But the group's first target would be sex education courses, which had proliferated along with these negative trends—and seemed to have perpetuated them, "exactly as the Communists have planned and intended."[17]

The organization proceeded to distribute instructional packets for starting local chapters, complete with leaflets, bumper stickers, sample news releases, and form letters to prospective members. It also produced a thirty-minute filmstrip on sex education, *The Innocents Defiled*, which activists could purchase for thirty dollars. Focusing mainly on Calderone and SIECUS, Birchite material besmirched them with the time-honored tactic of guilt by association: one SIECUS board member had been active in the "Communist-controlled" teachers' union in New York City, another signed the "Communist-inspired" Stockholm Peace Petition, and so on. Most of all, SIECUS's subversive intent was apparent in its own published doctrines and directives. Simply by raising sexual ethics as a "question for discussion," Birch Society members charged, SIECUS undermined those very ethics. The results could be seen and heard on any American streetcorner, in youths' "filthy language, squalid dress, lewd behavior, and disrespect for authority." The only remedy lay with American parents, who must seize back the moral authority they had mistakenly ceded to public schools. "I'm the person responsible for raising my children, not the principal," declared a suggested MOTOREDE script for addressing stubborn school officials. "And I certainly know more about what is best for them than he does."[18]

For the next several years Calderone and her supporters would blame the John Birch Society for the nationwide attack on sex education.[19] Just as SIECUS's critics exaggerated its scope and power, though, so did sex educators inflate the Birchites' influence. By the late 1960s the Birch Society was in disarray; plagued by paranoia and internal strife, it faded quickly from the scene. Across the political spectrum, meanwhile, Americans heaped ridicule upon the Birchites' accusation of "subversion" in sex education. The Chicago columnist Mike Royko jokingly suggested that Mao Tse-tung, Fidel Castro, Che Guevara, and Ho Chi Minh had sparked Communist revolutions by distributing sex pamphlets entitled "Let Mao Tell You How," "Hit the Hay, by Fidel and Che," and "Want to Know? Ask Ho!" In a more serious vein, the staunchly conservative American Medical Association published an impassioned attack on "the *extreme* right wing"—a code word for the John Birch Society—after the Birchites blasted the AMA for supporting "Communist" sex education.[20]

In the same editorial, however, the AMA acknowledged that the movement against sex education extended far beyond the Birch Society. Even as they rejected the society's claims of Communist intrigue, it seemed, thousands of "sincerely motivated but uninformed individuals" embraced the other two themes of the Birchite critique: moral degradation and parental rights. To put it differently, many Americans who scoffed at charges of subversion still rejected sex education as a blight on society and an insult to their own authority. "It's a red herring to label opponents as the far right," warned an Illinois school superintendent who supported sex education. Instead, he added, most critics of sex education were simply parents who were concerned about the moral well-being of their children. More precisely, most of them were *mothers:* rejecting the content and sometimes the premises of sex education, they also bridled at any association with the "far-right"—and male-dominated—John Birch Society. "The [sex education] programs are springing up like crabgrass and dichondra," noted Dixie Ryan, the mother of three children in the California schools, "but the opposition to it is beginning to sear the grass roots like prairie fire." Hardly the seedlings of the Birch Society, foes of sex education sprouted independently across the American political landscape.[21]

At least a year before the Birchites appeared on the scene, for example, Ryan had forged a group called Parents United for a Responsible Education (PURE) to fight sex education in the Los Angeles area. In a veritable avalanche of acronyms, hundreds of other local groups across the country also attacked sex education. The most common symbol was "P," for "parent": from Parents Opposed to Sex Education (POSE) to Parents Against Universal Sex Education (PAUSE) to Citizens for Parental Rights (CPR), hundreds of citizens' groups demanded the halt—or at least the suspension—of sex education in their children's schools. Battering school boards and legislatures, they made sex instruction "the most hotly debated topic in American elementary education," as *Time* magazine reported in July 1969. With only a touch of hyperbole, another pair of observers deemed sex education the most explosive school issue since the *Scopes* trial of 1925. In a small Phoenix elementary school district, more than 1,500 spectators crammed into a school board meeting on the subject; in Kansas a school official supporting sex education received a death threat; and in Minnesota tear gas fumes interrupted legislative hearings on the issue.[22]

Minus charges of Communist subversion, most of the local protest groups echoed the Birchites' basic critique: sex education promoted a promiscuous, amoral conception of sex. At its root, indeed, much of the debate about sex education concerned rival views of the sex act itself. To Mary Calderone and her supporters, sex was not simply a means of procreation but an essential component of human pleasure and happiness. To sex education's critics, however, this so-called recreational philosophy *denigrated* what was truly unique about human beings. Animals copulated whenever they pleased, for no higher reason than pleasure; by acknowledging or even celebrating this principle, then, sex education reduced people to a "bestial" state.[23] At the same time, it exaggerated the importance of sex to human health and well-being. "What makes you so positive about sex, as if it were the only thing in life," began a Rhode Island critic in a lengthy letter to Calderone:

I am 71 years old, love to work hard, try to have a purpose in life, *other than sex*. Hate dirty nude pictures the body is *far from beautiful*, when there are no clothes on it. God gave us sex to have children, not to play around with the body. People should have interests, as they mature, not depend on sex. My brother had a business and still looked young at 65 a bacholor, no sex drives, too bussy for such. Sex is to bear children, *if you want them*. I had two and it was all I cared to have, but, I wouldn't allow my husband to maul me, and play around, and we are both healthy . . . What makes you think your cryterian is for every woman or man. The sex foolishness is getting too much out of control.[24]

Worse than nonprocreative sex between partners was masturbation, the *bête noire* of sex education opponents in the 1960s. Even sexual intercourse with contraceptives had the potential to create children, but masturbation's sole goal was gratification—and of the self, at that. Although sex educators never "taught" or "advocated" masturbation, as critics often claimed, some textbooks and course outlines did seek to correct the widespread notions that it caused pimples, warts, blindness, and especially insanity. "The commonly quoted medical consequences of masturbation are almost entirely fictitious," stated one California textbook. "Masturbation will not impair the mind." Actually, many doctors and psychiatrists still preached the alleged perils of "self-abuse." More to the point, millions of citizens still believed in these dangers. "At 67 my bodily powers ceased and family life hampered which should of continued for life had I not wasted my substance," wrote one. "So don't let the medical profession or anyone hoodwink you into believing that masturbation is harmless."[25]

By accepting or even promoting sexual hedonism, opponents emphasized, educators echoed the crass messages that children received from the mass media. "To me, the whole thing we witness today on sex, sex, sex, sex sex sex sex sex sex sex sex is revolting," one correspondent told SIECUS officials in 1968, in a typical jeremiad. Critics particularly targeted modern film and literature, each of which had become, another spokesman complained, "a mere vehicle for four-letter words and dreary sexual perversions." Schools should challenge this pervasive coarsening of popular culture, he continued, establishing at least one safe harbor from "the sexual Typhoid Marys of the Sick Sixties." Thanks to sex education, however, the same bawdy winds that swirled across the mass media also blew into the American classroom. In schools as on the streets, critics warned, children ingested "an unmixed diet of high-calorie, highly commercialized sex."[26]

Ironically, sex educators often shared their opponents' abhorrence of wanton sexual imagery in the media. From television and the movies, Planned Parenthood president Alan Guttmacher worried, students learned to "treat sex as a commodity" rather than as an expression of love, trust, and respect. But this problem demanded the *expansion*—not the elimination—of sex education. "It's time we acknowledged that most parents fail utterly to educate their children sexually," Guttmacher declared. Citing several well-documented studies, educators noted that only a slim fraction of American youngsters learned about sex in their homes. So schools needed to take up the slack, just as they did in other areas of the curriculum. "By state law, parents are not—except under exceptional circumstances—permitted to teach history, geography, mathematics or any other academic subject," a Chicago sex educator explained. "Yet consider the strange anomaly: every parent is expected to be an expert in the critical area of sex education." Actually, a Kansas City supporter admitted, sex education *did* take place in the home. But it was the wrong *kind* of education, she emphasized, conveying a host of inaccurate and even damaging lessons: "Psychiatrists, psychologists, and marriage counselors report vast human suffering derived from warped, confused, repressive attitudes and concepts learned from well intentioned but misguided parents . . . While healthy sex education in the home is a fine ideal, it does not occur in the majority of homes, and cannot occur until parents themselves are capable of providing it. Thus it becomes the province of the specialist to provide such vital services."[27]

Parents versus Experts

Such paeans to "specialists"—and insults to parents—sent critics of sex education into convulsions of rage. "I am tired of being told by 'leading' educators, psychologists, doctors, and clergymen that we do not know how to raise our children," wrote an angry mother in upstate New York. "Do you really think that Satan would hesitate to appear in a scholar's robe, a doctor's uniform or a clerical collar?" Critics reserved special distaste for prominent churchmen who supported sex education; like school prayer, the issue exposed huge chasms between Protestant leaders and their laities. Mary Calderone dated her own involvement in sex education to a conference in 1961 sponsored by the National Council of Churches, which became a prime target for prayer supporters and sex education opponents alike. The director of the NCC's Family Life Department, William Genne, served as a SIECUS board member and became one of Calderone's closest confidants. As early as 1963 other NCC leaders displayed disagreement—and skepticism—about traditional sexual mores. "On this subject of premarital chastity the problem of the churches is in not knowing what to say," observed one NCC spokesman. "We must be courageous enough to define our differences of opinion and let the world know our confusion . . . The time has come to be honest."[28]

To millions of parishioners, however, such matters caused little "confusion": scripture, after all, placed an ironclad prohibition on sex outside of marriage. The only real conundrum concerned the church leaders themselves, who had inexplicably strayed from "God's immutable laws," as one worshipper wrote. Controversy proved particularly sharp within the United Presbyterian Church, where in 1970 leaders endorsed state contraceptive services, legalized abortion, and "thoughtful programs of sex education." Refusing to condemn premarital sex, the church's general assembly simply called on couples to make "responsible decisions"; it also deemed masturbation "one of the earliest pleasurable experiences," deploring the "guilt and shame" that still surrounded the topic. Across the country, local churches reacted with shock and outrage. "Less politely put, the [general assembly] seems to say, 'Go to bed, kids, it's all right," an Illinois pastor fumed. "We are paying more attention to Masters and Johnson than to Moses and Jesus." Sexual sinners *should* feel "guilt and shame," another critic added, as should the national church leaders who abetted them. "Little did I dream that our once grand and glorious old church would ever sink to such a level as to approve immorality and filth!" exclaimed a Presbyterian in Minnesota, vilifying church leaders who supported sex education. "You are going against the teachings of Christ, and I pray he will reward you according to your works!"[29]

Aside from these allegedly apostate ministers, sex education opponents probably reserved their greatest ire for psychiatrists. In part, their enmity reflected psychiatrists' obvious prominence in—and support for—sex education programs. More than that, though, it reflected critics' fears of emotional manipulation or "mind control" in the schools. The "new" sex education emphasized students' emotions, feelings, and attitudes: its goal was not just to teach the mechanics of sex (often derided as "plumbing") but rather to transmit a "healthy view" of it. To critics, this objective conjured up what one frightened parent called "psychological brainwashing" in "permissive morality." In the guise of encouraging students to make decisions, opponents asserted, sex educators used sophisticated psychiatric techniques of "sensitivity training" (ST) to inscribe their *own* decisions upon students.[30]

In California fears of ST grew so rapidly that the state assembly held special hearings in December 1968 to investigate it. Critics testified that ST techniques had infected the entire curriculum, not just sex-related instruction: in the "new" English and the "new" social studies, too, teachers tried to elicit—and to alter—students' "innermost feelings." But ST was clearly most dangerous when applied to the "new" sex education, which sought to influence the deepest emotions and the most critical decisions that a child could confront. "The child should be considered an individual," insisted one opponent of

sex education, "not something to be standardized, plied with information as in computer programming, and/or wound up like a spring
with pre-set attitudes and behaviors."[31]

Several sharp ironies marked this campaign against "sensitivity training" and psychiatry. In most of their pronouncements, opponents
attacked sex education for promoting "pluralistic" or "situational"
ethics: on matters like premarital sex, one spokesman declared,
schools should inculcate "universal and immutable" principles rather
than encourage students to formulate their own. In their attacks on
ST, however, these same critics castigated sex education for imposing
"group control" or "group-think" on individual students. Here these
conservatives' rhetoric echoed the contemporary left-wing critique of
psychiatry by popular authors like R. D. Laing, who charged that the
discipline used pseudo-scientific terms and rationales to scapegoat
racial minorities and stamp out political dissent. At the height of California's ST debate, in fact, white foes of sex education quoted a radical black activist's attack on a study that alleged a high prevalence of
psychiatric illness among African-Americans: "It becomes clearer
what may be crazy about those people: they are black, and they act
differently than 'normal' people—that is, the white political psychiatrists." In a hopeful spirit, sex education critics even quoted the black
activist's concluding call to arms: "There is no reason why blacks,
Christians, conservatives, youth—all those alienated from the mental
hygiene establishment—cannot join, despite all their differences, in
demands for restraint of political psychiatrists."[32]

At the same time, though, opponents of sex education eagerly
invoked the handful of mental health professionals who shared their
position. The most popular such authority was the New York child
psychologist Rhoda L. Lorand, who decried sex education courses for
interfering with the "latency" period of development (ages six to ten)
that Sigmund Freud had described. "Sublimation of sexual curiosity
. . . is the price we must pay to live in a civilized society," Lorand proclaimed in a much-cited pamphlet that drew heavily on Freud.
"Cramming sex knowledge down kids' throats does not promote

healthy growth." (Lorand neglected to note that Freud himself supported sex education in schools, ridiculing "the customary concealment from children of everything connected with sex.") Critics also claimed that sex educators suffered from "neurosis," another Freudian term that had entered the vernacular. "Now you want us to believe that these neurotic [sex educators] should teach our kids about Sex?" an Oregon activist asked. "Well there are Psychiatrists of a different opinion and I will continue to listen to them."[33]

As in the controversy over the medical consequences of masturbation, however, most sex education opponents ignored these abstract, theoretical debates. In the final analysis, they argued, only one arbiter really mattered: the parent. "The basic issue at stake [is] USURPATION OF PARENTAL AUTHORITY," a Californian blared. "This is the real cause of the so-called generation gap." Across the country, shocked parents reported that sex education interfered with their own efforts to instill modesty and chastity. In Illinois a ten-year-old boy announced over dinner that he "had a good time discussing the penis in school today"; in California a second-grader dissected his breakfast egg "to find the thing the rooster put through the hen to make the egg fertile"; in New York a mother complained that her seven-year-old son asked his grandmother to lift her skirts so he could see her vagina—a term he had learned in school. "There was never any kind of talk like this or anything even near it when I was growing up," the despondent mother wrote to Mary Calderone. "I'm beginning to think that we just don't have much say for OUR childrens education or life anymore no matter how hard we try to bring them up decently."[34]

Apocryphal or not, such anecdotes accurately captured the moral challenge that sex education posed to parental control. Sex educators did believe that "most parents" were "reluctant" or "unqualified" to teach their children about sex, as one supporter noted in 1969; the entire subject, she admitted, rested on that very premise. Like Calderone's New York correspondent, some dejected foes simply conceded that schools would supplant their authority in this area. But others resolved to seize back their God-given rights. "Ever Hear of 'Parent Power'?" one critic wrote to Calderone in March 1969. "You Will!" In Portland, Oregon, members of the National Parents' League picketed a Calderone speech; near Buffalo, New York, the newly formed "Parents of New York United" urged citizens to "CHALLENGE YOUR PTA AND YOUR SCHOOL BOARD" on sex education; and across the state in Schenectady, members of Citizens for Parental Rights argued that taxpayers should not have to subsidize such "poison" for their children. "Hell hath no fury like a parent scorned, and you perverts have not heard the last from me," threatened a Michigan critic in a letter to SIECUS's board of directors. "Where the morals, religion, and upbringing of my children is concerned, I will fight you to the death."[35]

Many of the same Americans who fought sex education also deplored the removal of prayer from the schools. Like the Supreme Court's ban on prayer, they claimed, sex education demonstrated the overall degeneracy of the schools as well as educators' hostility toward the Christian faith. "The schools got into trouble when they took God out and put sex in," thundered the evangelist Billy Graham in an oft-quoted address in 1969. In each case, it seemed, citizens were forced to subsidize an initiative that ran directly counter to their spiritual beliefs. "Why must I as a taxpayer give money to a school system that is not allowed to teach about God," a Michigan mother asked, "but is allowed to teach, instruct, show filthy literature and movies on sex, family planning, sensitivity programs, etc.?" Both sex education and the ban on school prayer, a New York critic explained, violated a basic American freedom: the right of parents to transmit their religious values to their young. "My children belong to me," she insisted, "and I do not want the school involved in teaching [a] moral and religious subject."[36]

As other sex education critics quickly recognized, though, this argument almost exactly echoed the case *against* school prayer. According to prayer opponents, any classroom devotions would violate the rights of religious minorities—or of atheists—to uphold and transmit their own beliefs. Even as they condemned the prayer ban for "secularizing" education, critics often summoned that very principle to censure sex education. "If the teaching of religion is such an infringement on the rights of the individual, so, then, is the teaching of sex," declared one upstate New York citizen. As "a Christian thinking parent," she added, she certainly deplored the removal of prayer from the classroom. But now that the courts had barred religious instruction, any presentation of sexual issues was bound to occur within a materialist, "anti-religious" framework. "The government and the people have taken God out and Prayer out of the schools and now they want to teach sex . . . without the Book that invented or started sex," a Michigan couple complained. Better to bar all mention of the subject than to subject all children to a "secular" view of it.[37]

Nor would it suffice to excuse objecting families from sex education, as school officials frequently ordered. Here, too, sex education critics explicitly invoked the campaign against prayer and other religious exercises. "In the controversy over voluntary Bible reading in the schools we were told that it would do grave psychological harm to children if they were excused . . . for they would be set off from the other students and that would constitute punishment," a minister noted. "Now we are told that sex education is somehow different. We may excuse our children, but the program will continue." In fact, critics claimed, children who refused to take sex education faced far *greater* social censure than those who declined to pray. Given the rebellious spirit infecting many high schools, protesters against prayer might well win popular acclaim from their peers; but students boycotting sex education would simply be dismissed as "squares," prudish retrogrades whom the sexual revolution had left behind. In elementary schools, meanwhile, *any* exclusion—from prayer *or* sex education—could traumatize young minds. In a large California district, for example, students whose parents objected to sex education were sent to a study room or to the principal's office. One of these children spent the entire class period in tears, his mother reported, convinced that his removal implied some form of reproach.[38]

Thirteen years later, in February 1982, a group called the Coalition of Concerned Parents brought suit against a state-mandated sex education curriculum in New Jersey. Like earlier critics, the CCP attorney Joseph Shanahan appealed to the Supreme Court's bans on prayer and Bible reading: if spiritual exercises violated dissenters' freedom of religion, surely sex education did the same. But Shanahan also cited the Court's more recent ruling on abortion, *Roe v. Wade*, which ordained a constitutional "right to privacy." Just as prohibitions on abortions violated a woman's right to privacy, Shanahan argued, so did the state's sex education program inhibit a similar right between parents and children. "When you make a sword," he said, summarizing his strategy, "expect it to be used against you." Well into the 1980s, it seemed, sex education's right-wing foes were hoisting liberals on their own petard.[39]

Sex Education in the 1980s

Like the school prayer battle, the struggle over sex education cooled in the 1970s. By 1978 nearly half of American pupils reported that they had studied the subject. And a growing fraction of schools addressed the so-called Big Four topics of sexual controversy: masturbation, homosexuality, contraception, and abortion. Some curricula and textbooks deemed masturbation "an acceptable way to relax" or even a safe alternative to intercourse; some schools showed films describing homosexuality as normal. Many of these materials aimed explicitly at provoking student "discussion," a hallmark of the "new" sex education. Students in Richmond, Virginia, simulated a visit to Planned Parenthood, including a role-play pelvic exam in which male students placed their feet in stirrups; in Minneapolis they stood on a "Values Continuum" line representing their reactions to remarks like "young teenage women don't like sex"; and across the country girls carried an egg for a week to experience the responsibilities—and the difficulties—of young parenthood.[40]

Indeed, the issue of teen pregnancy played a key role in sex education's overall expansion in the 1970s. Contrary to many popular perceptions, the birth rate for teen women nearly *halved* from 1960 to 1975. But the widespread fear of an "epidemic" of teen pregnancy sparked a new infusion of funds for sex education, most notably from the federal government. Under the Adolescent Health Services and Prevention and Care Act of 1978, school districts could receive federal grants to develop sex education programs that provided birth control counseling. Two years later New Jersey became the first state to require sex education (as opposed to health instruction) in all of its public schools. Proponents played heavily on the rise of illegitimate births in the state, especially to teenage girls. They also emphasized the overwhelming support for "preventive" sex education among teens themselves, both in New Jersey and across America. "Maybe I'm in the 'Immoral Minority,'" quipped a teenager in Pittsburgh, "but I'd rather be informed than a FATHER."[41]

The teenager's comment alluded to the Moral Majority, the brain child of the preacher Jerry Falwell and the best-known component of the so-called New Christian Right. In 1980, just a year after its founding, the Moral Majority sued the Washington State Library in an attempt to learn which schools had borrowed a controversial sex education film. The following year the group was selected to rebut Mary Calderone in a much-discussed episode of the popular television show *60 Minutes*. Nearly eighty years old, the spry Calderone continued to insist that sex education sought to stem—not to encourage—premarital intercourse. Nonsense, replied Moral Majority vice-president Cal Thomas. Sex education in America resembled a driving teacher who announced to children, "Here is the wheel, here are the keys, here is the accelerator, but forget the brake, and for Heaven's sake, don't use reverse gear," Thomas told *60 Minutes*. Whatever its apologists said, in short, sex education encouraged youngsters to have sex—an act that true Christians reserved for marriage. "We are simply and *fundamentally*—if I may used that word—involved in a battle for the hearts and the minds of the American people," Thomas concluded.[42]

Hundreds of other organizations joined in the attack. As Thomas's pun implied, many sex education opponents belonged to fundamentalist Protestant churches. But many others were Catholics, who joined with conservative Protestants to fight sex education just as they had united in the struggle for school prayer. As in the prayer dispute, moreover, Catholics often found themselves at odds with their own leaders. To the alarm of many parishioners, for example, New Jersey's Catholic Conference supported the state's 1980 sex education mandate. "It is almost impossible for those of us who are Catholic to get any input even with our own Bishops," one worshipper complained. "This is a tragedy." Several lay Catholics wrote letters to the Pope, condemning their conference's position on sex education and pleading with the Vatican to intervene. Others flooded meetings of the state board of education, lest school officials conclude that Catholics stood united on the subject. "The Catholic Conference of New Jersey [has] absolutely no right to represent us," an angry parishioner told the board. "As a matter of fact, they better get themselves straightened out because they are going definitely against the Catholic faith."[43]

The same critics also blasted sex educators' "non-judgmental" approach toward homosexuality, which allegedly undermined "the traditional nuclear family" as well as the word of God. Ironically, they noted, New Jersey's sex education mandate was known as "family life" instruction. "We keep talking about family life, family life, family life," a grandmother complained. "There is no way you're going to teach [my] grandchild that homosexuals make a family. The sin of homosexuality is forbidden." Some opponents even suggested that classroom discussion of masturbation indirectly encouraged sexual abuse of children. After all, they reasoned, masturbation in childhood implied that the child was a sexual being. Sexual predators shared—and acted upon—this warped perspective. Here critics especially targeted the popular feminist health book *Our Bodies, Ourselves*, which was used as a reference text in a few school districts. By "normalizing" masturbation as well as homosexuality, foes alleged, the book also encouraged "public acceptance of pedophilia."[44]

Most important, critics now charged that sex education—formerly viewed as an enemy of religion—actually conveyed a religion of its own: "secular humanism." The charge dated to the 1960s, when a handful of opponents said that sex education reflected a "humanist" faith that elevated man over God.[45] By the early 1980s New Right groups like the Moral Majority had brought this argument into the popular lexicon. "Secular humanism . . . is an aggressive atheism which denies God, denies life after death, and shuns all moral absolutes," wrote one New Jersey activist. Moreover, she added, sex education was "the major transmission belt" for this religion in American schools. Just a few years earlier, she pointed out, Mary Calderone had received the "Humanist of the Year" Award from the American Humanist Association. But the real proof of "humanist indoctrination" lay in sex education curricula themselves, which consistently supplanted God's word with "godless ethics." In short, critics concluded, sex education violated the First Amendment's ban on the establishment of religion. Humanism *was* a religion, and sex education foisted it upon the public schools.[46]

Two very different corollaries flowed from this argument. Since humanism had already penetrated the public schools, some critics argued, their own religion should receive "equal time." Like advocates of school prayer and creationism, opponents of sex education often echoed the neutral, "impartial" cadences of liberal pluralism. "If we are to educate the whole child, practice democracy, stimulate critical thinking, then both sides of an issue must be presented," asserted one critic, demanding a "God-centered" perspective to complement the "humanist" faith. "Permitting one over the other is alien to everything a democratic society represents." To other activists, however, this very attempt to satisfy "both sides" reflected the loose, "situational" ethics of the humanist foe. "How can we give our children answers that we as a society are still in the process of arriving at?" asked another opponent of sex education. "Let's stick to things we do know about: reading, writing, arithmetic, the basics." Better to avoid the subject altogether than to confuse children with mixed, incoherent messages about morality and sexuality.[47]

By the mid-1980s conservatives began to formulate a third position. Rather than teaching "both sides" of sexual issues or eliminating them from the curriculum, they argued, schools should provide an entirely new brand of sex education with a single, unambiguous message: abstinence. Following their sweep of Congress and the White House in the 1980 elections, Republicans in Washington had required that federally funded sex education programs emphasize "self-discipline and responsibility in sexuality." But such programs did not become common at local levels until 1985 and 1986, thanks to the first stirrings of a new sexual crisis: AIDS. Conservatives were shocked when Surgeon General C. Everett Koop demanded broader sex education—including instruction about condoms—to fight the spread of the disease. Asked at a press conference in 1986 when such education should begin, Koop responded, "at the earliest age possible"; pressed to be more specific, he blurted, "third grade." Across the Christian Right, critics blasted Koop—a staunchly "pro-life" conservative—for his apostasy on sex education. According to the fundraiser Richard Viguerie, the surgeon general was "proposing instruction in buggery"; to Phyllis Schlafly, a longtime critic of sex education, Koop's report appeared to have been "edited by the Gay Task Force."[48]

Yet given the obvious threat of AIDS, even Schlafly could no longer oppose all forms of sex education. Instead, like other conservatives, she began to advocate "abstinence only" curricula. The same year as Koop's comments on AIDS, Christian Right activists started to tout a federally funded program called "Sex Respect"; six years after that, roughly 1,600 school districts had adopted it. In marked contrast to the surgeon general, "Sex Respect" made no mention of contraception. Instead, it focused obsessively on the supposed perils of even the "safest" premarital sex. "Schools ought to teach that the consequences of sex fall twice as heavily on girls as on boys," Schlafly declared, in support of the abstinence-only approach. "Little girls ought to be taught about . . . the side effects of contraceptives, of abortion and its trauma, venereal diseases, the poverty, the cervical cancer, the emotional and psychological trauma."[49]

In at least one suburban New York district, meanwhile, schools offered students a choice between "mainstream" sex education and a new abstinence-only curriculum. But such compromises were rare on the issue of sex education, which polarized Americans for the better part of two decades. "I think this country is very deeply split over morality," a California teenager observed in 1968. "What some parents consider an outrage seems rather tame, even quaint, to younger, more liberal parents." Twenty years later Americans were no closer to reaching an accord on the question; by some measures, indeed, they were much farther apart. Designed to elicit discussion of Americans' "values," sex education would remind Americans how sharply—and, it seemed, how irrevocably—these values clashed.[50]

Searching for Common Ground

In August 1994 the president of the United States invited a soft-spoken, bespectacled sociologist to a breakfast meeting at the White House. The sociologist was James Davison Hunter, and Bill Clinton wanted to talk to him about America's "culture wars." The author of an influential 1991 book by that title, Hunter claimed that Americans were most sharply divided not by economic or racial inequalities but rather by "worldviews"—that is, by "different and competing under-standings of what is good and true." Clinton concurred. Two years earlier he had ascended to the presidency by emphasizing bread-and-butter issues such as labor, foreign trade, and budget deficits: as his campaign aides were fond of repeating, "It's the economy, stupid." Now that Clinton was in office, however, he found that the most cru-cial issues dividing America were "primarily cultural in character": abortion, homosexuals in the military, and so on. How, he asked, could the nation resolve them?[1]

Clinton must have been disappointed by Hunter's response: that the culture wars *cannot* be resolved. By definition, Hunter argued, these conflicts involve fundamental beliefs and assumptions that simply do not allow for compromise—or even for dialogue. "Is it not impossible to speak to someone who does not share the same moral language?" Hunter would later write. "Gesture, maybe; pantomime, possibly. But the kind of communication that builds on mutual understanding of opposing and contradictory claims on the world? That would seem impossible." Much of this conflict quite naturally devolved upon the school, America's chief public institution for distilling and delivering moral values to its young. Indeed, the very term "culture wars" derived from the German *Kulturkampf,* which first referred to Protestant-Catholic battles over religion in school. But *Kulturkampf* also implied a struggle without end, because each side to the dispute claimed an absolute monopoly on truth. Especially in its fiery educational theater, then, America's own culture war showed little sign of cooling. From older issues like prayer in the classroom to the more recent controversy over "multiculturalism" in the curriculum, Hunter warned, the "school wars" reflected incompatible belief systems—and resisted common ground.[2]

Was Hunter right? As we have seen, the answer depends upon which war we mean. Too often lumped into a single drama, America's struggles over religion and history in the schools have followed two very different plots over the past century. Our "history wars" have usually surrounded the issue of "inclusion"—who gets into the national narrative, and who does not—rather than the structure of this narrative itself: each "race" gets to have its heroes sung, as the *New York Times* put it in 1927, but no group may question the melody of peace, freedom, and economic opportunity that unites them all. Dissidents from this narrative were sometimes silenced, as the saga of Harold Rugg's textbooks reminds us. More commonly, though, they simply developed separate texts and courses—think of white neo-Confederates in the early 1900s, or black militants in the 1960s—until their stories could be reconciled with the cheerful national vision. The price of diversity in American history has been banality in its tone, a single and often suffocating triumphalism that blots out most traces of misery, tragedy, and especially self-doubt. Careful to note America's occasional departures from its own civic creed, our textbooks remain confident that the country—like the creed—will continue on a straight line of progress and beneficence.

In battles over religious and moral subjects, by contrast, no such consensus has emerged. The midcentury system of "released time" aimed to mollify different faiths by welcoming all of them: just as each "race" won a place in the history textbooks, so would each religion receive a slot in the school day. The arrangement sparked bitter conflict between liberal and conservative Protestants, both groups hoping to instill their own views. This tension erupted into a full-scale war in the 1960s, when the Supreme Court barred religious exercises from the classroom. Mounting their own "massive resistance" to these rulings, white racists quipped that the Court "put the Negro into the schools, and took God out." In sex education classes, other conservatives complained, educators seemed to denigrate scripture's immutable sanctions in favor of a nondirective approach. Just as heaven and hell lacked any middle ground, it appeared, there was no room for compromise between a theistic worldview and a secular one.

Or was there? By the 1980s many Christian conservatives had renounced their explicit quest to restore "God" to the schools. Instead, mimicking multiculturalists on the left, they asked only that their distinct heritage and beliefs receive "respect" and "equal time" in the curriculum. Scholars who have noticed this shift have evaluated it very differently: some deride conservatives for adopting a disingenuous "victim" pose, while others praise their newfound tolerance for a variety of viewpoints.[3] In practice, however, this "compromise" was often unworkable. Different moral frameworks simply cannot be mixed into the curriculum like so many spices, enhancing its overall flavor. For as James Davison Hunter told Bill Clinton, these frameworks are fundamentally "incommensurable"—that is, each one presupposes the invalidity of the other. In this they differ sharply from racial and ethnic claims upon the history curriculum, which have generally been folded into a single overarching story.

Our popular discourse typically ignores this essential contrast, sliding easily from "culture wars" about prayer and sex education to "culture wars" about history. In the first two years after Hunter's *Culture*

Wars appeared, America's newspapers and magazines printed more than a thousand articles with this phrase in their text. Echoing Hunter, most of these early reports addressed conflicts in the moral or religious realm. So did conservative political figures such as Patrick Buchanan, who warned the 1992 Republican national convention of a "culture war" over abortion and gay rights. As Buchanan pointedly added, the "soul of America" lay in the balance.[4]

After 1994, however, "culture wars" increasingly connoted battles about race, ethnicity, and patriotism. One catalyst for this change was the controversy over national history standards in the schools, which burst across America's front pages in late 1994 and early 1995. From the former secretary of education William Bennett to the talk-show impresario Rush Limbaugh, conservatives charged that the proposed standards besmirched America's image by inflating both the achievements and the oppression of racial minorities and women. On the other side stood professional historians and schoolteachers, who argued that the new standards provided a more complete picture of the nation—and might even inspire students to address its persistent problems.[5] By 1996 an avalanche of new books had made "culture wars" nearly synonymous with this struggle over multiculturalism in schools and universities. Right-wing critics accused scholarly radicals of imposing an "anti-American" dogma of "political correctness" on the classroom.[6] On the left, some authors urged a revamped defense against the conservative challenge; others warned that the entire multicultural issue was diverting the country from more pressing matters, especially economic inequality.[7]

Whatever their ideological bent, commentators generally assumed that this controversy reflected an unprecedented grassroots activism and concern. As we have seen, however, citizens contested American history instruction throughout the twentieth century. Immigrant groups fought fervently for a voice in the curriculum in the years following World War I. Thanks to Polish and German pressure, textbooks added florid depictions of Thaddeus Kosciusko and Friedrich von Steuben; to meet black demands, Crispus Attucks received a similar place of honor. Nor did African-Americans in the civil rights movement ignore history instruction, as some scholars have suggested.[8] Instead, they fought for "integrated" curricula alongside "integrated" classrooms; as many activists insisted, blacks would never achieve equality in America so long as their textbooks remained "lily white."

Each one of these movements to change the teaching of history was larger and more influential than any battalion in today's "history wars." Compared to the conflicts that preceded them, indeed, our current struggles may not qualify as "wars" at all. As its closest chroniclers have acknowledged, the 1994–95 battle over national history standards was largely a "media event" fought by elite politicians, journalists, and professors rather than by citizens in local communities. The same account of the standards imbroglio connects it to the midcentury campaign against Harold Rugg's textbooks, which were also vilified as unpatriotic and un-American. But the resemblance ends there. The anti-Rugg campaign took hold at the grassroots, enlisting local activists and eventually removing Rugg's texts from thousands of school districts. The anti-standards "movement"— if we can even call it that—targeted a set of purely voluntary guidelines and left no lasting imprint on local curricula. Lacking a genuinely popular base, the issue of national standards subsided almost as soon as the U.S. Senate voted (by a 99–1 margin) to condemn them.[9]

By contrast, America's other culture war—over religion and morality—continues to plague the nation's public schools. At times, it is true, commentators have exaggerated the scope as well as the "polarized" nature of this conflict. As several recent studies make clear, the vast majority of Americans avoid battles over school prayer, sex education, or so-called humanistic literature; when pushed to take a position on these questions, moreover, they often uphold "conservative" and "liberal" views in the same breath.[10] Nevertheless, our "culture wars" on moral and religious subjects remain much more prevalent and much more polarized than our history conflicts. More people fight over religion than over history, in short, because they have more to fight *about*.

Consider the question of school prayer. As part of the same "Goals 2000" legislation, passed in 1994, that authorized the drafting of history standards, Senator Jesse Helms of North Carolina introduced a rider requiring schools to allow "voluntary" prayer. Although Helms's measure went down to defeat, school prayer entangled Congress well after the issue of standards had disappeared. Deeming prayer "one of the seminal fights of the decade," Speaker of the House Newt Gingrich revived the thirty-year-old campaign for a constitutional amendment guaranteeing students' "right" to engage in "voluntary" prayer. This "Religious Freedom Amendment," as it was dubbed, wound its way through various committees and finally reached the House floor in June 1998, where it garnered more than half of the lawmakers' votes—although not the two-thirds majority that constitutional changes require. Borrowing a strategy from the prayer advocates of the 1960s, some congressmen argued that the amendment would protect America's "Judeo-Christian heritage." Others were careful to craft their appeals in a pluralist idiom, simply demanding that schools grant the same respect and liberty to devout Christians as to other groups.[11]

Unlike the question of history standards, the prayer issue continued to embroil local communities as well. Especially in the South, school districts routinely flouted federal law by conducting prayers. When school officials or courts tried to bar this activity, angry citizens rose up against them. In Jackson, Mississippi, hundreds of black and white students walked out of class to protest the firing of an African-American principal for allowing the recital of a prayer on his school's public address system. Ostensibly "ecumenical," the prayer resembled "common denominator" devotionals that northern school systems had tried to institute in the 1950s: "Almighty God, we ask that you bless our parents, teachers and country throughout the day. In your name we pray. Amen." In its racial component, however, the protest in Jackson signaled a remarkable shift. Southern whites and African-Americans had long supported school prayer, albeit for very different reasons: whites viewed bans on prayer as an insult to "states' rights," reminiscent of federal doctrine on integration, while blacks saw prayer as a way to further racial justice. Now they marched side by side—in support of a black principal, no less—and in the name of a single, shared principle: believers should be "free" to pray. "Christians feel, rightfully so, that there has been an assault on our Christian commitment," explained one white activist.[12]

Four years later students in neighboring Alabama staged their own "prayer strike"—this time to protest a federal judge's injunction against student-led devotionals in school. "Having Jesus in our school is something that we need," one protester told reporters. "It gives us strength." Another student was more defiant in his assessment: "We can't let this judge keep us from praying." A similar chord of resistance was struck by citizens and school officials in Decatur, Georgia, who held a prayer service at the local high school to memorialize the stabbing death of a student. "We are here in defiance of the Supreme Court," one speaker proclaimed, "calling the name of Jesus Christ." In December 1997 the entire nation was forced to revisit the issue when a fourteen-year-old Kentucky boy fired a rifle into a prayer circle at his high school, killing three students. Although this was obviously an isolated episode, as one observer noted, the martyred students immediately became symbols of "a nation deeply and violently divided" over prayer in its schools.[13]

Across the curriculum, religion remained the most divisive issue in American education. School officials reported that the majority of parental complaints about local curricula concerned moral or religious subjects, not racial ones. Likewise, publishers found that textbooks in the so-called nonhistorical social studies—especially psychology and "family life," the most common site of sex education—drew much stronger public ire than regular history texts did.[14] Most of all, combatants on every side of these problems despaired of ever finding a practical solution to them. The generic liberal answer—

more conversation—seemed impossible, or at best implausible: "conversation" requires a minimal consensus on certain basic principles, but the school wars often stemmed from an *absence* of precisely this consensus. A 1997 debate between four South Carolina educators—Gary Burgess, James Carper, Carolyn Murphy, and Aretha Pigford—vividly captured the essence of this dilemma:

> *Burgess:* My concern is that there are people out there who are arrogant enough to think that is it [*sic*] their way or no way.
> *Carper:* But isn't it the very nature of moral commitment that it is not compromisable?
> *Murphy:* But that is for *you.* I am committed to a moral framework that does *not* allow me to impose my moral commitments on you.
> *Carper:* Can you compromise that? There are certain issues that I consider closed because they are true.
> *Pigford:* For example?
> *Carper:* The Bible is the infallible word of God . . . As a conservative Christian, how do I relate to a morally inclusive classroom when I do not believe in such inclusiveness? You see, institutions embody a particular moral framework. Whose is it going to be?

As the philosopher Richard Rorty summarized in 1994, religion more often operates as a "conversation-stopper" than as a spur to dialogue between adherents of different beliefs.[15]

Might America's culture war over race, ethnicity, and patriotism suggest some clues for alleviating its religious one? Rorty's remarks appeared in his review of a much-discussed book by the law professor Stephen L. Carter, who pleaded for the country to award religion the same "respect" and "dignity" that race and ethnicity routinely received. According to Carter, the very Americans who praised the nation's wide range of races and ethnicities often turned a blind eye—or even a disdainful frown—upon its equally rich variety of spiritual

beliefs. Nowhere was this contradiction clearer than in history textbooks, which too often ignored the religious impulses of figures such
as John Winthrop, Abraham Lincoln, and Martin Luther King Jr. "It
ought to be embarrassing, in this age of celebration of America's
diversity, that the schools have been so slow to move toward teaching
about our nation's diverse religious traditions," Carter wrote. Just as
texts extolled racial and ethnic "cultures," in short, so should they
laud spiritual ones.[16]

Yet as Carter acknowledged, textbook publishers were already taking steps to remedy this imbalance by the time his own book appeared in 1993. Since then, the material that texts devote to religious
topics has steadily expanded. Important gaps remain, especially in
the treatment of religion in recent American history.[17] When textbooks do pay attention to religion, however, they focus solely on its
"positive contributions" to national and world history. At a meeting
with educators in the early 1990s, several textbook publishers flatly
refused to print information about the role of religion in fostering prejudice, violence, and war. Although the historical record was
chock-full of such conflict, as one publisher admitted, any discussion
of the subject risked offending one religious group or another. Better
to gloss over inconvenient facts than to lose customers, especially in
an industry where the fate of a single textbook could determine the
life or death of a company.[18]

Here religion exactly echoed the pattern set by race and ethnicity
in America's texts. Since the 1920s each group that has gained admis-
sion to the grand national narrative has received the same fulsome
praise as the nation itself. True, groups that were excluded from this
story—especially African-Americans—were often horribly denigrated
or stigmatized. Once they earned a place in the pantheon, however,
they became as sacrosanct as any other god. For instance, today's
texts shy away from discussing the African role in the slave trade or
the human sacrifice practiced by some Native Americans prior to the
European conquest. These facts would temper the texts' image of
minority groups as uniformly peaceful and morally pristine. They

might also alienate big-city school boards, often the key constituency in determining the success of a history textbook.[19]

By the late 1990s one could detect the outlines of a classic American bargain—you get your heroes, I get mine—in history textbooks' discussion of race and religion. Insofar as it folded these characters into a triumphalist national narrative, though, the bargain violated the texts' own central theme: the freedom of the individual. Textbooks depict America as a beacon of personal liberty and opportunity, lighting the way for an often tyrannical and barbaric world. Yet by stressing this sunny story and downplaying darker ones—especially poverty, racism, and imperialism—the texts actually inhibit the very individualism that they venerate. If the books took personal freedom seriously, they would encourage students to develop their own perspectives about the nation *and* about its various races, ethnicities, and religions. You cannot praise America for cultivating individual freedom of thought, then proceed to tell every individual what to think. But that is exactly what most of our schoolbooks continue to do.

To be sure, every nation seems to invent certain parts of its history and to "forget" others.[20] Around the world, moreover, these "mythical" versions of nationhood have often inspired tremendous acts of courage and compassion.[21] As the eminent historian William McNeill explains, "An appropriately idealized version of the past may . . . allow a group of human beings to come closer to living up to its noblest ideals." Here McNeill cites the American civil rights movement, which called on the nation to fulfill its founding principles.[22] Yet black activists rarely idealized the actual history of these principles, as they were implemented—or ignored—by successive generations of Americans. Nor should we, if we truly believe in the free will and dignity of each individual. When we wrap American history in myth, we deny students the opportunity to wrestle with its real dilemmas.

Over the past thirty years, for example, historians have engaged in a rich debate about the "liberal" character of American society. Were slavery and nativism simply bumps in the road toward America's democratic destiny, brief interruptions of the parade of progress? Or did the traditions of liberalism and racism work in tandem, each one defining the content and contours of the other? Is America a "uniquely free" country, as its textbooks proudly proclaim? What does "free" mean, anyway?[23] Elementary school children are not mature enough to enter such discussions. But these are all questions that high school students *can* answer—indeed, that they *must* answer, if they are to develop the critical capacities that democratic citizenship requires. As the literature professor Gerald Graff has argued, "culture itself is a debate, not a monologue." So we should teach it *as* a debate, pressing our students to join America's arguments rather than pretending that we settled these differences long ago.[24]

Sadly, the historical record provides few precedents for this type of instruction: across the curriculum, our conflicts have generally stormed *over* the schoolhouse rather than inside it. Part of the reason lies in the institutional culture of high schools, where an overarching emphasis on "control" and "classroom management" quashes inquiry and investigation.[25] But in this book I have suggested a second obstacle to critical education in American public schools: the American public itself. From the Knights of Columbus and the Ku Klux Klan in the early twentieth century to the National Association for the Advancement of Colored People and the John Birch Society in more recent years, citizens have almost always sought to promote their own opinions rather than a discussion of competing ones. As one of my students once quipped, "You'll never see a parents' group called 'Americans in Favor of Debating the Other Side in Our Schools.'" Citizens enter the arena of curriculum so that a particular view or attitude will find a place within it. The last thing they want, it seems, is a multiplicity of perspectives.

Yet over the past two decades, as I have documented, citizens across the ideological spectrum have donned the mantle of cultural pluralism. Abandoning their former quest for a "Christian America," even self-described evangelicals now ask only that teachers present their "culture" alongside the many others that schools celebrate. In sex education as well as science classes, they demand "equal time" for what they call (in their less pluralist moments) the "Christian" point of view. To bolster their calls for school prayer, meanwhile, evangelicals note the worshipful attitude that accompanies the study of America's patriotic heroes. If schools can venerate Martin Luther King Jr.—a Christian preacher—why can't they venerate the God he followed?

The evangelicals have a point. Their argument echoes a long line of "me too" compromises in American education, whereby each successive group gets to have its heroes sung. Only this time their hero is God. Critics will quickly respond that students should be free to follow whatever creed they think fit, and that a school-sanctioned prayer to God—*any* God—violates that freedom. Of course it does. But our history curriculum violates it, too, by subjecting students to a daily catechism in the virtues of America and its diverse groups. So I would like to suggest a very different type of compromise: schools should not "celebrate" anyone, if by that verb we mean giving unconditional homage or reverence. Prayers would be barred under this stricture, because by their very nature they commit children to a certain deity or worldview: as the philosopher Warren Nord has noted, "to pray is to take sides."[26] But our history and social studies classes "take sides," too, sanctifying the heroes and demonizing the villains. This process represents its own form of quasi-religious indoctrination. It, too, must come to an end.

Would Christian conservatives agree to such a bargain? The answer, I think, depends on how far the rest of us are willing to extend it. If it allowed for real discussion across the curriculum, evangelicals might sign on. From literature and history to science and health, classes would examine—not mention or describe, but *examine*—religious perspectives. Biology courses would ask: What explains life on earth better, Darwinism or the various creation stories of world religions? Economics classes would evaluate the self-maximizing actor of utilitarian theory next to diverse religious critiques of private property and accumulation. In sex education, meanwhile, students would compare modern American images of sexuality with the teachings of different spiritual traditions, including Christianity.[27]

Admittedly, this new compromise would require an enormous change in the way America trains its public school teachers. I conceived of this book almost ten years ago, while working as a social studies educator at a large public university. Fresh from graduate school, where I received a doctorate in history, I implored prospective teachers to engage children in the timeless questions of the discipline: What is history? Does it move in a linear direction, a cyclical one, or neither? What separates historical fact from historical fiction? Most of all, what makes one version of history superior to another? As I quickly realized, however, I was urging students to ask questions that they had never addressed on their own. To most of these future teachers, history was simply "the facts"—a parade of names, events, and dates—rather than a continuing conversation about them. "What's all this business about debate?" one college senior asked me a few weeks before he began practice teaching. "There's nothing to debate in history. Either it happened or it didn't."

We can hardly institute a dialogic approach in American classrooms if our teachers remain ignorant of the dialogues that define their disciplines. My student seemed bright and capable, but he had taken only two history courses. That was enough to qualify him for teaching social studies in his state. Amazingly, some states certify social studies teachers who have taken *no* college history courses at all. Across the country, more than half of junior high and high school history students now learn the subject from a teacher with neither a major nor a minor in history. Not surprisingly, these students also tend to view history as a litany of unassailable truths rather than as a continuous—and contested—discussion.[28] If teachers are never exposed to historical debate, how can they expose their students to it?

True, we still lack strong evidence linking teachers' academic preparation to their instructional abilities. Already, academic classes take up between half and three-quarters of teacher candidates' postsecondary schooling; adding "more of the same" would improve nothing and might even make matters worse. But neither should we decrease teachers' academic course load, on the specious theory that they need only know "how to teach" a subject rather than the subject itself.[29] Future teachers need *better* academic training—not simply "more" of it—that focuses on the logic and debates within their respective subject areas, not merely on the "facts" that these subjects have generated. Only with such training will teachers be prepared to lead wide-ranging discussions among their wonderfully diverse students.

This dialogic ideal brings us back to Walter Lippmann, whose much less hopeful words I quoted in the Introduction. Writing in 1928, soon after the *Scopes* trial, Lippmann used an imagined conversation—featuring Socrates, William Jennings Bryan, and Thomas Jefferson—to argue that devout Christianity and liberal democracy were philosophically incompatible:

> *Socrates:* Well, how would you gentlemen compose your fundamental principles, if a majority, exercising its fundamental right to rule, ordained that only Buddhism should be taught in the public schools?
> *Bryan:* I'd move to a Christian country.
> *Jefferson:* I'd exercise the sacred right of revolution. What would you do, Socrates?
> *Socrates:* I'd re-examine my fundamental principles.

Lippmann expanded on this dilemma in a second imagined conversation, between a "fundamentalist" and a "modernist":

> *Fundamentalist:* You can say: Maybe Darwin is right . . . maybe Lamarck is right . . . perhaps Einstein is right . . . perhaps he

isn't. . . . That is your scientific spirit. But you can't say: Perhaps
the word of God is right and perhaps it isn't.

Modernist: Why can't you?

Fundamentalist: Because the authority of the Bible rests upon revelation, and if you are open-minded about revelation you simply
do not believe in it . . .

Modernist: I don't understand.

Fundamentalist: What do you mean by open-mindedness?

Modernist: A refusal to reach a conclusion on the ground that the
evidence is not conclusive.

Fundamentalist: Exactly. But those who believe in the divine
authority of the Bible believe it on grounds which are beyond
the reach of human inquiry and evidence . . .

Modernist: Is there no way out of this conflict?

Fundamentalist: That is not for me to say.[30]

I cannot prescribe a "way out" of this conflict, either—except to
suggest that the conflict itself might provide a partial solution to it.
At the level of logic, Lippmann was surely correct: the fundamentalist
worldview leaves little room for compromise or even for conversation
with nonbelievers. Yet as a practical matter, as I have demonstrated,
conservative Christians have come to accept the reality—if not the
philosophy—of modern American pluralism. The shift was cleverly
captured by the historian George Marsden, who updated Lippmann's
"Dialogue on Olympus" for the 1990s:

Socrates: So how is it, if you put loyalty to the bible first, you evangelicals are such American patriots? The fact is that you seem to
have tremendous loyalty to democracy and to the whole liberal
polity that Jefferson and his friends designed . . .

WJB: Ultimately we have to play by the rules of the system.

Socrates: Why is that? If the system tends to favor Godless materi-
alism—as clearly it does in some respects—why don't you try to
get a new system? . . . If you Christians are really committed to

your rhetoric of always putting God's will first, then why aren't you working to destroy your liberal political system and its phony neutrality, and trying to take over the government?

TJ: That's what they *are* trying to do. In my days you Presbyterians were always trying to take over.

WJB: That's a lie. We have always played by the rules of the country.

Socrates: By and large that seems to be true. But I wonder why . . .

WJB: The powers that be are ordained by God. We do not have to have a perfect system in order to have an obligation to play by its rules. Besides, the American system of democracy is the best thing that humans have come up with so far.[31]

In Lippmann's dialogues, Bryan played the stereotypical 1920s fundamentalist: dogmatic, unequivocal, and unyielding. Marsden's Bryan is closer to the spirit of present-day religious conservatives, who realize that they must "play by the rules" if they want to remain in the game. As Marsden has said elsewhere, orthodox believers may not always enjoy the contest or applaud its outcome. Yet "in a pluralistic society we have little choice but to accept pragmatic standards"—that is, the codes and procedures of liberal democracy.[32] The rest of us should seize this historic opportunity, showing the same willingness to enter into a dialogue with devout believers as they demonstrate toward us. In the end, debating our differences may be the only thing that holds us together.

Abbreviations • Notes • Acknowledgments • Index

Abbreviations

AHR	*American Historical Review*
BJCC	Boston Jewish Community Council Papers, American Jewish Historical Society, Waltham, Mass.
BLPP	Bessie Louise Pierce Papers, Joseph Regenstein Memorial Library, University of Chicago
CDER	California Department of Education Records, State Archives, Sacramento
CVTP	Claude Van Tyne Papers, Bentley Historical Library, Ann Arbor
DIS	Department Investigations Series, California Department of Education Records, State Archives, Sacramento
EDP	Everett M. Dirksen Papers, Dirksen Congressional Center, Pekin, Ill.
FPSB	*Friends of the Public Schools Bulletin*
ICRE	International Council of Religious Education
JCRCGP	Jewish Community Relations Council of Greater Philadelphia Records, Philadelphia Jewish Archives Center
JNH	*Journal of Negro History*
JWFI	Jewish Welfare Federation of Indianapolis Papers, Indiana Historical Society, Indianapolis
KCHC	Knights of Columbus Historical Commission files
LCCP	Lucille Cardin Crain Papers, Knight Library, University of Oregon, Eugene
MCP	Mary Steichen Calderone Papers, Arthur and Elizabeth Schlesinger Library, Radcliffe College

NAMP   National Association of Manufacturers Papers, Hagley Museum and Library, Wilmington, Del.

NCC   National Council of Churches Papers, Presbyterian Historical Society, Philadelphia

NCTE   National Council of Teachers of English Papers, University Archives, University of Illinois, Champaign

NHB   *Negro History Bulletin*

NJSBE   New Jersey State Board of Education Records, State Archives, Trenton

NYSASCE   New York State Assembly Standing Committee on Education, Incoming Correspondence Relating to Proposed Legislation, Collection LO129, State Library, Albany

NYT   *New York Times*

PPFA   Planned Parenthood Federation of America II Papers, Sophia Smith Collection, Smith College

SCF   Schomburg Center Clipping File, Schomburg Center for Research in Black Culture, New York Public Library

UO   Knight Library, University of Oregon, Eugene

UPCC   United Presbyterian Church in the USA, Board of Christian Education, Correspondence and Other Papers on Sexuality and the Human Community, Presbyterian Historical Society, Philadelphia

WP   *Washington Post*

WPF   Working Papers folder

WRE-NC   Weekday Religious Education Record Group, North Carolina Council of Churches Papers, Division of Archives and History, State Archives, Raleigh

Notes

Introduction: Beyond Dayton and Chicago

1. Walter Lippmann, *American Inquisitors* (New Brunswick, N.J.: Transaction, 1993 [1928]), 22–23.
2. See Todd Gitlin, *The Twilight of Common Dreams: Why America Is Wracked by Culture Wars* (New York: Henry Holt, 1995).
3. Jonathan Zimmerman, "Bible Can Be Tool to Further Agenda of Liberals, Too," *Denver Rocky Mountain News*, 9 July 2000, 3B.
4. Lippmann, *American Inquisitors*, 8.
5. George C. Wallace, "State of Alabama Proclamation by the Governor" (ms, 27 Nov. 1972), enclosed with J. Rupert Picott to "Executive Council Members," 2 Jan. 1973, folder 11, box 88, Raymond P. Alexander Papers, University of Pennsylvania Archives.
6. Lippmann, *American Inquisitors*, xxxv. On the supposed retreat from public affairs see George Marsden, *Fundamentalism and American Culture: The Shaping of Twentieth Century Evangelism, 1870–1925* (New York: Oxford University Press, 1980); Joel A. Carpenter, *Revive Us Again: The Reawakening of American Fundamentalism* (New York: Oxford, 1997).
7. Joan DelFattore, *What Johnny Shouldn't Read: Textbook Censorship in America* (New Haven: Yale University Press, 1992), 80–81.
8. On bland patriotism see James W. Loewen, *Lies My Teacher Told Me: Everything Your American History Textbook Got Wrong* (New York: Touchstone, 1995); Frances Fitzgerald, *America Revised* (New York: Vintage, 1979). But see Robert Lerner, Althea K. Nagai, and Stanley Rothman, *Molding the*

Good Citizen: The Politics of High School History Texts (Westport, Conn.: Praeger, 1995).

9. See Gary B. Nash, Charlotte Crabtree, and Ross E. Dunn, *History on Trial: Culture Wars and the Teaching of the Past* (New York: Knopf, 1997); Arthur M. Schlesinger Jr., *The Disuniting of America: Reflections on a Multicultural Society,* rev. ed. (New York: Norton, 1998).

10. Christian Smith et al., "The Myth of Culture Wars: The Case of American Protestantism," in *Culture Wars in American Politics: Critical Reviews of a Popular Myth,* ed. Rhys H. Williams (New York: Aldine De Gruyter, 1997), 175; Alan Wolfe, *One Nation, After All* (New York: Viking, 1998), 276–279; Christian Smith, *A Christian America? What Evangelicals Really Want* (Berkeley: University of California Press, 2000), 132.

11. See, e.g., Louise Adler, "Curriculum Challenges in California," *Record in Educational Administration and Supervision* 13 (Spring–Summer 1993): 10–20; idem., "Institutional Responses: Public School Curriculum and Religious Conservatives in California," *Education and Urban Society* 28 (May 1996): 327–346.

12. Testimony of Mary Flunn, Minutes of State Board of Education Hearing on Family Life Education Programs, 8 April 1980, II: 151, accession 1997.025, NJSBE.

13. David Miller, *On Nationality* (New York: Oxford University Press, 1995), 35–36; David Archard, "Myths, Lies, and Historical Truth: A Defense of Nationalism," *Political Studies* 43 (Sept. 1995): 472–481.

I. HISTORY WARS

1. Frederick Bausman, "Under Which Flag?" *American Mercury,* Oct. 1927; "The Spotlight Shifts from Tennessee to Chicago," *Chicago Tribune,* 25 Oct. 1927, both in "Chicago Text Book fight, Bill Thompson and burning of books" folder; "Those Chicago Textbooks," *Publishers Weekly,* 29 Oct. 1927, "Big Bill Thompson" folder, all in Arthur Schlesinger Jr. Papers (in Schlesinger's possession).

1. Ethnicity and the History Wars

1. Horace M. Kallen, "Culture and the Klan," in *Culture and Democracy in the United States* (New York: Arno, 1970 [1924]), 41–43.

2. "Patriotic Organizations Appeal for School History Bill" (ms, 1924), 2, "Chicago Text Book Fight, Bill Thompson and burning of books" folder, Arthur Schlesinger Jr. Papers (in Schlesinger's possession); M. S. Waters, "Urges Definite Action to Prevent Un-American Instruction of Youth," *Newark Evening News*, 29 Jan. 1924; Kallen, "Americanization and the Cultural Prospect," in *Culture and Democracy*, 132, 139. Dewey, "Nationalizing Education," in idem., *The Middle Works, 1899–1924*, ed. Jo Ann Boydston (Carbondale: Southern Illinois University Press, 1976), 10: 205.

3. "Patriotic Organizations Appeal for School History Bill," 1; "Denounce Efforts to Censor History," *Trenton Times*, 19 Feb. 1924, 3; D.A.P., "Maintains School History Revisers Will Be Guided by Study of Facts," *Newark Evening News*, 1 Feb. 1924, 13; "Steubenites Celebrate the Fourth," unidentified clipping enclosed with John Grossghbauer to George S. Silzer, 16 July 1923, box 26, folder 148C, George S. Silzer Papers, New Jersey State Archives.

4. See, e.g., Paul A. Carter, *Another Part of the Twenties* (New York: Columbia University Press, 1977); Stanley Coben, *Rebellion against Victorianism: The Impetus for Cultural Change in 1920s America* (New York: Oxford University Press, 1991); William E. Leuchtenberg, *The Perils of Prosperity, 1914–1932*, 2nd ed. (Chicago: University of Chicago Press, 1993). But see Lynn Dumenil, "The Tribal Twenties: 'Assimilated' Catholics' Response to Anti-Catholicism in the 1920s," *Journal of American Ethnic History* 11 (Fall 1991): 43.

5. William G. Ross, *Forging New Freedoms: Nativism, Education, and the Constitution, 1917–1927* (Lincoln: University of Nebraska Press, 1994), chs. 3–4, 7–8; David Tyack, "The Perils of Pluralism: The Background of the Pierce Case," *AHR* 74 (Oct. 1968): 74–98.

6. Edward F. McSweeney [hereafter EFM], "Address to Supreme Convention," 2 Aug. 1922, in "EFM, Address to Supreme Convention, August 1922" folder, KCHC; EFM, "Racial Contributions to America," *Columbia* 3 (June 1924): 8.

7. Harold Underwood Faulkner, "Perverted American History," *Harper's* 152 (Feb. 1926): 338.

8. David Saville Muzzey, *An American History* (Boston: Ginn, 1911), iii; idem., *An American History* (Boston: Ginn, 1925), iii, iv. See also James Harvey Robinson, *The New History: Essays Illustrating the Modern Historical Outlook* (New York: Macmillan, 1912).

9. Muzzey, *American History* (1911), 107; (1925), 90.

10. Ibid. (1911), 128, 130; (1925), 110–111.

11. Interviews with David S. Muzzey, Feb.–April 1956, p. 39, Oral History Research Office, Columbia University Libraries; Gary B. Nash et al., *History on Trial: Culture Wars and the Teaching of the Past* (New York: Knopf, 1997), 29; "History Inquiry Ordered by Hylan," *NYT*, 7 Dec. 1921, 36; "Hirshfield to Set Our History Right," *NYT*, 30 Dec. 1921, 20; "Hirshfield Finds Heroes for History," *NYT*, 4 Feb. 1922, 24; Bessie Louise Pierce, *Public Opinion and the Teaching of History in the United States* (New York: Knopf, 1926), 281; "There Need Be No Unwritten Chapters," *American Hebrew* 110 (10 Feb. 1922): 353.

12. EFM, "Memorandum to the Supreme Directors," 30 March 1923, "Subcommittee of Supreme Board On Historical Commission Report, Jan. 1923" folder, KCHC. Douglas Bukowski, *Big Bill Thompson, Chicago, and the Politics of Image* (Urbana: University of Illinois Press, 1998), ch. 7; Walter Lippmann, *American Inquisitors* (New Brunswick: Transaction, 1993 [1928]), 26–27.

13. See, e.g., Claude Van Tyne [hereafter CVT], "A Questionable History," *NYT*, 24 July 1925, 12; Faulkner, "Perverted American History," 344; "Historical News and Comments," *Mississippi Valley Historical Review* 14 (March 1928): 575.

14. CVT to Arthur Pound, 30 Nov. 1918; M. E. Osborne to Jessie McLean, 5 April 1918, both in folder 39, box 2, CVTP; John E. Moser, *Twisting the Lion's Tail: American Anglophobia between the World Wars* (New York: New York University Press, 1999), 4.

15. David Matteson to EFM, 20 Feb. 1922, "Report of Proceedings, Feb. 1922" folder, KCHC; Lippmann, *American Inquisitors*, 68.

16. Oliver L. Spaulding to CVT, 11 March 1928, folder 29, box 2, CVTP; Henrik Willem Van Loon, "'Big Bill' Thompson," *Outlook* 148 (8 Feb. 1928): 207; EFM to Luke Hart, 15 Jan. 1923, "Correspondence, 1923, Jan.–March" folder, KCHC; F. G. Wickware to CVT, 14 Dec. 1921, folder 21; Andrew C. McLaughlin to CVT, 2 Sept. 1923, folder 24, both in box 1, CVTP; Muzzey, *American History* (1911), 128; David Matteson to EFM, 20 Feb. 1922, "Report of Proceedings, Feb. 1922" folder, KCHC; *Official Bulletin of the National Society of the Sons of the American Revolution* 18 (June 1923): 67; Frances Fitzgerald, *America Revised* (New York: Vintage, 1979), 21, 107. In the preface to their 1925 edition the Beards boasted that they had omitted "biographies of heroes" and "all descriptions of battles," emphasizing instead the "causes and results of wars." But in fact

they excluded almost all economic analysis and provided graphic descriptions of Revolutionary heroes, especially of "Foreign Officers" who aided the American cause. Charles A. and Mary R. Beard, *History of the United States* (New York: Macmillan, 1925), v–vii, 118–121.

17. Fitzgerald, *America Revised*, 59; Theodore D. Gottlieb, "Patriot League for History Now Declared Vindicated," *Sunday Call*, 20 June 1926, "Miscellaneous Correspondence, Pre-WWII" folder, box 12, Carleton J. H. Hayes Papers, Manuscripts Collections, Columbia University Libraries; "Patriotic Organizations Appeal for School History Bill," 17, 14; "Chicago Buys History, Paying $1.50 a Word," *NYT*, 7 Dec. 1927, 29; Chicago Board of Education, *Lest We Forget: Lafayette, Von Steuben, Kosciusko, Pulaski, DeKalb, John Barry, The Distinguished Patriots from Europe Who Volunteered Their Services and Fought Valiantly in the Revolutionary War for the Liberty of America. Betsy Ross. The American Flag. Yankee Doodle* (Chicago, 1927); typescript of testimony by John J. Gorman, n.d. [1927], folder 7, box 10, BLPP.

18. "Witness Reveals Britain's Hand in School Histories," *Irish World and American Industrial Laborer*, 26 Nov. 1927, 2; Dixon Ryan Fox, "Mayor Thompson and the American Revolution," *Contemporary Review* 134 (Nov. 1928): 607; David Hirshfield, *Report on the Investigation of Pro-British History Text-Books in Use in the Public Schools of the City of New York* (n.p., 25 May 1923), 60–68; "Hirshfield Asks Ban on 8 Histories as Pro-British," *NYT*, 4 June 1923, 13; Andrew C. McLaughlin to Bessie Pierce, n.d. [May 1922], folder 8, box 13, BLPP; EFM, *Americans, Wake Up!* (n.p., [1921?]), cabinet Q-R, KCHC.

19. Arthur M. Schlesinger, *New Viewpoints in American History* (New York: Macmillan, 1922), ch. 1; William Morris, "Barring of Hayes' Text-Book of History Opens Up Big Question—What Is History? The Standard Should Be Truth, Not Prejudice," *Brooklyn Standard Union*, 3 May 1930, "Clippings on World History Textbook Controversy" folder, box 11, Hayes Papers; W. H. Thompson, "Are We Victims of British Propaganda? I—Patriots and Propagandists," *Forum* 79 (April 1928): 509. Schlesinger's *New Viewpoints* was not actually used in Chicago public schools. Yet the Thompson "trial" revealed that the book was on the reading list of a course for teachers at the University of Chicago, prompting at least one witness—herself a teacher—to suggest that Schlesinger "should be filling a cell in a Federal prison." Arthur M. Schlesinger, *In Retrospect: The History of a Historian* (New York: Harcourt, Brace, and World, 1963), 104–105; "Viereck Coadjutor to Thompson's Aid," *NYT*, 3 Nov. 1927, 2.

20. EFM to Burton J. Hendrick, 6 Nov. 1923, "Correspondence, Nov.–Dec. 1923" folder; Memorandum to the Supreme Board of the Knights of Columbus from the Knights of Columbus Historical Commission, 7 Oct. 1923, 3, "Subcommittee of Supreme Board on Historical Commission Report, Jan. 1923" folder, both in KCHC; EFM to Diarmuid Lynch, 22 June 1922, folder 1, box 11, Daniel F. Cohalan Papers, American Irish Historical Society, New York; "To Spur the Study of History," *NYT,* 29 May 1921, 5.

21. Bessie Pierce to Bruce Bliven, 4 June 1923, folder 5, box 8, BLPP; Frank Donnelly to "Reverend and Dear Father," 18 April 1919; Friends of Irish Freedom and Associated Societies, *America's Debt to Ireland* (n.p., n.d. [1919]), both in folder 11, box 7, Cohalan Papers; Edward Cuddy, "'Are the Bolsheviks any worse than the Irish?': Ethno-Religious Conflict in America during the 1920s," *Eire-Ireland* 11, no. 3 (1976): 15; Daniel T. O'Connell, "Senator Williams' False Statements Refuted," Irish National Bureau press release, 21 Oct. 1919, folder 12, box 12, Cohalan Papers: James Sullivan to CVT, 27 Feb. 1922, folder 44, box 2, CVTP.

22. Concord Society of America, *Year Book 1927* (Detroit: Herold Printing, 1928), 37–38; *Souvenir Program, Grand Ball and Pageant, Steuben Society of America for the Metropolitan District of New York* (n.p., 28 Jan. 1926), 21–23, both in scrapbook 8, box 2, Carl Ernest Schmidt Papers, Bentley Historical Library, Ann Arbor; Theo H. Hoffmann, "July Fourth" (ms, 1928), folder 2, box 1, Steuben Society of America Collection, Princeton University Libraries.

23. "History Must 'Go,'" *NYT,* 20 Nov. 1927, III: 4; "Handy History Seats Heroes in Wrong Pews," *Chicago Tribune,* 6 Feb. 1928, "Chicago Text Book Fight" folder, Schlesinger Papers; *Lest We Forget,* 8–9; "Dutch and Italians Ask History Change," *NYT,* 16 Nov. 1927, 11; *Souvenir Program,* 5, 2; Concord Society, *Year Book 1927,* 42.

24. "Thompson Will Get Indians' Complaint," *NYT,* 7 Nov. 1927, 25; "American Heroes," *Chicago Defender,* 10 Dec. 1927, II: 2; letter by Arnett Voneydoar Eskridge, "As Heroes Pass in Review," ibid., 17 Nov. 1927, II: 2.

25. Charles H. Wesley, *Negro History in the School Curriculum* (Washington: Howard University Press, 1925), 18; "Mayor Thompson in a War Dance," *NYT,* 2 Dec. 1927, 5; "History as It Is Written," *Negro World,* 19 Nov. 1927, 4; Floyd Logan to Edwin C. Broome, 19 Jan. 1932, folder 13, box 6, Floyd Logan Papers, Urban Archives, Temple University; Howard K. Beale, *Are American Teachers Free? An Analysis of Restraints upon the Freedom of*

Teaching in American Schools (New York: Scribner's, 1936), 197; William Pickens, "The Negro in American History," *New York Age*, 4 March 1922.

26. "Revising School Histories," *New York Age*, 26 Nov. 1927, 4; "Mayor Thompson in a War Dance."

27. "What Is Patriotism?" *New York Age*, 5 Nov. 1927, 4; M. S. Waters, "Urges Definite Action to Prevent un-American Instruction of Youth," *Newark Evening News*, 29 Jan. 1924, 13; Gail S. Carter, "'America First' Bluff Wrecks 'Big Bill,'" *Kourier* (June 1928): 29–32, folder 14, box 2, Crown Point Ku Klux Klan Collection, Indiana Historical Society, Indianapolis.

28. Morris, "Barring of Hayes' Text-Book."

29. W. I. Lincoln Adams, "The Proper Teaching of History," *Official Bulletin of the National Society of the Sons of the American Revolution* 17 (Dec. 1922): 18; Wallace McCammant, "Report of Committee on Patriotic Education," ibid. 18 (June 1923): 66.

30. J. L. O'Connor to EFM, 5 March 1923, "Correspondence, 1923, Jan.–March" folder, KCHC; Pierce, *Public Opinion*, 101; Albert Kerr Heckel, "Pure History and Patriotism," *Historical Outlook* 16 (March 1925): 106; EFM, *Attempt of British to "De-Americanize Americans"* (n.p., n.d. [1920]), folder 2, box 18, Cohalan Papers; EFM, *Americans, Wake Up*, 3.

31. EFM, address, 2 Aug. 1922, "EFM, Address to Supreme Convention, August 1922" folder, 10, KCHC; Charles Edward Russell, *Bare Hands and Stone Walls: Some Recollections of a Side-Line Reformer* (New York: Scribner's, 1936), 339–340; J. M. Wall, "Jefferson's Immortal Masterpiece," *Journal of the American-Irish Historical Society* 25 (Jan. 1926): 281–282.

32. Philip R. V. Curoe, *Educational Attitudes and Policies of Organized Labor* (New York: Arno, 1969 [1926]), 116; John H. Reddin, "The National History Movement," *Columbia* 1 (Nov. 1921): 21.

33. Wallace McCammant to Jesse A. Ellsworth, 16 June 1924, "World History Correspondence" folder, box 11, Hayes Papers; *Official Bulletin of the National Society of the Sons of the American Revolution* 18 (June 1923): 67; A. H. Conner, *Should the "History of the American People" by Willis Mason West Be Used as a School Text Book?* (n.p., n.d. [1923]), "Big Bill Thompson" folder, Schlesinger Papers.

34. "Cashman Speech Put in State Records," *Milwaukee Telegram*, n.d., enclosed with J. L. O'Connor to EFM, 5 March 1923, "Correspondence, 1923, Jan–March" folder, KCHC; Pierce, *Public Opinion*, 272–273.

35. See, e.g., George N. Fuller to CVT, 26 Sept. 1921, folder 21, box 1; Edith Scott to CVT, 20 Sept. 1927, folder 28, box 2; J. Holland Rose to CVT,

folder 28, box 2, all in CVTP; S. B. Duncan, "American-English History," *Oregon Teachers Monthly* 26 (April 1922): 1–3, "Chicago Text Book Fight" folder, Schlesinger Papers.

36. J.T., "Point as to Discoverer of America in Discussing History Text Books," *Newark Evening News*, 25 Jan. 1924, 13; clipping, n.p., n.d. [Boston], "Declaration Av Indipindense," folder 4, box 11, Cohalan Papers; "Introducing Abraham of House of Linkhorn," *Dallas News*, 26 Oct. 1924, scrapbook 9, box 8, Schmidt Papers.

37. "Loyal Coalition" leaflet, n.d., n.p., enclosed with Margaret Rooney to Daniel F. Cohalan, 29 April 1920, folder 13, box 10, Cohalan Papers; J.T., "Point as to Discoverer of America"; A Teacher, "School Books under Fire," *NYT*, 13 Dec. 1921, 18; H. H. Powers to CVT, 11 Nov. 1923, folder 24; M. M. Yates to Van Tyne, 15 Nov. 1921, folder 21, both in box 1, CVTP.

38. Carleton J. H. Hayes, *Essays on Nationalism* (New York: Russell and Russell, 1966 [1926]), 243.

39. Concord Society, *Year Book 1927*, 27.

40. Randolph Bourne, "Trans-National America," in idem., *History of a Literary Radical and Other Essays*, ed. Van Wyck Brooks (New York: B. W. Huebsch, 1920), 297; Kallen, *Culture and Democracy*, 124–125; Dewey, "School as a Means of Developing a Social Consciousness," in *Middle Works*, 155, 154, 153.

41. Gary Gerstle, "The Protean Character of American Liberalism," *AHR* 99 (Oct. 1994): 1060; idem., *Working-Class Americanism: The Politics of Labor in a Textile City, 1914–1960* (Cambridge: Cambridge University Press, 1989), 3–4; idem., "Liberty, Coercion, and the Making of Americans," *Journal of American History* 84 (Sept. 1997): 557n74.

42. "No Propagandist, Says Mrs. Stetson," *NYT*, 6 March 1924, 9; "Attacks Mrs. Stetson at Anthem Hearing," *NYT*, 21 March 1924, 9; Joseph T. Griffin to Augusta Stetson, 14 June 1922, "Correspondence—1922" folder, KCHC.

2. Struggles over Race and Sectionalism

1. "Minutes of the Meeting of the Board of Directors, Feb. 8, 1932," frames 430–431, reel 2, *The Papers of the National Association for the Advancement of Colored People*, part I (Frederick, Md.: University Publications of America, 1982); Charles Edward Russell to W. E. B. Du Bois, 12 Oct. 1932, frames 613–614, reel 37, *The Papers of W. E. B. Du Bois* (New York: Micro-

filming Corporation of America, 1980); Russell to James Weldon Johnson, 18 Oct. 1933, folder 3, box 17, Rachel Davis DuBois Papers, Immigration History Research Center, St. Paul, Minn.

2. "Muzzey's History, Adopted as Text Book in Virginia, Is Held Unfair to the South," *Richmond News Leader,* 23 Jan. 1932, book C-9, p. 98, Confederate Memorial Literary Society Scrapbooks, Museum of the Confederacy, Richmond, Va.; "John Tyler's Son," *NYT,* 18 Feb. 1932, 20; "Northern Idols Taken for a Ride in Muzzey Row," *Richmond Times-Dispatch,* 25 Feb. 1932, book C-9, p. 99, Confederate Memorial Literary Society Scrapbooks. For black attacks on Muzzey's *An American History,* see W. E. B. Du Bois, *Black Reconstruction* (Milwood, N.Y.: Kraus-Thomson, 1976 [1935]), 712; Charles Edward Russell, "Civil War History as Taught in Certain Textbooks" (ms, [1935?]), "Civil War History" folder, box 37, Charles Edward Russell Papers, Library of Congress.

3. See, e.g., Mary B. Poppenheim, "Objections to Eggleston's History" (ms, n.d.), enclosed with Martha B. Washington circular, 6 June 1905, "UDC" folder, box 1, James Mercer Garnett Papers, Alderman Library, University of Virginia; Mildred L. Rutherford [hereafter MLR], *Historical Sins of Omission and Commission* (n.p., 1915), vol. 4, item 47, MLR Scrapbooks, Museum of the Confederacy; typescript review of Muzzey, *American History,* n.d [1922], "Correspondence and Statements in re Controversy 'Muzzey's History' 1921–22" folder, box 1, Textbook Correspondence, Office of Superintendent, Records of the Dept. of Public Instruction, Division of Archives and History, North Carolina State Archives, Raleigh.

4. "History! Whose History? Written by Whom?" *The State* [Columbia, S.C.], 30 May 1914, "Miscellany" folder, box 2, United Daughters of the Confederacy Papers, Museum of the Confederacy.

5. Peter Novick, *That Noble Dream: The "Objectivity Question" and the American Historical Profession* (Cambridge: Cambridge University Press, 1988), 76; Michael Kammen, *Mystic Chords of Memory: The Transformation of Tradition in American Culture* (New York: Vintage, 1993), 416; Thomas J. Pressly, *Americans Interpret Their Civil War* (Princeton: Princeton University Press, 1954).

6. On the archival and monographic contributions of men like Du Bois, see, e.g., Jacqueline Goggin, *Carter G. Woodson: A Life in Black History* (Baton Rouge: Louisiana State University Press, 1993); August Meier and Elliott Rudwick, *Black History and the Historical Profession, 1915–1980* (Urbana: University of Illinois Press, 1986).

7. Many historians emphasize sectional reconciliation after the Spanish-American War; see, e.g., Gaines M. Foster, *Ghosts of the Confederacy: Defeat, the Lost Cause, and the Emergence of the New South* (New York: Oxford University Press, 1987), 145–191; Cecelia Elizabeth O'Leary, "'Blood Brotherhood': The Racialization of Patriotism, 1865–1918," in *Bonds of Affection: Americans Define Their Patriotism,* ed. John Bodnar (Princeton: Princeton University Press, 1996), 53–81; Nina Silber, *The Romance of Reunion: Northerners and the South, 1865–1900* (Chapel Hill: University of North Carolina Press, 1993), esp. 159–196. By contrast, I agree with Michael Kammen that beneath America's patina of sectional harmony lay "a roiling sea of inter-regional rivalries and resentments." Kammen, *Mystic Chords of Memory,* 376–377.

8. Fred Arthur Bailey, *William Edward Dodd: The South's Yeoman Scholar* (Charlottesville: University Press of Virginia, 1997), 81.

9. Angie Parrott, "'Love Makes Memory Eternal': The United Daughters of the Confederacy in Richmond, Virginia, 1897–1920," in *The Edge of the South: Life in 19th-Century Virginia,* ed. Edward L. Ayers and John C. Willis (Charlottesville: University Press of Virginia, 1991), 221.

10. *To Promote Patriotic Study in the Public Schools, Report of Special Committee Appointed by Col. Albert D. Shaw . . .* (n.p., 1897), folder 5, box 81, Grand Army of the Republic Papers, New York State Library, Albany; Stephen D. Lee, *History Committee, Interesting Report Submitted to United Confederate Veterans Yesterday . . .* (n.p., 1897), Broadsides Collection, Alderman Library, University of Virginia; "General Stephen D. Lee, Chairman, Presents the Report of the Historical Committee to Confederate Reunion" (n.p., 1898), book R-3, pp. 48–49, Confederate Memorial Literary Society Scrapbooks; James H. M'Neilly, "History as It Should Be Written," *Confederate Veteran* 30 (Jan. 1922): 13–14.

11. *Journal of the Thirty-Fourth National Encampment of the Grand Army of the Republic* (Philadelphia: Town Printing, 1901), 143; *Journal of the Thirty-Eighth Encampment of the Grand Army of the Republic* (Chicago: M. Umbdenstock, 1904), 245–246; George L. Christian, *Official Report of the History Committee of the Grand Camp, Confederate Veterans, Department of Virginia* (n.p., 1902), 28; Sophie Lea to Mrs. James Mercer Garnett, 10 May 1904, "UDC—Papers and Pamphlets" folder, box 1, Garnett Papers.

12. O'Leary, "Blood Brotherhood," 67; Foster, *Ghosts of the Confederacy,* 172; Parrott, "Love Makes Memory Eternal," 221; Mary D. Carter to Claude

Van Tyne [hereafter CVT], 13 Aug. 1925; Carter to CVT, 1 Aug. 1925, both in folder 47, box 2, CVTP.

13. Fred Arthur Bailey, "Mildred Lewis Rutherford and the Patrician Cult of the Old South," *Georgia Historical Quarterly* 77 (Fall 1994): 530–532; Grace Elizabeth Hale, "'Some Women Have Never Been Reconstructed': Mildred Lewis Rutherford, Lucy M. Stanton, and the Racial Politics of White Southern Womanhood, 1900–1930," in *Georgia in Black and White: Explorations in the Race Relations of a Southern State, 1865–1950*, ed. John Inscoe (Athens: University of Georgia Press, 1994), 182; MLR, *A Measuring Rod to Test Text Books . . .* (n.p., 1919), 5.

14. MLR, *An Open Letter to all State Historians, Chairmen of Historical Committees and Chapter Historians . . .* (Athens, Ga.: McGregor Co., n.d. [1911]), item 18; *Address Delivered by Miss Mildred L. Rutherford . . .* (n.p., 1914), p. 16, item 35, both in vol. 4, MLR Scrapbooks; "Confederates Assert Lincoln Forced War; Call for 'Fair' Schools Histories in South," *NYT,* 22 June 1922, 1; *Miss Rutherford's Scrap Book* 2 (Sept. 1924), 5; *Address Delivered by Miss MLR,* 28.

15. *Action of R. E. Lee Camp No. 1; Minutes of the Eleventh Annual Meeting of the UDC,* 198; "Report of Historical Committee of Louisiana Division United Confederate Veterans" (ms, 1904), "The Genesis of Secession" folder, box 1, Garnett Papers; Fred Arthur Bailey, "Free Speech and the 'Lost Cause' in Texas: A Study of Social Control in the New South," *Southwestern Historical Quarterly* 97, no. 3 (1994): 464.

16. *Proceedings of the Tenth Annual Meeting of the Grand Camp Confederate Veterans, Department of Virginia* (Richmond: William Ellis Jones, 1897), 27; Bailey, "Free Speech," 469; "Report of Historical Committee of Louisiana Division United Confederate Veterans"; Christian, *Official Report,* 27.

17. See, e.g., Adelia A. Dunovant, *Truthful History* (Houston: J. J. Pastoriza, 1898), "Address: Truthful Histories" folder, box 9, UDC Papers; Christian, *Official Report,* 27.

18. Christian, *Official Report,* 27; "Protest against False Histories," *Confederate Veteran* 21 (Jan. 1913): 38; *Minutes of the Thirtieth Annual Convention of the United Daughters of the Confederacy* (Jackson, Miss.: McCowat-Mercer, 1923), 165.

19. *Report of the Historian-General, Mrs. J. Enders Robinson, to the General Convention of the United Daughters of the Confederacy* (n.p., 1911), 8, "Report of the Historian-General" folder, box 6, UDC Papers; Mrs. B. M. Howorth to "Dear Sir," 15 Jan. 1912, item 83, vol. 3, MLR Scrapbooks; Elise Dodson,

The Story of Slavery in Virginia (n.p., 1915), 1, 11, "'Historical Work' of Rawley Martin Chapter, Daughters of Confederacy, for year 1914–1915" scrapbook, box 13, UDC Papers.

20. Pressly, *Americans Interpret Their Civil War*, 237–238; Novick, *That Noble Dream*, 229–230; Albert Bushnell Hart to MLR, 24 Jan. 1917; MLR to Hart, 29 Jan. 1917, both in "Rutherford, M" folder, box 22, accession 4448.6, Albert Bushnell Hart Papers, Harvard University Archives; Hale, "Some Women," 176. See also Mary D. Carter to CVT, 1 Aug. 1925; Carter to CVT, 13 Aug. 1925, both in folder 47, box 2, CVTP.

21. J. T. Jenkins to *The Independant*, 27 March 1905, accession 4448.27, box 1, Hart Papers.

22. R. H. Dabney et al. to History Committee, 11 April 1899, History Committee Records, Papers of the Grand Camp Confederate Veterans, Library of Virginia, Richmond; Howard K. Beale, *Are American Teachers Free? An Analysis of Restraints upon the Freedom of Teaching in American Schools* (New York: Scribner's, 1936), 177; Bessie Louise Pierce, *Public Opinion and the Teaching of History in the United States* (New York: Knopf, 1926), 265; Matthew Page Andrews to MLR, 5 July 1923, folder 15, box 1, Mildred Lewis Rutherford Papers, Hargrett Rare Book and Manuscript Library, University of Georgia, Athens; Arthur H. Jennings to Bessie Louise Pierce, 12 Aug. 1923; Jennings to Pierce, 2 Aug. 1923, both in folder 1, box 15, BLPP.

23. See, e.g., *Criticism of the History of the American People by Beard and Bagley* (n.p., n.d. [1921]), "Correspondence—1922" folder, box 2, Textbook Correspondence, Office of Superintendent, North Carolina State Archives.

24. Pressly, *Americans Interpret Their Civil War*, 207–208; Meier and Rudwick, *Black History and the Historical Profession*, 3; *Accomplishments and Program of the History Committee, Sons of Confederate Veterans* (n.p., 1938), 10–11.

25. *Criticism of the History of the American People by Beard and Bagley*, 2, 6; Du Bois, *Black Reconstruction*, 714–715.

26. Carter G. Woodson [hereafter CGW], "Negro History in Its Proper Setting," *New York Age*, 15 Feb. 1936, 6; "Negro History Week: The Eleventh Year," *JNH* 21 (April 1936): 106. See Goggin, *Carter G. Woodson*, ch. 6; Lorenzo J. Greene, *Working with Carter G. Woodson, the Father of Black History: A Diary, 1928–1930*, ed. Arvarh E. Strickland (Baton Rouge: Louisiana State University Press, 1989).

27. I have relied especially on Goggin, *Carter G. Woodson;* Wilson Jeremiah Moses, *Afrotopia: The Roots of African American Popular History* (Cambridge: Cambridge University Press, 1998); Meier and Rudwick, *Black History and*

the *Historical Profession;* and David Levering Lewis, *W. E. B. Du Bois: Biography of a Race, 1868–1919* (New York: Henry Holt, 1993).

28. F. L. Hoffman to CGW, 8 July 1925, frame 336, reel 3, Carter G. Woodson Papers, Library of Congress; Goggin, *Carter G. Woodson,* 22; Arthur A. Schomburg, "The Negro Digs Up His Past" [1925], in *Voices from the Harlem Renaissance,* ed. Nathan Irvin Huggins (New York: Oxford University Press, 1995), 221.

29. Agnes M. Roche, "Carter G. Woodson and the Development of Transformative Scholarship," in *Multicultural Education, Transformative Knowledge, and Action,* ed. James A. Banks (New York: Teachers College Press, 1996), 99–100; Goggin, *Carter G. Woodson,* 84–85; CGW, "The Celebration of Negro History Week, 1927," *JNH* 12 (April 1927): 105–107.

30. CGW, "Negro History Week: The Fourth Year," *JNH* 14 (April 1929): 113; Greene, *Working with Woodson,* xxvii, 203.

31. Greene, *Working with Woodson,* 225–226; idem., *Selling Black History for Carter G. Woodson: A Diary, 1930–1933,* ed. Arvarh E. Strickland (Columbia: University of Missouri Press, 1996), 56–57; "Negro History Week: The Tenth Year," *JNH* 20 (April 1935): 127; "S.C. Elementary Schools to Use Negro Text Books," *Call* [Kansas City], 25 Aug. 1939; "Negro Textbooks in the Public Schools," *Black Dispatch* [Oklahoma City], 26 Aug. 1939, both in frame 155, reel 63, Tuskegee Institute News Clipping File (Tuskegee, Ala.: Tuskegee Institute, 1978).

32. "Interracial Aspect of Historical Meeting Next Week Looms Large," *Journal and Guide* [Norfolk], 7 July 1931, file 000.362 1, SCF; "Negro History Week: The Tenth Year," 127; Luther P. Jackson, "The Work of the Association and Its People," *JNH* 20 (Oct. 1935): 390–391; "School News," *NHB* 1 (Nov. 1937): 3; "Books," *NHB* 2 (Oct. 1938): 6.

33. ASNLH press release, 8 Feb. 1937, folder 1, box 366, Claude A. Barnett Papers, Chicago Historical Society; "School News," *NHB* 1 (Feb. 1938): 7; Thomas L. Dabney, "The Study of the Negro," *JNH* 19 (July 1934): 270–274; "School News," *NHB* 1 (Oct. 1937): 8; "Negro History to Be Taught in Beaumont Colored School," *Informer* [Houston], 9 Feb. 1935, frame 259, reel 50, Tuskegee Clipping File.

34. CGW to Mary Church Terrell, 3 Feb. 1928, frame 279, reel 6, Mary Church Terrell Papers, Library of Congress; Greene, *Working with Woodson,* 391; CGW, "Only One in Ten Thousand Interested in Racial History," folder 1, box 370, Barnett Papers; "Selling the Negro to Negroes," *St. Louis Argus,* 11 Nov. 1932, file 005.861–1, SCF.

35. Ella W. Parker, "Suggestions for the Elementary School," *NHB* 2 (Feb. 1939): 40–41; Greene, *Selling Black History,* 200, 133; CGW, "Only One in Ten Thousand Interested," 11; CGW, *The Mis-Education of the Negro* (Washington: Associated Publishers, 1933), 132, 138; CGW, "Negro History Week, Negro History Year," *New York Age,* 21 Dec. 1935, 11.

36. "Minutes of the Meeting of the Board of Directors, Dec. 12, 1932," frame 506, reel 2, part I; William Pickens to Branch Officers, 17 Feb. 1938, frame 161, reel 1, part 19A; Pickens to "Branches and Youth Groups," 17 May 1939, frame 195, reel 1, part 19A, all in NAACP Papers; Helen Boardman to Charles Edward Russell, 26 Nov. 1937, pp. 3881–84, vol. 20, Russell Papers; "Textbook Survey for Youth Councils" (ms, n.d. [1938]), frame 169, reel 1, part 19A, NAACP Papers; NAACP, *Anti-Negro Propaganda in School Textbooks* (New York, 1939), 16.

37. See, e.g., Carleton Mabee, *Black Education in New York State: From Colonial to Modern Times* (Syracuse: Syracuse University Press, 1979), 273; Beale, *Are American Teachers Free,* 312; Michael Homel, *Down from Equality: Black Chicagoans and the Public Schools, 1920–1941* (Urbana: University of Illinois Press, 1984), 115.

38. Thomas F. Armstrong Jr., "The Public Educational Programs of Selected Lay Organizations in Pennsylvania" (Ph.D. diss., Temple University, 1947), 293; "Report of Miss Ovington on Textbook Investigation by Mr. Reddick" (ms, 4 April 1938), frame 558, reel 8, part 16A, NAACP Papers; Gloria Oden, "My Discoveries" (ms, 1939), folder 14, box 17, Rachel Davis DuBois Papers.

39. Lawrence D. Reddick, "Racial Attitudes in American History Textbooks of the South," *JNH* 19 (July 1934): 264–265; Frank Marshall Davis, "Now Is Strategic Time to Start Improving Our School Textbooks," *Call* [Kansas City], 6 Aug. 1943, frame 119, reel 83; "Fight for Negro History Course in California Schools," *Black Dispatch* [Oklahoma City], 27 Aug. 1938, frame 951, reel 58, both in Tuskegee Clipping File.

40. W. E. B. Du Bois to Charles Edward Russell, 7 Oct. 1932, frame 611, reel 37, *Du Bois Papers;* "Minutes of the Meeting of the Board of Directors, Sept. 12, 1933," frames 548–549, reel 2, part I, NAACP Papers; "Committee on What We Should Teach the Negro about Himself and about Others in Relation to Himself, Makes Report," *New York Age,* 23 Dec. 1933, file 005–861–1, SCF; "Timely Suggestions for Negro History Week," *NHB* 1 (Feb. 1938): 12; "History Week and What It Means," *Chicago Defender,* 23 Jan. 1932, file 003–562–1, SCF.

41. Willis N. Huggins and John G. Jackson, *An Introduction to African Civilizations, with Main Currents in Ethiopian History* (New York: Avon House, 1937), 143; Mrs. Booker T. Washington to Mary Church Terrell, 20 Sept. 1922, frame 384, reel 5, Terrell Papers; "Negro History Needed," *Amsterdam News,* 28 Feb. 1931; "Negro History Week," ibid., 9 Feb. 1931, both in file 003–562–1, SCF.

42. Although the term "Afrocentrism" was not coined until the early 1960s, I use it here as Wilson J. Moses does: to connote "the idea that African-Americans were essentially African, and that the solutions to their problems must be discovered within a Pan-African context." Moses, *Afrotopia,* 2, 13.

43. George Wells Parker, "Questions and Answers in Negro History," *Michigan State News,* 18 Oct. 1924, frame 18, reel 21, Tuskegee Clipping File.

44. Moses, *Afrotopia,* 89–91, 93–94; letter from James Patten, "Who Started Civilization," *Chicago Defender,* 5 Nov. 1927, II: 2.

45. Moses, *Afrotopia,* 88–89; CGW, *Negro Makers of History* (Washington: Associated Publishers, 1928), 12–13; idem., *The Story of the Negro Retold* (Washington: Associated Publishers, 1935), 14; CGW and Charles Wesley, *The Negro in Our History,* 11th ed. (Washington: Associated Publishers, 1966 [1922]); idem., *African Myths* (Washington: Associated Publishers, 1928), ix; "The Negro in Art from Africa to America," *NHB* 2 (March 1939): 49; "Africa in Discovery and Invention," *NHB* 3 (March 1940): 82; CGW, "Why the Negro Lacks His Tenth," *New York Age,* 4 Jan. 1936, 6; "Committee on What We Should Teach the Negro," 3.

46. Schomburg, "The Negro Digs Up His Past," 220; "Negro History Week: The Eleventh Year," 106–108; Robert G. Weisbord, *Ebony Kinship: Africa, Africans, and the Afro-American* (Westport, Conn.: Greenwood, 1973), 89, 98–99; J. A. Rogers, "The Suppression of Negro History" [1940], in *Modern Black Nationalism: From Marcus Garvey to Louis Farrakhan,* ed. William L. Van Deburg (New York: New York University Press, 1997), 71.

47. Lorenzo J. Greene, "Dr. Woodson Prepares for Negro History Week, 1930," *NHB* 28 (May 1965): 175; Goggin, *Carter G. Woodson,* 152–153; "The Declaration of Rights of the Negro Peoples of the World" [1920], in *Marcus Garvey and the Vision of Africa,* ed. John Henrik Clarke (New York: Vintage, 1974), 446, 451; Marcus Garvey, "History and the Negro" (1925?), in *The Marcus Garvey and Universal Negro Improvement Association Papers,* ed. Robert A. Hill (Berkeley: University of California Press, 1984), 6: 226; UNIA Convention Report, 17 Aug. 1922, ibid., 4: 897–898.

48. Marcus Garvey to Earnest S. Cox, 8 Aug. 1925, *Garvey and UNIA Papers,* 6: 224–226 (italics added).
49. Eleanor Roosevelt to Charles Edward Russell, 9 Feb. 1939, p. 4117, vol. 22, Russell Papers.

3. Social Studies Wars in New Deal America

1. Harold Rugg, *That Men May Understand: An American in the Long Armistice* (New York: Doubleday, Doran, 1941), 139, 241; idem., "This Has Happened Before," *Frontiers of Democracy* 7 (15 Jan. 1941): 106–107; idem., "A Study in Censorship: Good Concepts and Bad Words," *Social Education* 5 (March 1941): 179. Rugg's analysis neglected the degree to which the "new historians" had changed their textbooks to meet popular challenges; see Chapter 2.
2. Amos A. Fries to "Editor, Evening Star, Washington, D.C.," 23 June 1925, folder 6, box 2, Amos A. Fries Papers, UO; letter from Marie J. Andrus, *WP,* 27 Nov. 1935, 8; "The Revision of Histories Began Twenty Years Ago," *FPSB* 2 (March 1940): 3; Lizabeth Cohen, *Making a New Deal: Industrial Workers in Chicago, 1919–1939* (Cambridge: Cambridge University Press, 1990), 287; Rugg, *That Men May Understand,* 252.
3. See, e.g., Harold Rugg, "The American Way of Progress," *Scholastic,* 13 April 1935, item 124; "Teaching Americanism," *St. Louis Dispatch,* n.d. [Feb. 1940], item 147, both in vol. 2154, reel 179, *American Civil Liberties Union Papers* (Wilmington, Del.: Scholarly Resources, 1996).
4. See Alan Brinkley, *The End of Reform: New Deal Liberalism in Recession and War* (New York: Knopf, 1995).
5. *Bergen [N.J.] Evening Record,* 26 Aug. 1940, 22, quoted in Marian C. Schipper, "The Rugg Textbooks Controversy: A Study in the Relationship between Popular Political Thinking and Educational Materials" (Ph.D. diss., New York University, 1979), 159; George E. Sokolsky, "Our Children's Guardians," *Liberty* 17 (April 1940): 36.
6. See Warren Susman, "The Culture of the Thirties," in idem., *Culture as History: The Transformation of American Society in the Twentieth Century* (New York: Pantheon, 1984), 150–183, esp. 153–154; Robert M. Collins, *The Business Response to Keynes, 1929–1964* (New York: Columbia University Press, 1981), 45–46.
7. Christopher J. Kauffman, *Faith and Fraternalism: A History of the Knights of Columbus, 1882–1982* (New York: Simon and Schuster, 1992), 261–

286; William Pencak, *For God and Country: The American Legion, 1919–1941* (Boston: Northeastern University Press, 1989), 275–277; Hamilton Hicks, "Ours to Reason Why," *American Legion Magazine* 50 (May 1941): 54.

8. Gary Gerstle, "The Protean Character of American Liberalism," *AHR* 99 (Oct. 1994): 1063; Brinkley, *End of Reform*, 165–166.

9. In *Introduction to the Problems of American Culture* (Boston: Ginn, 1931), e.g., Harold Rugg included lengthy chapters entitled "The Immigrant in Community and Neighborhood Life" and "Assimilation of Different Nationalities and Races."

10. Catholics, especially, praised the textbooks' denunciation of laissez-faire economics; see, e.g., Joseph J. Panzer, "Rugged Collectivism," *Catholic School Journal* 41 (Sept. 1941): 228.

11. Howard K. Beale, *Are American Teachers Free? An Analysis of Restraints upon the Freedom of Teaching* (New York: Scribner's, 1936), 304–305; "Hayes-Moon History Stigmatized as Unfit," unidentified clipping, 17 Oct. 1927; "English Union World Menace, Says Russell," *New York Herald Tribune*, 17 Nov. 1927; "Hayes History Used in Chicago, Board Is Told," ibid., 18 Nov. 1927, all in "Clippings on World History Textbooks Controversy" folder, box 11, Carleton J. H. Hayes Papers, Manuscript Division, Columbia University Libraries.

12. J. H. Beers to Carleton J. H. Hayes, 29 April 1930; "City Bars Professor Hayes' History," *NYT*, 2 May 1930; "Memorandum of conversation" (ms, 3 May 1930), all in "Miscellaneous Correspondence, Pre-WWII" folder, box 12, Hayes Papers.

13. "Memorandum of conversation"; "Fears Red Theories in Hayes History," *NYT*, 7 May 1930; "History Course Altered as Book Ban Is Defended," *New York Herald Tribune*, 7 May 1930, all in "Miscellaneous Correspondence, Pre-WWII" folder, box 12, Hayes Papers.

14. See John Higham, *Strangers in the Land: Patterns of American Nativism, 1860–1925* (New York: Atheneum, 1965 [1955]), chs. 8–10.

15. David Tyack et al., *Public Schools in Hard Times: The Great Depression and Recent Years* (Cambridge, Mass.: Harvard University Press, 1984), 63; "McCarl Shuts Off Pay of All 'Red' Teachers 'In or Out of Schools,'" *WP*, 16 Nov. 1935, 1; Carl L. Becker to W. Stull Holt, 26 Nov. 1935, in *"What Is the Good of History?" Selected Letters of Carl L. Becker, 1900–1945* (Ithaca: Cornell University Press, 1973), 232; "Board to Scan School Books for Red Views," *WP*, 21 Nov. 1935, 1.

16. L. B. Shippie to Bessie Louise Pierce, 2 Dec. 1935, folder 1, box 15, BLPP; Arthur M. Schlesinger, *In Retrospect: The History of a Historian* (New York: Harcourt, Brace, and World, 1963), 106; Burleigh Taylor Wilkins, *Carl Becker: A Biographical Study in American Intellectual History* (Cambridge, Mass.: MIT Press, 1961), 171–172; "Historians Hit 'Red' Charges against Book," *WP*, 4 Nov. 1935, 1; Carl L. Becker to Editor, *Washington Herald*, 26 Nov. 1935, in *"What Is the Good of History,"* 232–234; "Board Clears Four School Books of Red Charges," *WP*, 19 Dec. 1935, 1.

17. Letter from Marie Graves Bonham, *WP*, 27 Nov. 1935, 8; letter from Grover Ayres, *WP*, 1 Dec. 1935, B9; letters from Alexander Sidney Lanier, *WP*, 16 Nov. 1935, 6, and 26 Nov. 1935, 8.

18. George Wolfskill and John A. Hudson, *All but the People: Franklin D. Roosevelt and His Critics, 1933–39* (New York: Macmillan, 1969), 193, 186–187; Wolfskill, *Happy Days Are Here Again! A Short Interpretive History of the New Deal* (Hinsdale, Ill.: Dryden, 1974), 120; Bernard Sternsher, *Rexford Tugwell and the New Deal* (New Brunswick, N.J.: Rutgers University Press, 1964), 348–353.

19. Beale, *Are American Teachers Free*, 310; "The Changing Scene," *Social Frontier* 3 (Dec. 1936): 67–68; "State Board Bans Tugwell's Book," *Wilmington Morning News*, 16 Oct. 1936, 12.

20. Ruth Wood Gavian, *Society Faces the Future* (Boston: D. C. Heath, 1938), 27–28, quoted in Ralph West Robey, *Abstracts of Secondary School Social Science Text Books* (New York: National Association of Manufacturers, 1941), item 172. And see Susman, "Culture of the Thirties," 156.

21. Hiram Caton, "Progressivism and Conservatism during the New Deal," in *The New Deal and Its Legacy: Critique and Reappraisal,* ed. Robert Eden (Westport, Conn.: Greenwood, 1989), 182; "Business Men Awake!" *America in Danger!* no. 43 (29 Nov. 1936): 2, "America in Danger" folder, box 17, Henry Bourne Joy Papers, Bentley Historical Library, Ann Arbor.

22. O. K. Armstrong, *Treason in the Textbooks* (n.p., 1940), 3, 5, item 173, vol. 2154, reel 179, ACLU Papers.

23. Ibid., 12, 4–5.

24. Rugg, *That Men May Understand*, 74–75; *Proceedings of the Twenty-Fourth Annual Convention of the American Legion* (1942), 18.

25. Herbert M. Kliebard, *The Struggle for the American Curriculum, 1893–1958,* 2nd ed. (New York: Routledge, 1995), 175; Elmer Arthur Winters, "Harold Rugg and Education for Social Reconstruction" (Ph.D. diss., University of Wisconsin, 1968), 185; Edgar Bruce Wesley, *Teaching the Social Studies,* 2nd

ed. (Boston: D. C. Heath, 1942), 56, 199; Harold Rugg to Walter Lippmann, 24 Nov. 1924, folder 1077, box 29, series I, Walter Lippmann Papers, Yale University Library; Rugg, *That Men May Understand*, 44.

26. Bertie C. Forbes, "Treacherous Teachings," *Forbes* 44 (15 Aug. 1939): 8; "The Battle of the Books," *American Legion Magazine* 29 (Nov. 1940): 68; "Sons of the American Revolution Also Interested in Rugg Books," *FPSB* 4 (Aug. 1941): 2; Alonzo F. Meyers, "The Attacks on the Rugg Books," *Frontiers of Democracy* 7 (15 Oct. 1940): 19–20; "State Your Text" (ms, n.d. [1940]), "Social Science Textbook Investigation" folder, box 4, Merwin K. Hart Papers, UO; "Progress Report on Suggested Project to Stimulate Consideration of Textbooks Used in Various Public School Systems" (ms, 11 Sept. 1940), "Robey Textbook Survey" folder, box 847, NAMP.

27. Rugg, "Study in Censorship," 176–178. The ensuing account relies on internal correspondence reproduced in Orville Eastland Jones, "Activities of the American Legion in Textbook Analysis and Criticism, 1938–51" (Ed.D., University of Oklahoma, 1957). Since the Legion appears to have destroyed this correspondence—and since Jones copied it verbatim—I have treated his dissertation as a separate manuscript source, hereafter cited as Jones Papers.

28. Augustin C. Rudd to Stephen Chadwick, 18 Feb. 1939, p. 12; Rudd to Chadwick, 6 March 1939, p. 13; Homer L. Chaillaux to Rudd, 9 May 1939, p. 15, all in Jones Papers. See also Pencak, *For God and Country*, 273.

29. Garden City Post 265 Resolution, 1940, pp. 26–27; Chaillaux to Rudd, 22 June 1940, p. 25, both in Jones Papers; "The Battle of the Books," *American Legion Magazine* 29 (Nov. 1940): 2.

30. Talbot J. Taylor to Anthony S. Stumpp, 7 July 1941, p. 41; "Report of the Special Committee of Members of The American Legion and American Legion Auxiliary of North Canton Post No. 419 . . .," 14 Oct. 1940, p. 33; Walter McDonald to Milo J. Warner, 17 June 1941, p. 39; J. W. Getsinger to Warner, 25 Nov. 1940, pp. 62–63; C. B. Smith to Elmer W. Sherwood, 26 Jan. 1941, p. 76, all in Jones Papers.

31. Editorial by Earl Elhart in *Retail Executive*, 28 July 1939, quoted in Helen Sorenson, *The Consumer Movement: What It Is and What It Means* (New York: Harper and Bros., 1941), 162–163; editorial in *American Business Survey*, Jan. 1940, quoted in Meyers, "Attacks on the Rugg Books," 21–22.

32. Rugg, "Study in Censorship," 177–178; "Confidential Analysis of the Current (1939–1940) Attacks on the Rugg Social Science Series, Prepared by Harold Rugg in May–June 1940" (ms, 1940), "Harold Rugg" folder, box

58, William F. Russell Papers, Milbank Library, Teachers College; Winters, "Rugg and Education for Social Reconstruction," 149; Rugg, *That Men May Understand*, 77.

33. American Legion National Publicity Division, *News Bulletin*, 15 April 1941, p. 74; "What Is Taught in the Schools," *New York Sun*, 19 Oct. 1940, p. 77, both in Jones Papers; "Un-American Tone Seen in Textbooks on Social Sciences," *NYT*, 22 Feb. 1941, 6.

34. Schipper, "Rugg Textbook Controversy," 130; George E. Sokolsky, "Propaganda in Our Schoolbooks," *Liberty* 16 (30 Dec. 1939): 18; Fulton Oursler, "Introduction," in George E. Sokolsky, *The American Way of Life* (New York: Farrar and Rinehart, 1939), xiii.

35. "Professor H. O. Rugg on Carpet in Row over 'Radical' Texts," *Newsweek*, 4 Sept. 1939, 47; "Textbooks Brought to Book," *Time*, 3 March 1941, 40; "Attacks on Social Studies Textbooks," *High Points* 23 (June 1941): 6–7; "Historical News," *AHR* 46 (July 1941): 1004; William G. Carr, "This Is Not Treason," *Journal of the National Education Association* 29 (Nov. 1940): 237.

36. Wesley Mitchell, "General Statement on Social Science Textbooks" (ms, 1941), enclosed with M. I. Finkelstein to National Executive Committee and Committee on Textbooks, 15 March 1941, ACDIF folder 12; "Open Letter to Vierling Kersey, Superintendent of Schools, Los Angeles" (n.d. [May 1941]) enclosed with W. C. Mitchell to "Dear Colleague," 6 May 1941, ACDIF folder 5, both in Franz Boas Papers, American Philosophical Society, Philadelphia.

37. "What Do We Want Taught to Our Children?" *FPSB* 3 (Jan. 1941): 1; Amos Fries to Lowell Mason, 29 Dec. 1942, folder 27, box 2, Fries Papers; *Why Partisan Opinionated Textbooks for Vermont School Youngsters? Review of School Texts of Harold Ordway Rugg* (Burlington, Vt.: Free Press Association, 1940), 4, 24.

38. George H. Sabine et al., *The Text Books of Harold Rugg* (New York: American Committee for the Defense of Intellectual Freedom, 1942), 26–27, "Harold Rugg" folder, box 58, Russell Papers; Rugg, *That Men May Understand*, 251–252; Panzer, "Rugged Collectivism," 228.

39. Sokolsky, *American Way of Life*, vii; S. Alexander Rippa, *Education in a Free Society*, 3rd ed. (New York: David McKay, 1976), 291, 294; "Official Draft of a Memorandum of Industry's Recommendations for the Improvement of American Educational Methods in the Preparing of Students for Citizenship in a Republic" (ms, 29 June 1939), 1; "N.A.M. Educational Cooperation Meeting" (ms, 22 April 1940), 10, both in "Robey Textbook Survey"

folder, box 847, NAMP; "Un-American Tone Seen in Textbooks on Social Sciences," 1.

40. Richard Feier, *Elements of Economics,* quoted in "Excerpts from Various Textbooks Criticized in the Survey," *NYT,* 22 Feb. 1941, 6; Emory S. Bogardus and Robert H. Lewis, *Social Life and Personality* (New York: Silver Burdett, 1938), 239, quoted in Robey, *Abstracts,* item 53; James Truslow Adams and Charles Garrett Vannest, *The Record of America* (New York: Scribner's, 1938), 11, quoted ibid., item 5; Merwin K. Hart, "Let's Discuss This on the Merits," *Frontiers of Democracy* 7 (15 Dec. 1940): 85; Guardians of American Education, *Undermining Our Republic* (New York, 1941), 13; *Why Partisan Opinionated Textbooks for Vermont School Youngsters,* 9.

41. "SAR Also Interested in Rugg Books," *FPSB* 4 (Aug. 1941): 2; "Textbooks Brought to Book," 39; Harold Underwood Faulkner, *Economic History of the United States* (New York: Macmillan, 1938), 57–58, quoted in Robey, *Abstracts,* item 148; Leon H. Canfield et al., *The United States in the Making* (Boston: Houghton Mifflin, 1940), 169–170, quoted ibid., item 82.

42. George E. Sokolsky, "Hard Boiled Babes," *Liberty* 17 (16 March 1940): 50; idem, *American Way of Life,* vii; idem, "Is Your Child Being Taught to Loaf?" *Liberty* 17 (4 May 1940): 42.

43. Bertie C. Forbes to President, Board of Education, Englewood, N.J., 7 May 1940, "Correspondence—1940" folder, Bertie Charles Forbes Papers, George Arents Research Library, Syracuse University; Armstrong, *Treason in the Textbooks,* 4; Charlotte Wettrick, *Stable Government Relies upon Theory of Education* (Seattle: Patriotic Laymen's Education Association, n.d. [1941]), p. 80, Jones Papers; "What Is Taught in Schools," *Lyndonville [Vt.] Union Journal,* 30 Oct. 1940, rpt. from *New York Sun,* n.d. [Oct. 1940], "Harold Rugg" folder, Faculty Files, box 39, Public Relations Office Papers, Milbank Library.

44. Harold O. Rugg, *America's March toward Democracy* (New York: Ginn, 1937), 173; Hart, "Let's Discuss This on the Merits," 86.

45. "Textbooks Brought to Book," 37; W. N. Davis to Miss McCarthy, 8 Dec. 1940, enclosed with V. Sauer to Philip W. Haberman, 11 Dec. 1940, "Rapp-Coudert Committee: Correspondence, Dec. 1940" folder, box 14, Frederic Coudert Jr. Papers, Columbia University Libraries; Sokolsky, "Propaganda in Our Schoolbooks," 18.

46. Rugg, *That Men May Understand,* 268; "Extract from Remarks of Roger N. Baldwin before the PEA Conference" (ms, 29 Nov. 1940), item 87, vol. 2306, reel 197, ACLU Papers; "Roger Baldwin Replies," *Frontiers of*

Democracy 7 (15 Dec. 1940): 88; "Educators in Row over Rugg Books," *Philadelphia Inquirer,* 23 Feb. 1941, 1; Harold Rugg, *Now Is the Moment* (New York: Duell, Sloan and Pearce, 1943), 20.

47. Brinkley, *End of Reform,* 7; E. T. Meredith Jr. to Nicholas Murray Butler, 9 June 1939, "Harold Rugg" folder, box 58, Russell Papers.

48. Rugg to William F. Russell, 11 July 1939, "Harold Rugg" folder, box 58, Russell Papers; "Book Burnings," *Time* 36 (9 Sept. 1940): 64; Schipper, "Rugg Textbook Controversy," 221; R. Worth Shumaker to John E. Thomas, 4 Aug. 1943, p. 82, Jones Papers; Richard Seelye Jones, *A History of the American Legion* (Indianapolis: Bobbs-Merrill, 1946), 277; Jack Nelson and Gene Roberts Jr., *The Censors and the Schools* (Westport, Conn.: Greenwood, 1963), 39; interview with R. Bruce Raup (1963), pp. 192–196, Oral History Research Office, Columbia University Libraries.

49. Max Lerner, *Ideas for the Ice Age: Studies in a Revolutionary Era* (New York: Viking, 1941), 360; "In This Issue," *American Legion Magazine* 29 (Nov. 1940): 2; John C. Gebhard to W. B. Weisenburger, 11 July 1940; C. E. Harrison Jr. to Weisenburger, 25 June 1940; W. D. Fuller to Edmund deS. Brunner, 5 March 1941; "The N.A.M. Textbook Survey" (ms, n.d. [1941]), all in "Robey Textbook Survey" folder, box 847, NAMP.

50. "Indoctrinating Ideas," *Burlington Free Press,* n.d. [1950], "Harold Rugg" folder, Faculty Files, box 39, Public Relations Office Papers.

4. The Cold War Assault on Textbooks

1. Lucille Cardin Crain [hereafter LCC] to William F. Buckley Jr., 14 Aug. 1952, folder 25, box 26, LCCP; "A Declaration," *Educational Reviewer* 1 (15 July 1949): 1; William F. Buckley Jr., *God and Man at Yale: The Superstitions of "Academic Freedom"* (Chicago: Henry Regnery, 1951).

2. Buckley Jr. to Frank Adams, 28 Aug. 1952; LCC to William F. Buckley Sr., 27 Sept. 1951; Buckley Sr. to Merrill, Lynch, Pierce, Fenner, and Beane, 18 Oct. 1951; Robert L. Donner to Edward Allan Pierce, 5 Jan. 1952, all in folder 25, box 26, LCCP.

3. James Truett Selcraig, *The Red Scare in the Midwest, 1945–1955: A State and Local Study* (Ann Arbor: UMI Research Press, 1982), 79.

4. See, e.g., Ellen Schrecker, *Many Are the Crimes: McCarthyism in America* (Boston: Little, Brown, 1998).

5. See Jerome L. Himmelstein, *To the Right: The Transformation of American Conservatism* (Berkeley: University of California Press, 1990), 13–62; William

B. Hixon Jr., *Search for the American Right Wing: An Analysis of the Social Science Record, 1955–1987* (Princeton: Princeton University Press, 1992), 3–48.

6. Glen Warren Adams, "The UNESCO Controversy in Los Angeles, 1951–53: A Case Study of the Influence of Right-Wing Groups on Urban Affairs" (Ph.D. diss., University of Southern California, 1970), 47.

7. See Robert Griffith, "Dwight D. Eisenhower and the Corporate Commonwealth," *AHR* 87 (Feb. 1982): esp. 91–92; Himmelstein, *To the Right*, 24–25. Ralph W. Gwinn to LCC, 12 Oct. 1948, folder 4, box 37, LCCP.

8. "Houston Parents Read Students' Textbooks," *FPSB* 12 (Dec. 1949): 7; Amos A. Fries to J. Howard Rhoades, 7 June 1949, folder 44, box 2, Amos A. Fries Papers, UO.

9. James Alan Lufkin, "A History of the California State Textbook Adoption Program" (Ed.D., University of California at Berkeley, 1968), 143–144; Trustees of Americanism Fund, California Society, Sons of the American Revolution, *The Betrayal of America: Complaint to California Legislature* (San Francisco, n.d. [1947]), 2–3; G. E. Oaks to Roy E. Simpson, 7 Aug. 1947, folder 686; Frances M. Foster to Whom It May Concern, 26 Feb. 1947, enclosed with Gordon N. Mackenzie to the Members of the Committee on Education of the California State Senate (n.d. [1947]), folder 689; Mrs. W. J. Ravenscroft to Roy E. Simpson, 25 Feb. 1948, folder 683, all in DIS F3752, CDER.

10. Aaron M. Sargent, "Complaint," 21 Feb. 1947, 3, folder 676, DIS F3752, CDER; Roy E. Simpson to Earl Warren, 20 Jan. 1947, folder 1166, Earl Warren Papers, California State Archives; "Jack B. Tenney, California Legislator" (Oral History Program interview, University of California at Los Angeles, 1969), 1327, Bancroft Library, University of California at Berkeley; *The Facts* 6 (May 1951): 3, folder 16, box 61, LCCP; "Reports of the Senate Committee on Education," 20 June 1947, 14, folder 680, DIS F3752, CDER.

11. Roy E. Simpson to Emmett R. Berry, 11 March 1948, folder 686, DIS F3752; Edna Lonigan, "Broadcasting Collectivist Propaganda," *Educational Reviewer* 1 (15 July 1949): 3.

12. May Erwin Talmadge [hereafter MET], "Macgruder's Ghost walks again" (ms, n.d. [1951]), folder 12, box 30; idem, "If This Be Treason," *Atlanta Constitution*, 11 July 1951, folder 7, box 50; State Board of Education Minutes, 27 June 1951, folder 3, box 32, all in May Erwin Talmadge Papers, Hargrett Rare Book and Manuscript Library, University of Georgia, Athens; Jack Nelson and Gene Roberts Jr., *The Censors and the Schools* (Westport, Conn.: Greenwood, 1963), 42.

13. John T. Wood, "The Greatest Subversive Plot in History—Report to the American People on UNESCO," *Congressional Record,* 18 Oct. 1951, 82nd Cong., lst sess., folder 22, box 50, LCCP; Don Carleton, *Red Scare! Rightwing Hysteria, Fifties Fanaticism and Their Legacy in Texas* (Austin: Texas Monthly Press, 1985), 167; Adams, "UNESCO Controversy in Los Angeles," 50, 59; "Ford Foundation Plan Thrown Out by School Board," *Brooklyn Tablet,* 18 July 1953; "Los Angeles: Pink Ford?" *Time,* 27 July 1953, both in folder 12, box 17, Paul Blanshard Papers, Bentley Historical Library, Ann Arbor.

14. Adams, "UNESCO Controversy in Los Angeles," 56; Senate Committee on Education, State of California, "In the Matter of the Investigation in re Textbooks and Educational Practices in Public Schools" (ms, 8 April 1947), folder 698, DIS F3752; "Books Burned in Oklahoma Town," *NYT,* 12 Feb. 1952, folder 11, box 17, Blanshard Papers; Gordon D. Hall, *The Hate Campaign against the United Nations: One World under Attack* (Boston: Beacon, 1952), 27.

15. Sons of the American Revolution, *Betrayal of America,* 16–17; "Examination of Lucille Cardin Crain," *Educational Reviewer, Inc. and Lucille Cardin Crain, Plaintiffs, against McCall Corporation . . .* (Supreme Court of the State of New York, 6 April 1955), 66; J. H. von Sprecken to Herman Talmadge, 7 Aug. 1950, enclosed with Charles P. Whitman to MET, 25 Sept. 1950, folder 12, box 30; Gordon Persons to Herman Talmadge, n.d., enclosed with Herman Talmadge to MET, 5 June 1952, folder 5, box 8, both in MET Papers; Alabama Act. no. 888. H. 644 (ms, 19 Sept. 1953), folder 10, box 17, Blanshard Papers.

16. Ruby Hurley to Gordon Persons, 27 May 1952, enclosed with Herman Talmadge to MET, 5 June 1952, folder 5, box 8, MET Papers; "How Pure Is Pure?" *Business Week,* no. 1288 (8 May 1954): 178–179; "Update," ibid., no. 1290 (22 May 1954): 132.

17. "The Crisis in American Education," in *Freedom and Public Education,* ed. Ernest O. Melby and Morton Puner (New York: Praeger, 1953), 184–185, 192; Stuart John Foster, "Red Alert! The NEA's National Commission for the Defense of Democracy through Education Confronts the 'Red Scare' in American Schools, 1945–1955" (Ph.D. diss., University of Texas–Austin, 1996), ch. 4; Robert A. Skaife, "Groups Affecting Education," in *Forces Affecting American Education* (Washington: Association for Supervision and Curriculum Development, 1953), 53.

18. "Crisis in American Education," 185, 184, 197; "The Pasadena Case," *News and Views,* March 1951, 4, folder 16, box 36; "McCall's Lays Three Eggs," *Firing Line,* 1 Dec. 1952, 1, folder 15, box 61, both in LCCP; "Teaching Politics 'In Accordance with High Professional Standards,'" *FPSB* 13 (June 1951): 7.

19. Ethel M. Morrow to Greta Deffenbaugh, 14 Dec. 1944, folder 38; Deffenbaugh to Fries, 29 July 1943, folder 37, both in box 1, Fries Papers.

20. Deffenbaugh to Fries, 13 Jan. 1943; Fries to Deffenbaugh, 18 Jan. 1943, both in folder 37, box 1; Chance B. Humphrey to Fries, 14 Oct. 1952, folder 15, box 2; Amelia Murray to Fries, 9 Sept. 1949, folder 32, box 2; Grace I. Schneider to Fries, 13 May 1950, folder 49, box 2; J. Howard Rhoades to Fries, 31 Aug. 1949, folder 44, box 2, all in Fries Papers.

21. LCC to John Flynn, 1 Sept. 1950, "Communism in Schools and Textbooks" folder, box 26, John T. Flynn Papers, UO; Lewis Haney to LCC, 4 Nov. 1949; LCC to "Dr. Haney, Prof. Meyers, Prof. Saxton," 11 Nov. 1949, both in folder 17, box 53, LCCP; LCC to Rose Wilder Lane, 25 April 1951, folder 2, box 43, LCCP.

22. Rose Wilder Lane to LCC, 4 Nov. 1949, folder 2, box 43, LCCP; John E. Miller, *Becoming Laura Ingalls Wilder: The Woman behind the Legend* (Columbia: University of Missouri Press, 1998), 254; Roger Baldwin, "Gilt-Edged Patriots: Presenting the New York State Economic Council and Its Presiding Genius, Merwin K. Hart," *Frontiers of Democracy* 7 (15 Nov. 1940): 45–47; Mary Ann Raywid, *The Ax-Grinders: Critics of Our Public Schools* (New York: Macmillan, 1962), 115–116.

23. Allen Zoll, *Organized Attack on Schools Is Seen* (New York: National Council of American Education, 1951), "National Council of American Education: Miscellaneous, 1950–54" folder, box 38, Jewish Community Relations Council of Minnesota Papers, Minnesota Historical Society, St. Paul; Arthur D. Morse, "Who's Trying to Ruin Our Schools," in Melby and Puner, eds., *Freedom and Public Education,* 170–171; Frederick Woltman, "Wainwright Quits Educational Council with Fascist Taint," *New York World-Telegram,* 7 Oct. 1948, "National Council of American Education: Miscellaneous, 1947–49" folder, box 38, Jewish Community Relations Council of Minnesota Papers; William F. Buckley Jr. to C. H. Huvelle, 13 Dec. 1951, folder 2, box 27, LCCP.

24. "Examination of LCC," 8, 55; Verne Kaub, "A Critic," *Saturday Review of Literature* 35 (Dec. 1952): 16.

25. Selcraig, *Red Scare in the Midwest,* 77; Frank Hughes to Fries, 14 April 1948, folder 25, box 1, Fries Papers; LCC to Hughes, 5 Jan. 1950; Hughes to LCC, 7 Jan. 1950; Hughes to LCC, 4 May 1951, all in folder 14, box 39, LCCP.

26. "Excerpt from Broadcast of Fulton Lewis, Jr.," 27 Nov. 1950, folder 14, box 43, LCCP; Michael Kazin, *The Populist Persuasion: An American History* (New York: Basic, 1995), 173; Foster, "Red Alert," 109–110; John T. Flynn to LCC, 28 April 1950, "Communism in Schools and Texts" folder, box 26, Flynn Papers; Carleton, *Red Scare,* 165; Selcraig, *Red Scare in the Midwest,* 79–80; MET to Edgar C. Pulliam, 17 Jan. 1952, folder 5, box 8, MET Papers.

27. Foster, *Red Alert,* 109; Flynn to LCC, 26 March 1951, folder 21, box 34, LCCP; J. B. Withee to LCC, 3 April 1951, enclosed with LCC to Flynn, 11 April 1951, "Communism in Schools" folder, box 25, Flynn Papers; Emily P. Morse to Friends of the Public Schools, 14 Dec. 1950, folder 27, box 2, Fries Papers; W. A. McClenaghan, "An Author," *Saturday Review of Literature* 35 (Dec. 1952): 17.

28. Kazin, *Populist Persuasion,* 178–183, 332n; Robert W. Iversen, *The Communists and the Schools* (New York: Harcourt Brace, 1959), 241–242; Flynn to LCC, 26 March 1951; LCC to Flynn, 31 March 1951, both in folder 21, box 34, LCCP.

29. Roy E. Simpson to Harry L. Foster, 20 Feb. 1947; William J. Bauer to Richard Chamberlain, 3 March 1947; Foster to Simpson, 16 April 1947, all in folder 683, DIS F3752, CDER; C. H. Munson to Julian A. Todd, 4 April 1949, folder 20, box 1, Fries Papers; "Evaluation of Instructional Materials" (ms, 1948), folder 13, box 17, Blanshard Papers; "Transcript of the Proceedings and Transactions of the 31st Annual Convention of the American Legion . . ." (ms, July 1949), 115–117, box 2, American Legion—Michigan Papers, Bentley Historical Library.

30. Irene Corbally Kuhn, "Your Child Is Their Target," *American Legion Magazine* 52 (June 1952): 18–19, 54–60; "Transcript of the Proceedings and Transactions of the 34th Annual Convention" (ms, Aug. 1952), 140–141, box 2, American Legion—Michigan Papers; letter from C. Conrad Schneider, *American Legion Magazine* 52 (June 1952): 4–5.

31. "Transcript of the Proceedings and Transactions of the 34th Annual Convention," 142; Harold Benjamin, "Communication Affecting Education," in *Forces Affecting American Education,* 111–113; "UNESCO Absolved in Legion Inquiry," *NYT,* 11 Sept. 1955, folder 14, box 17, Blanshard Papers; Philip John Zorich, "Lawrence Timbers and the American Legion: The Crusade against UNESCO and UNICEF" (M.A. thesis, University of Ore-

gon, 1978), 19–43; "The Road to Reason," *Reporter,* 2 June 1955, folder 12, box 17, Blanshard Papers.

32. *Third Report of Joint Fact-Finding Committee on Un-American Activities* (Sacramento: California Senate, 1947), 322.

33. "Is the Head of the Carnegie Foundation Communistic?" *FPSB* 11 (Sept. 1948): 3–4; Skaife, "Groups Affecting Education," 63–64; Dorothy Dunbar Bromley, "The Battle for the Schools," in Melby and Puner, eds., *Freedom and Public Education,* 208–209; "Who's Trying to Control Our Schools?" *FPSB* 15 (Oct. 1952): 7; Augustin G. Rudd to Fries, 18 Jan. 1950, folder 47, box 2, Fries Papers; W. T. Couch to LCC, n.d. [1953], folder 12, box 29, LCCP.

34. Elizabeth Fones-Wolf, *Selling Free Enterprise: The Business Assault on Labor and Liberalism, 1945–1960* (Urbana: University of Illinois Press, 1994), 190, 200; "Minutes of the Joint Session of the NAM Educational Advisory Committee and NAM Educational Advisory Council," 12 April 1951, 6, "Educational Advisory Council 1956–1951, Minutes" folder, box 65; NAM Educational Advisory Committee and NAM Educational Advisory Council, "This We Believe about Education" (ms, 1953), 39, "Education Dept., General, Oct–Dec. 1953" folder, box 62; "Education Appraises the NAM," *Times-Advocate* [Norfolk, Va.], 5 March 1953, "Education Dept., General, Jan–Sept. 1953" folder, box 62; F. Kenneth Brasted to Coordinating Committee, 8 April 1954, 7, "Education—Memorandum, General, 1954" folder, box 62, all in NAMP; Raywid, *Ax-Grinders,* 237n36, 117.

35. LCC to Lane, 13 Sept. 1950; Lane to LCC, 30 Sept. 1950; Lane to LCC, 22 March 1950, all in folder 2, box 43, LCCP.

36. "Examination of LCC," 70; James Cope to LCC, 19 July 1950, folder 2, box 29, LCCP; Wilbur Helm to "Dear Friends," 8 Dec. 1953, folder 17, box 2, Fries Papers; William Buckley Sr. to LCC, 27 April 1951, folder 24, box 26, LCCP.

37. Mrs. G. V. McCombs to Fries, 17 Dec. 1948, folder 27, box 2, Fries Papers; Adelbert W. Lee to MET, 19 March 1951, folder 4, box 8, MET Papers; James A. Gannon, n.t. (ms, 5 April 1951), folder 9, box 43, LCCP.

38. Charles Albert Adams and Melbert B. Adams, "Confidential, before the State Board of Education, Answer to the Protest of California Sons of the American Revolution" (ms., n.d. [1946]), enclosed with Roy E. Simpson to Earl Warren, 20 Jan. 1947, folder 1166, Warren Papers.

39. *Intellectual Freedom* 1 (May 1953): 4, folder 11, box 17, Blanshard Papers; Georgia State Board of Education minutes, 12–13 Aug. 1952, 7, folder 4,

box 32, MET Papers; "Houston Again," *New Republic,* 7 Dec. 1953, folder 12, box 17, Blanshard Papers.

40. "Statement by Senator Jack B. Tenney" [April 1947?], 4, folder 1166, Warren Papers; Ingrid Winther Scobie, "Jack B. Tenney and the 'Parasitic Menace': Anti-Communist Legislation in California, 1940–1949," *Pacific Historical Review* 43 (1974): 202, 204–205; *American Book Publishers' Council Bulletin* press release, 3 Jan. 1954, 3–5, folder 2; ACLU, "Report on Censorship, Sept. 1952–June 1953," 12, folder 3, both in box 3, Blanshard Papers.

41. Walter Gellhorn, "A General View," 375; William B. Prendergast, "Maryland: The Ober Anti-Communist Law," 169, 180; Vern Countryman, "Washington: The Canwell Committee," 285, 326–327; E. Houston Harsha, "Illinois: The Broyles Commission," 80–84, all in *The States and Subversion,* ed. Walter Gellhorn (Ithaca: Cornell University Press, 1952); M. J. Heale, *American Anti-Communism* (Baltimore: Johns Hopkins University Press, 1990), 184.

42. Walter Goodman, *The Committee: The Extraordinary Career of the House Committee on Un-American Activities* (New York: Farrar, Straus and Giroux, 1964), 274n; Aaron M. Sargent, "Overthrowing the Constitution with Propaganda," *Americans, Speak Up,* [1949?]; idem., *A Socialistic Public School System* (n.p., May 1950), both in folder 8, box 55, LCCP; "Congressional Investigation of Textbooks," *FPSB* 14 (Aug. 1951): 2; Fries to Grace H. De Fremery, 26 Sept. 1951, folder 61, box 2, Fries Papers.

43. "Conversation with Leo Blaisdell, Nov. 1954," folder 10, box 17; Harold Rugg to Paul Blanshard, 13 Sept. 1955, folder 60, box 2, both in Blanshard Papers; Virgil M. Rogers, "Textbooks under Fire," *Atlantic* 195 (Feb. 1955): 47.

44. My argument here echoes M. J. Heale, *McCarthy's Americans: Red Scare Politics in State and Nation, 1935–1965* (Athens: University of Georgia Press, 1998), esp. pt. 4.

45. E. Merrill Root, *Brainwashing in the High Schools: An Examination of American History Textbooks* (New York: Devin-Adair, 1958), 3, 11; Ginn and Co., "A Candid Evaluation of E. Merrill Root's *Brainwashing in the High Schools*" (n.d. [1959]), 1–3, enclosed with Jerry Cordrey to *Human Events,* 11 April 1960, folder 5, box 1, E. Merrill Root Papers, UO; Nelson and Roberts, *Censors and the Schools,* 69, 75–76.

46. Nelson and Roberts, *Censors and the Schools,* 91–95; "Mississippi Mud," *Time* 75 (16 May 1960): 65.

47. Nelson and Roberts, *Censors and the Schools*, 78–90, 15–16; Gertrude Stephens to MET, 7 May 1959, folder 2, box 10, MET Papers; "A D.A.R. Textbook Study," *Weekly Crusader* 5 (22 Oct. 1965): 3, Collection HH36, folder 7, box 1, Hall-Hoag Collection, John Hay Library, Brown University.

48. M. F. Peterson to Alexander C. Burr, 1 June 1962, folder 21, box 11, Alexander C. Burr Papers, State Historical Society of North Dakota, Bismarck; Fred M. Hechinger, "On Teaching about Communism," *NYT,* 19 Dec. 1962, 6; "Florida Statute, Chapter 61–77, House Bill no. 26 (Approved by Governor, 27 May 1961)," folder 1, box 12, Burr Papers; Shelby M. Jackson, "Studying Communism in Louisiana Schools," *American Legion Magazine* 72 (April 1962): 45.

49. Betty E. Chmaj, "Paranoid Patriotism: The Radical Right and the South," *Atlantic* 21 (Nov. 1962): 93; L. Edward Hicks, *"Sometimes in the Wrong, but Never in Doubt": George S. Benson and the Education of the New Religious Right* (Knoxville: University of Tennessee Press, 1994), 77; "Mississippi Mud," 65.

5. Black Activism, White Resistance, and Multiculturalism

1. James Alan Lufkin, "A History of the California State Textbook Adoption Program" (Ed.D. diss., University of California at Berkeley, 1968), 253–254; Harry N. Scheiber, "The California Textbook Fight," *Atlantic Monthly* 220 (Nov. 1967): 38–39; John W. Caughey, John Hope Franklin, and Ernest R. May, *Land of the Free: A History of the United States* (New York: Benziger, 1966), 3.

2. Lufkin, "California State Textbook Adoption Program," 273; letter from Mr. and Mrs. Serge R. Ballif, "Criticism of Land of the Free" (ms, 25 July 1966), 142, folder 842, CDER; Ford Sammis, *The Story behind "Land of the Free," A Controversial History Textbook* (n.p., 1967), 38–39; letter from Elsie P. Lodge, "Criticism of Land of the Free," 158.

3. "Police Rout 3500 Unruly Pupils at Black Power School Protest," *Philadelphia Inquirer,* 18 Nov. 1967, 1; John T. Gillespie, "Negro Students Explain Objections to Schools," *Philadelphia Evening Bulletin,* 21 Nov. 1967, "Schools—Philadelphia—African-American Studies" folder; "Pupils High: Officials," ibid., 15 Oct. 1968, "Schools, Philadelphia, Blacks, Disorder, 1968" folder; "Ten Days of Disorders: Pupils, Neighbors and Faculty Describe Crisis," ibid., 20 Oct. 1968, "Schools, Philadelphia, Blacks, Disorder,

1968" folder, all in box 204, Philadelphia Evening Bulletin Collection, Urban Archives, Temple University.

4. See esp. Gary B. Nash, Charlotte Crabtree, and Ross E. Dunn, *History on Trial: Culture Wars and the Teaching of the Past* (New York: Knopf, 1997).

5. Sammis, *Story behind "Land of the Free,"* 39.

6. Office of Research and Evaluation, School District of Philadelphia, *The Teaching of African and Afro-American Studies in the Philadelphia Public Schools, 1968/69 Academic Year* (Philadelphia, 1969), 6–8, "Black History" folder, box 4, Citizens Committee on Public Education Papers, Urban Archives; Letitia W. Brown, "Why and How the Negro in History," *Journal of Negro Education* 38 (Fall 1969): 448; William Loren Katz, "Black History in Secondary Schools," ibid., 431, 433.

7. Shirlee Smith, "Black History Months Have Not Sufficiently Inspired Our Youth," *Newsday,* 24 Feb. 1983, fiche 480, SCF.

8. Langston Hughes, "Simple on Negro History Week," *Chicago Defender,* 13 Feb. 1960, 10; *Thirty-Third Annual Celebration of Negro History Week* (Washington: Association for the Study of Negro Life and History, 1958), 3, folder 9, box 179–35, H. Council Trenholm Papers, Moorland-Spingarn Research Center, Howard University.

9. Mrs. E. K., "A Textbook in Race Hate," *Daily Worker,* 17 Feb. 1950, fiche 004.909–1, SCF; untitled manuscript, [1948?], folder 39, box 2, Faith Rich Papers, Special Collections, Harold Washington Library, Chicago Public Libraries; Samuel Eliot Morison and Henry Steele Commager, *The Growth of the American Republic,* 4th ed., vol. 1 (New York: Oxford University Press, 1950), 537; Neil Jumonville, *Henry Steele Commager: Midcentury Liberalism and the History of the Present* (Chapel Hill: University of North Carolina Press, 1999), 146–147.

10. Most accounts of intergroup education trace its origins to Rachel Davis DuBois, who designed school assemblies and curricula in the 1920s and 1930s to underscore the cultures and achievements of different racial and ethnic groups. The movement boomed during World War II, when Nazi propaganda abroad and racial violence at home dramatized the need to teach "tolerance" in the schools. DuBois corresponded frequently with George Washington Carver and with NAACP officials, who appointed a field secretary to traverse the country on behalf of intergroup education in the 1940s. Within this biracial coalition, however, only blacks placed a primary emphasis on revising history textbooks. George Washington Carver to Rachel Davis DuBois, 31 July 1927, folder 3; Rachel Davis

DuBois, *Some Racial Contributions to America: A Study Outline for Secondary Schools* (Philadelphia: Committee on Interests of the Colored Race, Philadelphia Yearly Meeting of Friends, [1927?]), folder 5, both in box 2, Rachel Davis DuBois Papers, Immigration History Research Center, St. Paul, Minn.; Noma Jensen, "Annual Report, Jan. 1, 1945—Jan. 1, 1946" (ms, 1946), frame 796, reel 6, pt. 17, NAACP Papers; Earl Conrad, "Official Defends Distorted Texts," *Chicago Defender,* 4 May 1946, 13.

11. "Little Black Sambo," *WP,* 30 Sept. 1947, folder 871, box 78–44, Papers of the NAACP—Washington D.C. Branch, Moorland-Spingarn Research Center.

12. Samuel Eliot Morison and Henry Steele Commager, *The Growth of the American Republic,* 5th ed., vol. 1 (New York: Oxford University Press, 1962), 527–529.

13. Mervyn M. Dymally, "The Struggle for the Inclusion of Negro History in Our Textbooks—A California Experience," *NHB* 33 (Dec. 1970): 190; Jack Nelson and Gene Roberts Jr., *The Censors and the Schools* (Westport, Conn.: Greenwood, 1963), 169; "UL Warns of 'Squandering' Child Potentials" (press release, 3 April 1963), fiche 004.909–3; "The CORE Southern Education Project Proposals for a Core Negro Culture Program" (ms, n.d. [1965]), fiche 003–560–8; National Urban League, *Textbooks, Civil Rights, and the Education of the American Negro* (New York, 1965), 2, fiche 004.909–4, all in SCF.

14. Nelson and Roberts, *Censors and the Schools,* 168–169; Albert E. Stone, *The Return of Nat Turner: History, Literature, and Cultural Politics in Sixties America* (Athens: University of Georgia Press, 1992), 299; African-American Heritage Association, "Operation: End Racist Poison in School Books" (ms, 11 Feb. 1962), frame 386, reel 4, series I, pt. III, Claude A. Barnett Papers (Frederick, Md.: University Publications of America, 1986); Hillel Black, *The American Schoolbook* (New York: William Morrow, 1967), 109–113; "Negro Culture Given Short Shrift in Many Histories in School Today," *Philadelphia Evening Bulletin,* 22 Oct. 1963, "Schools—Philadelphia—Text Books—1961 to" folder, box 209, Philadelphia Evening Bulletin Collection; Minutes of the Detroit School Board, 18 Dec. 1962, 317–320, "Task Force—Readings" folder, box 2, Racism and Bias Task Force File, NCTE.

15. Minutes of the Detroit School Board, 22 Jan. 1963, 388–392; ibid., 26 May 1964, 570, both in "Task Force—Readings" folder, box 2, Racism and Bias Task Force File, NCTE; "'Huck Finn' Barred as Textbook by City," *NYT,*

12 Sept. 1957; Nelson and Roberts, *Censors and the Schools,* 167–168; Everett T. Moore, "Censorship in the Name of Better Relations," *A.L.A. Bulletin,* July–Aug. 1961; "Still Missing," *New York Teacher News,* 10 Feb. 1962, both in fiche 004.909–3, SCF.

16. Raymond Pace Alexander to *Philadelphia Inquirer,* 17 Aug. 1964, folder 54, box 98, Raymond Pace Alexander Papers, University of Pennsylvania Archives; Nassau County NAACP to J. E. Allen, 31 Oct. 1965, "Intercultural Relations—General, July 1965–June 1966" folder, box 31, Collection 15080–69/77, Commissioner's Files, New York State Dept. of Education Records, State Library, Albany; *Report of the Special Committee on Non-discrimination of the Board of Public Education of Philadelphia, Pennsylvania* (n.p., 1964), 107, folder 18, box 19, Floyd Logan Papers, Urban Archives; "Negro Editor Scores 'Segregated' Texts," *NYT,* 1 Sept. 1966, fiche 004.909–4, SCF.

17. Martin Luther King Jr., *Where Do We Go from Here: Chaos or Community?* (Boston: Beacon, 1968), 41–44. For others who emphasized textbooks' "damage" to whites as well as to blacks, see, e.g., Floyd Logan to Helen C. Bailey, 8 July 1960, folder 16, box 12, Logan Papers; Gerald Grant, "Seven Texts Criticized for Negro Omissions," *Philadelphia Inquirer,* 13 Aug. 1964, folder 29, box 13, Alexander Papers; Hoyt Gimlin, "American History: Reappraisal and Revision," *Editorial Research Reports* 2 (5 Nov. 1969): 818, fiche 003–560–8, SCF.

18. "Vice President Humphrey Advocates the Study of Negro History by All Americans," *Congressional Record* 113, pt. 3 (15 Feb. 1967): 3487–88; Lerone Bennett Jr., "Reading, 'Riting and Racism," *Ebony* 22 (March 1967): 135; Dorothy Sterling address, n.t. (ms, 26 July 1967), 16, fiche 003.560–5; "House Committee Studies Treatment of Minorities in Text and Library Books," *Publishers Weekly,* 19 Sept. 1966, fiche 004.909–4, both in SCF.

19. "Negro Image Seen Blurred in Textbooks," *New York Post,* 24 Aug. 1966, fiche 004.909–4, SCF; Bennett, "Reading, 'Riting and Racism," 135; "House Committee Studies Treatment of Minorities."

20. National Urban League, *Textbooks, Civil Rights,* 5; Henry Wilkinson Bragdon, "Dilemmas of a Textbook Writer," *Social Education* 33 (March 1969): 297–298.

21. Bennett, "Reading, 'Riting, and Racism," 136; letter from Andrew Blunt, *Richmond Times-Dispatch,* 26 Feb. 1970, "Virginia: The New Dominion" folder, accession 7690-ac, Virginius Dabney Papers, Alderman Library,

University of Virginia; H. J. Lipham to Raymond Pace Alexander, 24 Aug. 1964, folder 1, box 88, Alexander Papers.

22. Here I rely heavily on Ronald P. Formisano, *Boston against Busing: Race, Class, and Ethnicity in the 1960s and 1970s* (Chapel Hill: University of North Carolina Press, 1991).

23. *Report of the National Advisory Commission on Civil Disorders* (New York: Dutton, 1968), 434; Richard E. Schermerhorn to Edwald B. Nyquist, 1 Feb. 1971, "Intercultural Relations—General. 11/69" folder, box 11, collection 15080–80, Commissioner's Files, New York State Dept. of Education Records; Gary B. Nash, "Multiculturalism and History: Historical Perspectives and Present Prospects," in *Public Education in a Multicultural Society: Policy, Theory, Critique,* ed. Robert K. Fullinwider (Cambridge: Cambridge University Press, 1996), 193.

24. Letter from Leslie S. Robison, "Criticism of Land of the Free," 161; Sammis, *Story behind "Land of the Free,"* 27; letter from Viola McLain, "Criticism of Land of the Free," 149; letter from Mrs. G. Hinton, ibid., 155.

25. Lufkin, "California State Textbook Adoption Program," 296, 307, 268–270; Sammis, *Story behind "Land of the Free,"* 9–12; Juel Janis, "Textbook Revisions in the Sixties," *Teachers College Record* 72 (Dec. 1970): 293; "New U.S. History Textbooks Putting Stress on Minorities' Contribution to Building Nation," *NYT,* 28 April 1974, fiche 004.909–4, SCF.

26. "New U.S. History Textbooks Putting Stress on Minorities' Contribution."

27. "Integrating the Texts," *Newsweek* 67 (7 March 1966): 94; American Indian Historical Society Executive Council, "Corrections Required in Textbooks Proposed for Adoption by the State of California" (ms, May 1966), folder 841, CDER; letter from Manuel H. Guerra, "Criticism of Land of the Free," 176; Nanci L. Gonzalez, "Positive and Negative Effects of Chicano Militancy on the Education of the Mexican-American," in *Student Dissent in the Schools,* ed. Irving G. Hendrick and Reginald L. Jones (Boston: Houghton Mifflin, 1970), 266; Robert K. Fullinwider, "Multicultural Education: Concepts, Policies, and Controversies," in Fullinwider, ed., *Public Education,* 7.

28. "Negro History Courses Set," Associated Press, 30 Jan. 1968, fiche 003.560–6, SCF.

29. "Boycott in Plainfield," *NYT,* 17 Feb. 1968, 30; Susan Snow, "My Teacher Is a Racist," in *The High School Revolutionaries,* ed. Marc Libarle and Tom Seligson (New York: Vintage, 1970), 94; "What's Wrong with the High Schools?" *Newsweek* 75 (16 Feb. 1970): 66; Mark Shedd, "The Curriculum

of Reality," *Integrated Education* 6 (May–June 1968): 9; "Black Culture Courses, More Negro Officials Asked for City Schools," *Philadelphia Evening Bulletin,* 26 Dec. 1968, "Schools—Philadelphia—African-American Studies" folder, box 204, Philadelphia Evening Bulletin Collection.

30. Raymond H. Giles, *Black Studies Programs in Public Schools* (New York: Praeger, 1974), 110; "Black Peacestone Rangers Rap to MSA," *Open Door* [Milwaukee], quoted in *Our Time Is Now: Notes from the High School Underground,* ed. John Birmingham (New York: Praeger, 1970), 161; *How Old Will You Be in 1984? Expressions of Student Outrage from the High School Free Press,* ed. Diane Divoky (New York: Avon, 1969), 75.

31. James Brown, "The Black Athlete," in Libarle and Seligson, eds., *High School Revolutionaries,* 50; Brumsic Brandon Jr., "Readin' 'Ritin' 'Rithmetic Racism," in *Harlem: A Community in Transition,* ed. John Henrik Clarke (New York: Citadel, 1969), 224.

32. *Malcolm X on Afro-American History* (New York: Pathfinder, 1970), 68–69; Daniel U. Levine, "Differences between Segregated and Desegregated Settings," *Journal of Negro Education* 39 (Fall 1970): 143.

33. "The Program of the Black Youth Alliance," in Divoky, ed., *How Old Will You Be in 1984,* 172, 174; Giles, *Black Studies Programs,* 112; Jean Dresden Grambs, Larry Cuban, and James A. Banks, "Black versus Negro History: What Are the Issues?" in *Black Image: Education Copes with Color: Essays on the Black Experience,* ed. Jean Dresden Grambs et al. (Dubuque, Ia.: William C. Brown, 1972), 28–29.

34. Kenneth L. Fish, *Conflict and Dissent in the High Schools* (New York: Bruce, 1970), 115.

35. See, e.g., letter from James Clayton to *Champaign-Urbana Courier,* 31 March 1969, "Censorship May 1969" folder, box 1, Censorship File, NCTE; Giles, *Black Studies Programs,* 123–128. For white attacks on Baldwin, see, e.g., "New Jersey, Nebraska, and Detroit Feature Negro History Projects," *Library Journal* 90 (15 March 1965): 2345; on Brown, Elizabeth G. Whaley to Peter Marsh, 6 Nov. 1972, "Censorship 1970–1974" folder, box 1, Censorship File, NCTE; on Cleaver, Mel Ash to Max Rafferty, 8 Sept. 1969, folder 743, CDER; and on Hughes, "City School Board Rejects WCTU Offer to Screen Books," *Columbus [Oh.] Citizen Journal,* 16 Oct. 1963, "Censorship Materials 1960–1963" folder, box 1, Censorship File, NCTE.

36. Robert Bone, "Negro Literature in the Secondary Schools: Problems and Perspectives," *English Journal,* n.d. [1968], "Censorship 1967–68" folder, box 1, Censorship File, NCTE.

37. Rose Marie Walker Levey, *Black Studies in Schools* (Washington: National School Public Relations Association, 1970), 20, 17; Karen Branan and Mary Kay Murphy, "Answering the Black's 'WHO AM I?'" *Scholastic Teacher*, 5 Jan. 1970, fiche 003–560–8, SCF; Giles, *Black Studies Programs*, 98, 101.

38. William L. Van Deburg, *New Day in Babylon: The Black Power Movement and American Culture, 1965–1975* (Chicago: University of Chicago Press, 1992), 17; John Brown Society, *An Introduction to the Black Panther Party* (n.p., 1969), 2, "Black Power" General File, Vertical Files, Tamiment Library, New York University; Levey, *Black Studies*, 3–4.

39. "Nichols Says Gratz Plan Is like South African," 12 Dec. 1967, "Schools—Philadelphia—African-American Studies" folder, box 204, Philadelphia Evening Bulletin Collection; "NAACP Unit Issues New Multi-Racial History Syllabus," *NHB* 33 (Nov. 1970): 167; Mark M. Krug, "Freedom and Racial Equality: A Study of 'Revised' High School History Texts," *School Review* 78 (May 1970): 303; Julius Hobson, "A Search for Identity," *Integrated Education* 7 (March–April 1969): 25; Van Deburg, *New Day in Babylon*, 27; Giles, *Black Studies Programs*, 9.

40. Katz, "Black History in Secondary Schools," 433; David Kirp, *Just Schools: The Idea of Racial Equality in American Education* (Berkeley: University of California Press, 1982), 182.

41. Benjamin L. Hooks, "A New Day Begun," *Journal and Guide* [Norfolk, Va.], 15 Dec. 1978, A9; Jim Cleaver, "How Easily We Forget What We Should Remember," *Los Angeles Sentinel*, 28 June 1979, A7; idem., "Remember When It Was Negro History?" ibid., 4 Feb. 1982, A7.

42. Levey, *Black Studies*, 5; George C. Wallace, "State of Alabama Proclamation by the Governor" (ms, 27 Nov. 1972), enclosed with J. Rupert Picott to "Executive Council Members," 2 Jan. 1973, folder 11, box 88, Alexander Papers; "Black History's History," *WP*, 28 Jan. 1987, fiche 484, SCF, pt. II.

43. James T. Patterson, *Brown v. Board of Education: A Civil Rights Milestone and Its Troubled Legacy* (New York: Oxford University Press, 2001), 176; Jeffrey Mirel, *The Rise and Fall of an Urban School System: Detroit, 1907–1981*, 2nd ed. (Ann Arbor: University of Michigan Press, 1999), 297.

44. Black, *American Schoolbook*, 114; Minutes of the Detroit School Board, 23 June 1964, 685–686, "Task Force—Readings" folder, box 2, Racism and Bias Task Force File, NCTE; Mirel, *Rise and Fall*, 307; "Recommended Guidelines for Multi-Ethnic Publishing in McGraw-Hill Book Co." (ms, n.d. [1969]), fiche 004.909–5, SCF.

45. Black, *American Schoolbook*, 119; R.H.S., "Implications of the Powell Hearings," clipping, n.t., n.d. [1966]), fiche 004.909–5, SCF; Gary Orfield, "Turning Back to Segregation," 7; idem, "The Growth of Segregation," 58, both in *Dismantling Desegregation: The Quiet Reversal of* Brown v. Board of Education, ed. Gary Orfield and Susan Eaton (New York: New Press, 1996); Marvin W. Schlegel, "What's Wrong with Virginia History Textbooks," *Virginia Journal of Education*, Sept. 1970; "Virginia Will Update History Courses," *WP*, 23 Jan. 1972; "New Texts Use More Negroes," *Richmond News-Leader*, 13 Jan. 1971, all in "Virginia: The New Dominion" folder, accession 7690-ac, Dabney Papers.
46. Frances Fitzgerald, *America Revised* (New York: Vintage, 1979), 94, 100.
47. James Baldwin, "The Nigger We Invent," *Integrated Education* 7 (March–April 1969): 18–20.

II. GOD IN THE SCHOOLS

1. Edward J. Larson, *Summer for the Gods: The Scopes Trial and America's Continuing Debate over Science and Religion* (New York: Basic, 1997), 198, 193, 201.
2. Ibid., 230–234.
3. Jonathan Zimmerman, "Relatively Speaking," *New Republic*, 6 Sept. 1999, 13–14.

6. Religious Education in Public Schools

1. Erwin L. Shaver [hereafter ELS], "Weekday Religious Education in Champaign Declared Legal," ICRE press release, 28 Jan. 1946, folder 14, box 28, RG 19, NCC; Walter M. Howlett to Richard Welling, "Released Time for Education" folder, box 69, National Self-Government Committee Papers, New York Public Library.
2. ELS, "Movement toward Cooperation among Conservative Christian Groups" (ms, n.d. [1946]), 4–5; ELS to "Dr. Ross and Dr. Sweet," 17 May 1945, both in folder 24, box 28, RG 19, NCC.
3. *McCollum v. Board of Education*, 333 U.S. 203 (1948); *Released Time Weekly Herald* [Pasadena, Calif.] 1 (Sept. 1949), 2; Felix Manley, "Weekday Christian Education in Pasadena" (ms, 26 Oct. 1949), enclosed with Manley to ELS, 18 Nov. 1949, both in folder 2, box 29, RG 19, NCC.
4. C. W. Schowengerdt, *Guideposts to Church-Public School Cooperation* (Missouri Council of Churches, n.d. [1948–49]), folder 17; ELS, "Interim Plans

for Weekday Religious Education," 10 Jan. 1949, folder 2, both in box 29, RG 19, NCC; Frank E. Gaebelein, *Christian Education in a Democracy* (New York: Scribner's, 1951), 81, quoted in John Q. Schisler, "Religion and the Public Schools," *Religion in Life* 21 (Winter 1951–52): 6, folder 37, box 32, RG 9, NCC. Since combatants in the struggle over religious education used the labels "fundamentalist" and "evangelical" interchangeably, I do the same here. To quote a self-avowed fundamentalist (and evangelical), the terms connoted Christians who "hold that the essence of the gospel consists mainly in its doctrines of man's sinful condition and need of salvation, the revelation of God's grace in Christ, the necessity of spiritual renovation, and participation of the experience of redemption through faith." Paul J. Andreasen, "An Appeal for Evangelical Released-Time Education," *United Evangelical Action* 5 (1 April 1946): 4.

5. See, e.g., Donald E. Boles, *The Bible, Religion, and the Public Schools* (Ames: Iowa State University Press, 1961); Robert Michaelsen, *Piety in the Public School* (New York: Macmillan, 1970); Robert Wuthnow, *"Quid Obscurum:* The Changing Terrain of Church-State Relations," in *Religion and American Politics: From the Colonial Period to the 1980s,* ed. Mark A. Noll (New York: Oxford University Press, 1990), 337–354.

6. Minor C. Miller, *Teaching the Multitudes: A Guidance Manual in Weekday Religious Education* (Bridgewater, Va.: Beacon Publishers, 1944), 132–133.

7. See Naomi Cohen, *Jews in Christian America: The Pursuit of Religious Equality* (New York: Oxford University Press, 1992); Stephen M. Feldman, *Please Don't Wish Me a Merry Christmas: A Critical History of the Separation of Church and State* (New York: New York University Press, 1997); and esp. Gregg Ivers, *To Build a Wall: American Jews and the Separation of Church and State* (Charlottesville: University Press of Virginia, 1995).

8. J. Ronald Oakley, *God's Country: America in the Fifties* (New York: Dembner, 1986), 319–321; Will Herberg, *Protestant-Catholic-Jew* (New York: Doubleday, 1955), 84.

9. Mary Dabney Davis, *Weekday Classes in Religious Education* (Washington: Govt. Printing Office, 1941), 1; Frank E. Karlesen, "The Coudert-McLaughlin Bill" (radio transcript, Station WQXR, 14 Jan. 1941), "Released Time for Religious Education" folder, box 69, National Self-Government Committee Papers; "Teaching Bible in the Public Schools of North Carolina," *North Carolina Christian Advocate,* 15 March 1941, 10, "WRE Clippings (Misc.)" folder, box 1, WRE-NC.

10. "Released Time Has Vast Gain," *NYT,* 16 Jan. 1942, "Released Time for Religious Education" folder, box 69, National Self-Government Committee Papers; Ruth G. LeValley, "A Study of Weekday Religious Education in North Carolina Public Schools" (M.A. thesis, University of North Carolina–Chapel Hill, 1946), 23, 42, 47; Walter M. Howlett, "Released Time for Religious Education in New York City," *Religious Education* 37 (1942): 106; *A Report to You on the Teaching of the Bible to the Boys and Girls in Our Mount Pleasant High School* (n.p., [1946?]), "Publicity" folder, box 2, WRE-NC.

11. Leo Pfeffer, *Church, State, and Freedom* (Boston: Beacon, 1953), 315–316; Davis, *Weekday Classes,* 27; Barbara Kae Bellefeuille, "The History of the Bluefield Bible Program, 1939–1989" (Ed.D., Virginia Tech University, 1989), 84–85; J. P. McCallie, "Teaching the Bible in Chattanooga's Schools," *United Evangelical Action* 10 (1 March 1946): 7; Alice Treuschel, "Report of the Weekday Church School Directed by the Community Council of Christian Education, Fremont, Ohio, 1944–45" (ms, 1945), folder 5, box 1, Fremont Council of Christian Education Papers, Rutherford B. Hayes Presidential Library, Fremont, Oh.; Z. B. Edworthy to ELS, 19 March 1948, folder 19, box 28, RG 19, NCC; ELS, "Weekday Religious Education in Champaign Declared Legal."

12. Frances C. Query, "Bulletin to Chairmen of Local Committees Responsible for Bible in North Carolina Public Schools," 15 March 1947, "Memorandums to Bible Teachers, 1946–47" folder, box 1, WRE-NC; Interfaith Council of Weekday Religious Education of Allegheny County, *The Kind of Life You Want Depends on How You Prepare for It* (n.p., [1948?]), folder 14, box 29, RG 19, NCC; "Did you Say 'Take Bible'?" (ms, [1946?]), "Publicity" folder, box 2, WRE-NC.

13. "Annual Meeting, North Dakota Council of Christian Education" (ms, 9 Jan. 1941), 12, folder 6, box 2, North Dakota Conference of Churches Papers, State Historical Society, Bismarck; LeValley, "Study of Weekday Religious Education," 58–71; *Sharing* [Bible Teachers of North Carolina], Nov.–Dec. 1943, 3; ibid., May 1943, 2, both in "NCEA Publications" folder, box 1, WRE-NC.

14. *Sharing,* March 1943, 3, "NCEA Publications" folder; John A. MacLean, "The Prayer of a Modern Pharisee, By One of Them" (n.p., [1948?], enclosed with Memorandum no. 17, 15 Jan. 1949, "Memorandums to Bible Teachers, 1948–1949" folder, both in box 1, WRE-NC.

15. Week Day Church School Section, ICRE, "Interpreting and Publicizing the Week Day Church Schools" (ms, Feb. 1941), 16, folder 15, box 29; Frank

Jennings to Minor C. Miller, 19 March 1948, in Virginia Council of Churches, *Weekday Religious Education in Virginia: Opinion of the Attorney General of Virginia* (n.p., 1948), appendix 6, folder 8, box 28; *Weekday Professional Advisory Section Newsletter* [ICRE], Nov. 1946, 4–5, folder 5, box 30, all in RG 19, NCC; Alice Treuschel, "Report of the Weekday Church School" (ms, Feb. 1944), folder 5, box 1, Fremont Council of Christian Education Papers.

16. Week Day Church School Section, "Interpreting and Publicizing," 5–6; James Banford McKendry, "Religious Education in Oak Park," *Religious Education* 37 (1942): 26–27.

17. Robert E. Segal, notes of meeting, 11 Dec. 1945; Segal to Herman H. Rubenovitz, 26 Nov. 1945; Henry Levy to Eugene Block, 8 Dec. 1942; Benjamin J. Shevach, "Comments on Released-Time in Boston" (ms, Dec. 1947), all in "Religion in the Schools—Released Time—1941–48" folder, box 177, BJCC.

18. Angus C. Hull, "The Supreme Court and Religion in the Schools," *First Baptist News* [Peoria] 7 (11 March 1948), enclosed with Idalee L. Woodson to ELS, 18 March 1948, folder 12; "Northern Baptists Have Not Acted in Champaign Case," *Taylorville [Ill.] Daily Breeze Courier*, 22 Nov. 1947, enclosed with ELS to John L. Franklin and Owen Rall, n.d. [1947], folder 15; ICRE, Children's Work Professional Advisory Section, "Report of Committee on Child Evangelism" (ms, Feb. 1942), folder 24, all in box 28, RG 19, NCC.

19. Lucille B. Milner, "Church, State, and Schools," *New Republic*, 13 Aug. 1945, folder 14, box 28, RG 19, NCC; Public Education Association, "Released Time for Religious Education in New York City's Schools" (ms, 30 June 1943), 3, "Released Time for Religious Education" folder, box 69, National Self-Government Committee Papers; "Sue to Ban City Schools' 'Bible Hour,'" *Chicago Sun Times*, 26 Oct. 1945, folder 20, box 28, RG 19, NCC; J. Lynwood Smith to Stanley B. Hyde, n.d. [1944]; Roger W. Fitzgerald to Hyde, n.d. [1944]; Jennie K. Sherman to Hyde, n.d. [1944], all in folder 17, box 7, Vermont Council of Churches Papers, Bailey-Howe Library, University of Vermont.

20. Cohen, *Jews in Christian America*, 131–143; Ivers, *To Build a Wall*, 63, 73–77; Synagogue Council of America, "Conference on Religious Education and Public School . . ." (ms, 29 March 1944), 12, "Church/State/ School, 1944–1956" folder, box 6, Jewish Community Relations Council of Pittsburgh Papers, Hillman Library, University of Pittsburgh.

21. Synagogue Council, "Conference on Religious Education and Public School," 2, 15; Shevach, "Comments on Released-Time"; American Association for Jewish Education, *Religious Education and the Public Schools* (n.p., n.d. [1942]), 32, folder 17, box 29, RG 19, NCC.

22. Synagogue Council, "Conference on Religious Education and Public School," 15, 17; "Excerpts from Published Statements for Use of Champaign Case Lawyers in Preparing Brief" (ms, 1947), 1, folder 15, box 28, RG 19, NCC; "Summary of Statement Made by Rabbi Herman H. Rubenovitz, President of Rabbinical Association of Greater Boston" (ms, 4 March 1941), "Religion in the Schools—Released Time—1941–48" folder, box 177, BJCC.

23. Synagogue Council, "Conference on Religious Education and Public School," 24, 26; Jewish Community Center of Metropolitan Boston, "Released Time Fact Sheet" (ms, 9 June 1948), 3, "Religion in the Schools—Released Time—1941–48" folder, box 177, BJCC; Shevach, "Comments on Released-Time."

24. Shevach, "Comments on Released-Time"; Walter A. Lurie to Mortimer Brenner, 11 April 1949, "Joint Advisory Committee on Religion and the Public Schools, 1947–49" folder, box 7, Synagogue Council of America Papers, American Jewish Historical Society; Synagogue Council, "Conference on Religious Education and Public School," 25; American Association for Jewish Education, *Religious Education and the Public Schools,* 23.

25. "Week-Day Religious Education," *United Evangelical Action* 3 (Nov. 1943): 3.

26. ICRE, "Report of Committee on Child Evangelism," 6–14.

27. "Buffalo Fundamentalists Organize for Week-Day Christian Education," *United Evangelical Action* 5 (1 Nov. 1944): 12; Archer E. Anderson, "Week-Day Christian Education in Duluth," ibid. 5 (15 March 1946): 9; "A Report from Gerald Knoff to the other Members of the Staff . . ." (ms, 4 May 1945), 2, folder 24, box 28, RG 19, NCC; Andreasen, "Appeal for Evangelical Released-Time Education," 4.

28. ICRE, "Report of Committee on Child Evangelism," 1–5, 13–16.

29. Ibid., 2–3; Stanley Borden to ELS, 20 Feb. 1946, folder 12, box 29; Carroll H. Lemon to ELS, 19 March 1948, folder 12, box 28, RG 19, NCC.

30. W. T. Smith, "What's Happening," *Herald* [First Methodist Church, Peoria, Ill.] 8 (12 March 1948), enclosed with Idalee L. Woodson to ELS, 18 March 1948, folder 12, box 28, RG 19, NCC.

31. James O'Neil, "Church-State Relationships" (ms, 27 July 1948), folder 1, box 29; "Is This a Distortion?" *Daily Oklahoman,* 16 March 1948, enclosed

with E. R. Reno to ELS, 16 March 1948, folder 12, box 28, both in RG 19, NCC; James R. Walter, "The U.S. Supreme Court and Religion in Public Schools," *First [Presbyterian] Church Messenger* [Fremont, Oh.] 22 (11 July 1948), folder 11, box 1, Fremont Council of Christian Education Papers; "The Supreme Court Decision," *Progress* [International Reform Federation] 48 (April 1948): 2, folder 12; Frank S. Mead, "Go Chase Yourself, Youngster," *Christian Herald*, June 1949, folder 14, both in box 29, RG 19, NCC.

32. See, e.g., Millie F. Stanley to ELS, 18 March 1948; Harriet Blanding to ELS, 18 March 1948, both in folder 12, box 28, RG 19, NCC; "A Brief Summary of Legal Opinions and Decisions of State Departments of Education Regarding Weekday Religious Education," in Virginia Council of Churches, *Weekday Religious Education*, app. 2.

33. Lois McClure to Rice Lardner, 28 July 1948, folder 16; O. Bronsletter to ELS, 19 March 1948, folder 12, both in box 28, RG 19, NCC.

34. Lillian White Shepard to E. E. Zimmerman, 8 Dec. 1950, folder 3, box 1, Fremont Council of Christian Education Papers; Frank J. Sorauf, "*Zorach v. Clauson:* The Impact of a Supreme Court Decision," *American Political Science Review* 53 (1959): 782, 780; "Survey of Weekday Religious Education Situation" (ms, 1 Feb. 1949), folder 19, box 28, RG 19, NCC; ELS, "A Statement Regarding the Decision of the United States Supreme Court in the Brooklyn Weekday Religious Education Case" (ms, n.d. [1952]), 2; ELS to Morton Kurtz, 19 Nov. 1952, both in "Weekday Religious Education" folder, box 4, WRE-NC.

35. National Council of Churches of Christ, "Study Document on Weekday Religious Education" (ms, 1959), 2, "Weekday Religious Education" folder, box 4, WRE-NC; John S. Groenfeldt, "The Weekday Movement Moves Ahead," *International Journal of Religious Education* 32 (May 1956): 17; Friends of Bible Teaching in the Public Schools, *The Fifty-Nine Year Miracle: The History of Bible Teaching in the Public Schools of Charlotte (1925–1984)* (n.p., [1984?]), 23, North Caroliniana Collection, University of North Carolina Library, Chapel Hill; ELS, "A Look at Weekday Church Schools," *Religious Education* 51 (Jan.–Feb. 1956): 20; "Editor's Notes," *Catholic Standard and Times* [Philadelphia], 10 Sept. 1954, p. 229, vol. 71, Archdiocesan Scrapbooks, Philadelphia Archdiocesan Historical Research Center; Seymour Gorchoff to Arthur Gilbert, 18 Feb. 1957, enclosed with Gilbert to ELS, 5 March 1957, folder 8, box 32, RG 9, NCC; Everett E. Levi to Albert Chernin, 14 Oct. 1955, folder 6, box 188, JWFI.

36. Catherine H. Smith, untitled report on Lyndonville Area Rural Project (n.d. [1954]), folder 1, box 33, RG 9, NCC; Milner, "Church, State, and Schools"; Ernst Christian Helmreich, *Religion and the Maine Schools: An Historical Approach* (Brunswick, Me.: Bureau for Research in Municipal Government, 1960), 59; Carl R. Key to Alice L. Goddard, n.d. [1960]; Goddard to Paul King, 7 Sept. 1960, both in folder 22, box 31, RG 9, NCC; "St. Louis Area: Religion in the Schools," *Christian Century* 76 (26 Aug. 1959): 980.

37. "That Supreme Court Decision," *Progress* [International Reform Federation] 48 (April 1948): 4, folder 12, box 29, RG 19, NCC; Richard B. Dierenfield, *Religion in American Public Schools* (Washington: Public Affairs Press, 1962), 34.

38. Michaelsen, *Piety in the Public School*, 168–169; "Annual Meeting, North Dakota Interchurch Council" (ms, 1949), folder 8; "Biennial Meeting, North Dakota Interchurch Council" (ms, 22 Jan. 1957), folder 11; North Dakota Interchurch Council, *Bible Reading in the Public Schools of North Dakota* (n.p., n.d. [1956]), folder 11, all in box 2, North Dakota Conference of Churches Papers; Elizabeth W. Wesson to Robert Segal, 5 Feb. 1953; Segal to Benjamin J. Shevach, 23 Oct. 1952; "Cambridge Housewife's Book Guides Teachers in Bible Readings," *Boston Daily Globe*, 22 Feb. 1957, all in "Religious Observances in Schools—Wesson, Elizabeth M." folder, box 180, BJCC.

39. Boles, *Bible, Religion, and Public Schools*, 86–87; Cohen, *Jews in Christian America*, 189–190; "Analysis of Religious Practices in the Indianapolis Public Schools" (ms, 1959), folder 13, box 203, JWFI; *The Regents Statement on Moral and Spiritual Training in the Schools* (n.p., 30 Nov. 1951), "Dr. Allen—Moral and Spiritual Values 1951–53" folder, box 2, Commissioner's File BO459-69, New York State Dept. of Education Records, State Library, Albany; Bruce J. Dierenfield, "Secular Schools? Religious Practices in New York and Virginia Public Schools since World War II," *Journal of Policy History* 4 (1992): 366; "Prayer in School Still State Issue," *NYT*, 3 March 1954, folder 3, box 23, Paul Blanshard Papers, Bentley Historical Library, Ann Arbor.

40. "San Diego, California: A Guide to Moral and Spiritual Education in Elementary Schools" (ms, n.d. [1953]), 2–3, enclosed with R. L. Hunt to "Dear Friends," 1 March 1955, folder 4, box 1, Presbyterian Board of Christian Education Papers, Presbyterian Historical Society, Philadelphia; Dierenfield, *Religion in American Public Schools*, 43–44; "Weymouth Teach-

ers Prepare Fifth Student 'Trust in God' Contest," *Patriot* [Quincy, Mass.], 18 Jan. 1958; Weymouth Moral and Spiritual Values Committee to "Dear Friends," 3 Jan. 1958; "The Workshop of Freedom" (ms, n.d. [1958]), all in "Religious Observances in Schools (General Files) 1956–1960" folder, box 179, BJCC.

41. Dierenfield, "Secular Schools?" 365; Ruth Fairbanks, "Chaff and Chatter," *Fargo Forum,* 24 Sept. 1950, 28, scrapbook 6, Bertha R. Palmer Papers, State Historical Society of North Dakota; John A. LaCoste, "Discussion on Problem of Religion and Public Education" (ms, n.d. [1955]), folder 3, box 1, Presbyterian Board of Christian Education Papers.

42. LaCoste, "Discussion on Problem of Religion"; "Religion in Schools—NCC's Plan," *Christian Beacon* 22 (11 April 1957): 1.

43. Louis Cassels, "Place of Religion in Public School Likely to Boil into Public Debate," unidentified clipping, n.d. [1956], folder 4, box 23; "'Hybrid Religion' Laid to Schools," *NYT,* 8 May 1957, folder 4, box 23; Mr. and Mrs. James E. Ghio to Paul Blanshard, 3 Oct. 1957, folder 22, box 3, all in Blanshard Papers; Robert Segal to Jason R. Silverman, 24 Dec. 1958, "Religious Observances in Schools (General Files) 1956–1960" folder, box 179, BJCC; "Broad Ripple High School Good Friday Program" (ms, 1961), folder 4, box 188, JWFI; Deborah Dash Moore, *To the Golden Cities: Pursuing the American Jewish Dream in Miami and L.A.* (Cambridge, Mass.: Harvard University Press, 1994), 182; Joseph W. Feldman to Earl Dimrick, n.d. [1956], folder 18, box 36, National Council of Jewish Women—Pittsburgh Section Papers, Hillman Library, University of Pittsburgh.

44. Robert Segal to Jason R. Silverman, 2 Dec. 1958; Louise M. Rodenhiser to Segal, 5 May 1960, both in "Religious Observances in Schools (General Files) 1956–1960" folder, box 179, BJCC.

45. "Memorandum Regarding Chelsea Christmas Carol Problem" (ms, 8 Dec. 1949); copies of letters of Abraham Wolper family, Dec. 1949, both in "Religious Observances in Schools, Chelsea Christmas Carol Problem, 1948–1950" folder, box 180, BJCC.

46. Isadore Zack to Robert Segal, 13 Feb. 1957; Jules Cohen to Louis Ruchames, 15 Jan. 1958, both in "Religious Observances in Schools (General Files) 1956–60" folder, box 179, BJCC; Marshall Cohen to Jules Cohen, 14 April 1958, folder 6, box 188, JWFI; Sidney Z. Vincent to G. Goodwin, 16 Nov. 1949, folder 93, box 6, Jewish Welfare Federation of Cleveland Papers, Western Reserve Historical Society, Cleveland; Jewish Community Council of Cleveland and Bureau of Jewish Education, *The*

Hanukkah Manual for Public School Teachers (ms, [1948?]), 1, General Collection, Balch Institute for Ethnic Studies, Philadelphia.

47. "Working Draft, Christmas-Hanukkah Celebrations" (ms, 1950); Raymond L. Spoerri to Sidney Z. Vincent, 20 Dec. 1948, both in folder 93, box 6, Jewish Welfare Federation of Cleveland Papers.

7. School Prayer and the Conservative Revolution

1. Leo Pfeffer, "Who's Who in the Prayer Controversy," *CLSA Reports* No. 6 (15 Aug. 1962), "Prayer in Schools—1961" folder, box 23, Leo Pfeffer Papers, George Arents Research Library, Syracuse University. See David J. Garrow, *Bearing the Cross: Martin Luther King, Jr., and the Southern Christian Leadership Conference* (New York: Vintage, 1986), 211.

2. Garrow, *Bearing the Cross*, 269; William M. Beaney and Edward N. Beiser, "Prayer and Politics: The Impact of *Engel* and *Schempp* on the Political Process," *Journal of Public Law* 13 (1964): 486; *The Dialogue* [National Conference of Christians and Jews] no. 29 (May 1964), folder 8, box 1, RG 9, NCC.

3. Samuel L. Scheiner to JCRM et al., 23 July 1962, "Prayer in Schools—1961" folder, box 23, Pfeffer Papers.

4. Dan T. Carter, *The Politics of Rage: George Wallace, the Origins of the New Conservatism, and the Transformation of American Politics* (New York: Simon and Schuster, 1995), 207; Arnold R. Hirsch, "Massive Resistance in the Urban North: Trumbull Park, Chicago, 1953–1966," *Journal of American History* 82 (Sept. 1995): 522–550; Thomas J. Sugrue, "Crabgrass-Roots Politics: Race, Rights, and the Reaction against Liberalism in the Urban North, 1940–1964," ibid., 551–578.

5. Conference of the Joint Advisory Committee of the Synagogue Council of America and the National Community Relations Advisory Council, "Reactions to Supreme Court Decision in Regents Prayer" (ms, 16 July 1962), 1, box 130, accession 184, JCRCGP; James P. Mullane, "J. P. Mullane Terms Court Contemptible," *Indianapolis News*, 1 July 1963, folder 6, box 187, JWFI; Emery S. Quimby to Everett Dirksen [hereafter ED], 28 April 1969, WPF 2127, EDP.

6. See Rebecca E. Klatch, *A Generation Divided: The New Left, the New Right, and the 1960s* (Berkeley: University of California Press, 1999), 2; James T. Patterson, *Grand Expectations: The United States, 1945–1974* (New York: Oxford University Press, 1996), ch. 21; and esp. Maurice Isserman and

Michael Kazin, *America Divided: The Civil War of the 1960s* (New York: Oxford University Press, 2000).

7. See Doug Rossinow, *The Politics of Authenticity: Liberalism, Christianity, and the New Left in America* (New York: Columbia University Press, 1998); Isserman and Kazin, *America Divided*, ch. 13.

8. See Patterson, *Grand Expectations*, esp. chs. 19 and 21; Matthew C. Moen, *The Transformation of the Christian Right* (Tuscaloosa: University of Alabama, 1992); Justin Watson, *The Christian Coalition: Dreams of Restoration, Demands for Recognition* (New York: St. Martin's, 1997).

9. Leo Pfeffer, *The Supreme Court's Bible-Prayer Decision . . .* (New York: Joint Advisory Committee of the Synagogue Council of America and the National Community Relations Advisory Council, 18 June 1963), 7–8, folder 7, box 203, JWFI.

10. "Uproar over School Prayer—and the Aftermath," *U.S. News and World Report* 53 (9 July 1962): 44.

11. See Bruce J. Dierenfield, "'Somebody Is Tampering with America's Soul': Congress and the School Prayer Debate," *Congress and the Presidency* 24 (Autumn 1997): 188; David E. Kyvig, *Explicit and Authentic Acts: Amending the United States Constitution, 1776–1995* (Lawrence: University Press of Kansas, 1996), ch. 16.

12. Dierenfield, "Somebody Is Tampering," 179, 176; "Does Schoolroom Prayer Require a New Amendment?" *Time* 83 (8 May 1964): 62; "The Court Decision—And the School Prayer Furor," *Newsweek*, 9 July 1962, 44, folder 1, box 188, JWFI; *The Dialogue*, no. 29 (May 1964), 2, folder 8, box 1, RG 9, NCC; Kenneth M. Dolbeare and Phillip E. Hammond, *The School Prayer Decisions: From Court Policy to Local Practice* (Chicago: University of Chicago Press, 1971), 32.

13. Dolbeare and Hammond, *School Prayer Decisions*, 32; Edward V. Brooke, "Findings, Rulings, and Order" (ms, 17 Dec. 1963); Morris Michelson to Brooke, 6 Sept. 1963, both in "Religious Observances in Schools (General Files), 1963–64" folder, box 179; "Sudbury Schools to Mark Christian, Jewish Holidays," *Boston Globe*, 27 Aug. 1964, "Religious Observances—Sudbury, Mass." folder, box 180, all in BJCC.

14. "Bah, Humbug, Virginia—We Don't Know: Christmas Poses Dilemma for the Schools," *American Education* 3 (Dec. 1966–Jan. 1967): 14–17; Isaiah Terman, "Christmas in the Public Schools, 1963" (ms, 8 Nov. 1963), folder 5, box 188; "Christmas Practices by Residence" (ms, 1966), enclosed with

Philip D. Pecar to "Dear Friend," 20 Jan. 1966, folder 3, box 177, both in JWFI; "Jewel" to "Dearest darling Beenie hillers" [Paul Blanshard], 9 Jan. 1963, folder 10, box 4, Paul Blanshard Papers, Bentley Historical Library, Ann Arbor.

15. Charles W. Winegarner to James G. O'Hara, 5 Jan. 1966, "Prayer in Schools" folder, box 12, James G. O'Hara Papers, Bentley Historical Library; "Some Second Thoughts on Moments of Silence," *NYT*, 4 March 1984, "School Prayer Legislation 1984" folder, box 7, accession 1991, JCR-CGP; Clarence W. Hall, "Is Religion Banned from Our Schools?" *Reader's Digest* 86 (Feb. 1965): 50; Bruce J. Dierenfield, "Secular Schools? Religious Practices in New York and Virginia Public Schools since World War II," *Journal of Policy History* 4 (1992): 371; Mel Carbonell to ED, 29 June 1966; *National Champions, Miami High "Stingarees," America's Outstanding Athletes Speak Up!* (Miami: Christian Youth Ranch, n.d. [1966]), both in WPF 2075, EDP.

16. Naomi Cohen, *Jews in Christian America: The Pursuit of Religious Equality* (New York: Oxford University Press, 1992), 212; James W. Fraser, *Between Church and State: Religion and Public Education in a Multicultural America* (New York: St. Martin's, 1999), 149; Samuel S. Wiley to Carlton Joiner, 29 June 1967; Wiley to "Dear Friend," 7 June 1967, both in "Week-Day Religious Educational Committee" folder, box 3, WRE-NC; Friends of Bible Teaching in the Public Schools, *The Fifty-Nine Year Miracle: The History of Bible Teaching in the Public Schools of Charlotte (1925–1984)* (n.p., [1984?]), 28, North Caroliniana Collection, University of North Carolina Library, Chapel Hill.

17. Samuel S. Wiley to Donald A. Lau, 18 May 1967, "Weekday Religious Educational Committee" folder, box 3, WRE-NC; *How We Teach the Bible in Public Schools* (Wheaton, Ill.: Religious Instruction Association, 1967), folder 19, box 3, North Dakota Conference of Churches Papers, State Historical Society, Bismarck; Samuel S. Wiley to "Mrs. Gwynn," 17 March 1967, "Weekday Religious Educational Committee" folder, box 3, WRE-NC.

18. James L. Hicks, "A Personal Thing," *Amsterdam News*, 7 July 1962, 10; Melvin Tapley, "Standing in the Way" [cartoon], ibid.

19. Fannie Ledbetter, "School Prayer," *Amsterdam News*, 4 Aug. 1962, 10; Mrs. Wellington Drexler to James G. O'Hara, 8 March 1963, "Prayer in Schools" folder, box 12, O'Hara Papers; "Sorry, This School's Segregated" [cartoon], *Indianapolis News*, 19 June 1963, folder 6, box 187, JWFI.

20. "Six Local Pastors View School Prayer Ruling," *Philadelphia Tribune,* 30 June 1962, 1; "Baptist Ministers Hit Court Prayer Edict," ibid., 7 July 1962, 11.

21. "Extracts from Statements of Denominational Bodies . . ." (ms, July 1962), 9, folder 32, box 32, RG 9, NCC; James C. O'Connor, "On the Issue of School Prayers," *Journal and Guide* [Norfolk, Va.], 14 July 1962, 7.

22. "Extracts from Statements of Denominational Bodies," 9; Vanessa Siddle Walker, *Their Highest Potential: An African American School Community in the Segregated South* (Chapel Hill: University of North Carolina Press, 1996), 109; Mrs. Paul F. Whitaker to L. H. Fountain, 24 Feb. 1967, enclosed with Whitaker to ED, 24 Feb. 1967, WPF 2104, EDP; "Gary Ministers' Opinions Vary on Prayer Ban," *Gary Post-Tribune,* 18 June 1963, folder 6, box 187, JWFI; Dierenfield, "Secular Schools?" 375.

23. "Bishop Scully's Statement," *Evangelist* [Albany], 29 June 1962, "Prayer in the Schools—News Clippings" folder, box 20, New York State Council of Churches Papers, Arents Research Library, Syracuse University; "After the Decision," *Criterion* [Indiana], 6 July 1962, folder 1, box 188, JWFI; *Congressional Record,* 9 June 1964, 12579–580, "Prayer (1)" folder, box 63, Alvin M. Bentley Papers, Bentley Historical Library; "Message by the Committee on Religion and Public Education" (ms, 24–27 June 1962), folder 28, box 28; "Pronouncement on the Churches and the Public Schools" (ms, 7 June 1963), folder 10, box 31, both in RG 4, NCC; Arlene and Howard Eisenberg, "Why Clergymen Are against School Prayer," *Redbook,* Jan. 1965, 97, Chicago Office File 5359, EDP.

24. "The Greater Evil," *WP,* 21 Jan. 1966, WPF 2067, EDP; "Nearer, My God, to Thee . . ." [cartoon], *St. Louis Globe-Democrat,* Sept. 1966, WPF 2068, EDP.

25. Allen J. Matusow, *The Unraveling of America: A History of Liberalism in the 1960s* (New York: Harper and Row, 1984), 95, 184, 207; Patterson, *Grand Expectations,* 543–544; Garrow, *Bearing the Cross,* 531; "The Greater Evil."

26. Eugene L. Heath to ED, 23 Sept. 1966; Berenice M. Storey to ED, 23 Sept. 1966, both in WPF 2083, EDP; Kenneth McFarland to ED, 7 Sept. 1966, WPF 2082, EDP; "Text of Address given by the Reverend George T. Cook . . ." (ms, 22 Sept. 1963), "Rev. George T. Cook" folder, box 2, Series IV, Frank J. Becker Papers, Arents Research Library; Norman Vincent Peale, "Superduper Liberals See Prayers as Corny—Is It 'Goodbye, Chaplains'?" *Congressional Record,* 4 June 1964, 12272, "Prayer (1)" folder, box 63, Bentley Papers.

27. Dierenfield, "Somebody Is Tampering," 198n10; Dean M. Kelley, "Analysis of Hearings on Constitutional Amendments to Permit Prayer and Bible-Readings in Public Schools" (ms., April 1964), "Prayer in the Schools—Miscellaneous" folder, box 20, New York State Council of Churches Papers; J. Goodloe Jackson, "Bible Reading and Prayer in Public Schools" (ms, 1964), enclosed with Jackson to Frank Becker, 1 Aug. 1964, "J. Goodloe Jackson" folder, box 6, Series IV, Becker Papers.

28. "Halt Prayers, Town Warned," *Herald-Traveler*, n.d. [1969], enclosed with William X. Wall to ED, 6 June 1969, WPF 2128, EDP.

29. See Michael Kazin, "The Grass-Roots Right: New Histories of U.S. Conservatism in the Twentieth Century," *AHR* 97 (1992): 136–155; Leonard J. Moore, "Good Old-Fashioned New Social History and the Twentieth-Century American Right," *Reviews in American History* 24 (1996): 555–573.

30. "A Prayer Amendment?" *America* 107 (8 Sept. 1962): 685–686; "Congress Considers Prayer Decision," *Congressional Record*, 15 June 1964, 13271, "Prayer (1)" folder, box 63, Bentley Papers; "Return of Bible to Schools Aim of Youth Group," *Christian Beacon* 28 (24 Oct. 1963): 5; "Carl Thomas McIntire, Larry Miller Testify on Behalf of Becker Amendment," ibid. 29 (14 May 1964): 1; "Film Stars Fight Court Ban on Prayer," *Shreveport Journal*, 6 July 1964, rpt. in *Congressional Record*, 27 July 1964, A3902, "Prayer (3)" folder, box 63, Bentley Papers; Drew Pearson column, *Newport News Daily Press*, 14 May 1964, rpt. in *Christian Beacon* 29 (21 May 1964): 1.

31. "Prayer-In-School Petitions Submitted," *Flint Journal*, 20 Oct. 1965, "Prayer (2)" folder, box 63, Bentley Papers; "RSVP, Goals and Guidelines" (ms, n.d. [1966]), enclosed with Ralph B. Vandenberg to "Honorable Sir," 29 March 1966, "Federal Miscellaneous, 1966, Prayer in Schools" folder, box 165, George Romney Papers, Bentley Historical Library; Rita Warren with Dick Schneider, *Mom, They Won't Let Us Pray* (Old Tappan, N.J.: Chosen Books, 1975), 14–16, 156; Rita Warren to Hugh L. Carey, 10 Dec. 1975, reel 41, Hugh L. Carey Office Records, Microfilm Copy, New York State Library, Albany; Dierenfield, "Somebody Is Tampering," 180–183; "Attacks on Integrity," *Augusta [Ga.] Herald*, 16 Nov. 1971, folder 11, box 122, William Jennings Bryan Dorn Papers, Modern Political Collections, University of South Carolina, Columbia.

32. Pfeffer, "Who's Who in the Prayer Controversy"; Conference of Joint Advisory Committee, "Reactions to Supreme Court Decision in Regents Prayer"; "Religious Reactions to the Regents' Prayer Decision," *Interreli-*

gious Newsletter 7 (Feb. 1963), 2–4, folder 12, box 203, JWFI; Edwin J. Lukas to Paul Blanshard, 12 Sept. 1962, folder 7, box 4, Blanshard Papers. To be sure, some Catholics—most notably the United States Catholic Conference—supported the Supreme Court's prayer decisions. But the USCC also became a favorite target for Catholic prayer advocates, who—like Protestant critics of the National Council of Churches—insisted that it did not speak for the majority of believers. William F. Buckley Jr., "The Prayer Amendment," *National Review* 23 (3 Dec. 1971): 1375.

33. "Bishop Kenrick and the Public Schools," *Philadelphia Catholic Standard and Times,* 7 Sept. 1962, "Discussion Papers, Policy Statements, Fact Sheets, Books I, II, II, IV 1962–1963" bound vol., box 122, accession 184, JCRCGP; "Who Made the Secularist School?" *New Mexico Register,* 28 Sept. 1962, "Prayer in Schools—Miami" folder, box 22, Pfeffer Papers; "Prelate Warns of Anti-Church Forces; Deplores High Court's Prayer Decision," *Catholic Standard and Times,* 20 July 1962, 5, vol. 85, Archdiocesan Scrapbooks, Philadelphia Archdiocesan Historical Research Center; William Ball to Clarence Manion, 1 Aug. 1973, folder 7, box 77, Clarence Manion Papers, Chicago Historical Society.

34. Jerry Falwell, *Strength for the Journey: An Autobiography* (New York: Simon and Schuster, 1987), 290; Joann Davis, "The Cross at Evans Jr. High," *Ottumwa Courier,* n.d. [1968], enclosed with Davis to ED, 17 May 1968, WPF 2115, EDP.

35. Jerome L. Himmelstein, *To the Right: The Transformation of American Conservatism* (Berkeley: University of California Press, 1990), 113–114; Robert Wuthnow, *The Restructuring of American Religion: Society and Faith since World War II* (Princeton: Princeton University Press, 1988), 189–190.

36. Louis Cassels, "Churches Join in Efforts to Halt Racial Injustices in Religion," *Chicago Defender,* 30 June–6 July 1962, 8; James E. Adams, "Let's Keep the Bible in Our Schools," *United Evangelical Action* 21 (July 1962): 6; "The Supreme Court Breaks with History," ibid. (Aug. 1962): 18; "What Did the Supreme Court Really Say," ibid. (Sept. 1962): 20.

37. "The Supreme Court," *Christian Beacon* 27 (5 July 1962): 1, 8; American Jewish Congress, "Public Reaction to the Engel v. Vitale Decision on the New York Regents' Prayer" (ms, 11 Sept. 1962), 13, folder 5, box 23, Blanshard Papers; "Statement by the Editor," *Christian Beacon* 28 (20 June 1963): 1; "The Supreme Court Decision," ibid. (27 June 1963): 1.

38. Margaret Ryersau to William Ford, 25 June 1968, "School Prayer" folder, box 4, William Ford Papers, Bentley Historical Library; Howard W. Kacy,

Wake Up, America (n.p., [1966?]), WPF 2077, EDP; Jean A. Polus to James G. O'Hara, n.d. [Nov. 1971], "School Prayer Amendment" folder, box 20, O'Hara Papers.

39. See, e.g., Joann Davis to ED, 17 May 1968, WPF 2115, EDP; Mildred Baker to James G. O'Hara, Nov. ? 1971, "School Prayer Amendment" folder, box 20, O'Hara Papers; Clara Comer to Paul Douglas, 10 June 1966, "Religion (2)" folder, box 482, pt. I, Paul Douglas Papers, Chicago Historical Society.

40. David G. Joyner to ED, 4 Oct. 1968, WPF 2120, EDP; Helen Bohn to James J. Kilpatrick, 8 Dec. 1972, "Religion" folder, box 7, accession 6626-e, James J. Kilpatrick Papers, Alderman Library, University of Virginia; Billy James Hargis, "The Need for a Constitutional Amendment Now!" (ms, Nov. 1963), HH36/2/1, Hoag-Hall Collection, John Hay Library, Brown University.

41. Charles Lamb to Lyman Taylor, 27 May 1963; Lamb to Theodore L. Conklin, 16 Jan. 1964, both in "Prayer in the Schools—Correspondence" folder, box 20, New York State Council of Churches Papers; "Bible Protests Growing; More Schools Defy Ban; Student Cards, Prayers Protest Ky. Bible Ban," *Cincinnati Post Times and Star,* 11 Sept. 1963, 1, rpt. in *Christian Beacon,* 31 Oct. 1963, 5; "Students Revolt against Prayer Ban," *Register* [Newport, Ky.?], 22 Sept. 1963, "Prayer—Newport, KY HS" folder, box 2; "Student 'Prayer Rebellion' Sweeps through High Schools," *Long Island Press,* 16 May 1964, "Prayer—Hicksville, L.I. Schools" folder, box 5; "Students Bow to School Authority, Refrain from Prayer Recitation," ibid., 19 May 1964, "Prayer—Hicksville, L.I. Schools" folder, box 5, all in Series IV, Becker Papers.

42. Chester and Millie Castle to ED, 28 Dec. 1966, WPF 2093, EDP; Twentieth Century Reformation Hour, *The Crusade to Put Prayer and Bible Reading Back in Schools* (n.p., [1966?]), WPF 2071, EDP.

43. Peale, "Superduper Liberals"; Mrs. Paul Wheeler to ED, 2 Feb. 1967, WPF 2102, EDP.

44. Eleanore Bowman to George Romney, 11 Nov. 1965, "Federal Miscellaneous, 1965, Prayer in Schools" folder, box 129, Romney Papers; Gladys Scesney to ED, 10 June 1969, WPF 2128, EDP; "Proud Christian," "Minority Reminded That Majority Has Rights," *Indianapolis News,* 22 Dec. 1962, folder 5, box 188, JWFI.

45. "Swapping Strategies at Forum on Family," *NYT,* 2 Aug. 1982, A13.

46. Falwell, *Strength for the Journey,* 298, 337–338, David Edwin Harrell Jr., *Pat Robertson: A Personal, Religious, and Political Portrait* (San Francisco: Harper and Row, 1987), 206–207; Dierenfield, "Somebody Is Tampering," 184;

Kenneth J. Heineman, *God Is a Conservative: Religion, Politics, and Morality in Contemporary America* (New York: New York University Press, 1998), 81–82; Jerry Falwell, *Listen, America!* (New York: Doubleday, 1980), 223.

47. Reagan to Kenneth J. Bialkin, 2 Sept. 1984, "School Prayer Legislation 1984" folder, box 7; "Reagan Draws Deeply on Religion in Speech," *Philadelphia Inquirer,* 31 Jan. 1984, "Reagan on Religion" folder, box 9; "President Reasserts His Faith," ibid., 7 March 1984, "Reagan on Religion" folder, box 9, all in accession 1991, JCRCGP.

48. William T. Martin, *With God on Our Side: The Rise of the Religious Right in America* (New York: Broadway Books, 1996), 204–205, 233; Ben Brodinsky, "The New Right: The Movement and Its Impact," *Phi Delta Kappan* 64 (Oct. 1982): 87–88; Matthew C. Moen, *The Christian Right and Congress* (Tuscaloosa: University of Alabama Press, 1989), 133.

49. "Public School Prayer in Spotlight Again," *Catholic Standard and Times,* 5 June 1980, "Helms Bill" folder, box 5, accession 923, JCRCGP; "Amendment Drive on School Prayer Loses Senate Vote," *NYT,* 21 March 1984; Arlen Specter to I. David Pincus, 29 March 1984; "One Leader Calls for Retribution, Others for Accord on Prayer Issue," unidentified clipping, n.d. [March 1984], all in "School Prayer Legislation 1984" folder, box 7, accession 1991, JCRCGP; Dierenfield, "Somebody Is Tampering," 188; "But Parental Objections Remain," *Suburban and Wayne [Pa.] Times,* 21 Dec. 1978, "Religion and the Public Schools 1978–79" folder, box 9, accession 1991, JCRCGP; Albert J. Menendez, *The December Wars: Religious Symbols and Ceremonies in the Public Square* (Buffalo: Prometheus, 1993), 98; Rita Warren to Wilma Belcourt, 4 March 1980, Book III, Wilma Belcourt Papers, Elwyn B. Robinson Department of Special Collections, Chester Fritz Library, University of North Dakota, Grand Forks.

50. "Louisiana Schools Challenge Supreme Court on Voluntary Prayer," *Philadelphia Inquirer,* 22 Feb. 1982, "School Prayer—Local" folder; "Prayer in Many Schoolrooms Continues Despite 1962 Ruling," *NYT,* 11 March 1984, "School Prayer Legislation 1984" folder, both in box 7, accession 1991, JCRCGP; "Reading Daily Devotions Common in Area Schools," *News and Record* [Greensboro, N.C.], 25 March 1984, p. 501, vol. 62, North Caroliniana Collection Clipping File, University of North Carolina Library, Chapel Hill.

51. "Ministers Split in Support, Opposition of Prayer Plan," *News and Observer* [Raleigh, N.C.], 24 May 1982, p. 553, vol. 62, North Caroliniana Collection Clipping File; "Prayer in Many Schoolrooms Continues

Despite 1962 Ruling"; Willie L. Maye to Hugh L. Carey, 7 Sept. 1978, reel 41, Carey Office Records; "Reading Daily Devotions Common in Area Schools."

52. North Carolina Project of People for the American Way, *Religion in North Carolina's Schools: The Hidden Reality* (Winston-Salem, 1983), 6; Dierenfield, "Secular Schools?" 380; "Suit Tests N.D. 'Commandments' Law," *Minneapolis Tribune*, 30 Dec. 1979, Book II; Edith Jones to Wilma Belcourt, 15 Jan. 1979, Book II; "Petitions Oppose Posting Tablets," *Grand Forks Herald*, n.d. [March 1979], Book I, all in Belcourt Papers.

8. The Battle for Sex Education

1. "Area Drive Opens to Fight Sex Education in Schools," *Kalamazoo Gazette*, 5 March 1969, "Sex Education—Correspondence—From 1963" folder, box 111, PPFA; Gordon V. Drake, *Is the Schoolhouse the Proper Place to Teach Raw Sex?* [1968], in *Sex, Schools, and Society,* ed. Stewart E. Fraser (Nashville: Aurora, 1972), 184.

2. "Attack on Sex Education 'Distorted,' Margolis Says," *Kalamazoo Gazette*, 16 Feb. 1969; "An Expert Speaks Out on Sex Education," ibid., 19 Feb. 1969, both in "Sex Ed—Corresp—From 1963" folder, PPFA.

3. Letter from George H. Huesman, *Kalamazoo Gazette*, 14 March 1969; letter from Shannon McManus, ibid., 10 March 1969; letter from Joan Long, ibid., 13 March 1969, all in "Sex Ed—Corresp—From 1963" folder, PPFA.

4. Testimony of Mary Baird, Minutes of State Board of Education Hearing on Family Life Education Programs, 4 April 1980, III: 10, accession 1997.025, NJSBE.

5. Envelopes to Mary Calderone [hereafter MC], both postmarked 1 Aug. 1969, New Orleans, "Crank Correspondence, 1968" folder, accession 73.150, MCP.

6. Douglas R. Mackintosh et al., "Sex Education in New Orleans: The Birchers Win a Victory," *New South* 25 (Summer 1970): 46, 55; Mary Breasted, *Oh! Sex Education!* (New York: Praeger, 1970), 269; _____ to MC, 12 Sept. 1969, "Crank Corresp, 1968" folder, MCP; Tom Anderson, "Straight Talk," *Southern Farm Publications,* June 1969, "Sex Education" folder, box 7, William Ford Papers, Bentley Historical Library, Ann Arbor; Mr. and Mrs. M. A. Gettman to Constance E. Cook [hereafter CEC], 25 March 1969, "Sex Education" folder, box 1, NYSASCE; _____ to SIECUS, 22 June 1969, "Crank Correspondence, 1969–1975" folder, accession 73.150, MCP. Under the terms of Calderone's bequest, the

Schlesinger Library bars researchers from identifying most of the correspondents in her papers. In such cases I have substituted a blank for the name of the correspondent.

7. Jeffrey P. Moran, *Teaching Sex: The Shaping of Adolescence in the Twentieth Century* (Cambridge, Mass.: Harvard University Press, 2000), chs. 1–5.

8. See ibid., ch. 6; Breasted, *Oh! Sex Education!*

9. Beth Bailey, *Sex in the Heartland* (Cambridge, Mass.: Harvard University Press, 1999), 137.

10. See, e.g., David Allyn, *Make Love, Not War: The Sexual Revolution: An Unfettered History* (Boston: Little, Brown, 2000), esp. 272–273.

11. Moran, *Teaching Sex,* 166, 163; Breasted, *Oh! Sex Education,* 208, 233; "Playboy Interview: Dr. Mary Calderone," *Playboy,* April 1970, reel 9, Women and Health Collection, microfilm ed. (Berkeley: Women's History Research Center, 1975); John D. Rockefeller III to MC, 9 June 1969, folder 230, box 14, collection 179, MCP.

12. Moran, *Teaching Sex,* 162; MC to _____, 9 Aug. 1968, "Crank Corresp, 1968" folder, MCP; Allyn, *Make Love, Not War,* 179, 154, 170, 173.

13. John Kobler, "Sex Invades the Schoolhouse" [1968], in *Sex, Schools, and Society,* 133, 137; Breasted, *Oh! Sex Education,* 233; Marjorie F. Iseman, "Sex Education" [1968], in *Sex, Schools, and Society,* 159.

14. Iseman, "Sex Education," 143; Robert Eberwein, *Sex Ed: Film, Video, and the Framework of Desire* (New Brunswick, N.J.: Rutgers University Press, 1999), 118–119; Breasted, *Oh! Sex Education,* 63; Kobler, "Sex Invades the Schoolhouse," 129–131; Victoria Brittain, "Unpermissive America," *New Statesman,* 10 Oct. 1969, reel 9, Women and Health Collection.

15. Jeffrey P. Moran, "'Modernism Gone Mad': Sex Education Comes to Chicago, 1913," *Journal of American History* 83 (Sept. 1996): 502–506; Eberwein, *Sex Ed,* 116; "Sex in the Schoolroom," *Time* 51 (22 March 1948): 71–72; "Sex Education," *Life* 24 (24 May 1948): 56; "Sex Education," *FPSB* 12 (May 1950): 8; *Third Report of Joint Fact-Finding Committee on Un-American Activities* (Sacramento: California State Senate, 1947), 353.

16. Gene Birkeland, "Deliver Us from Evil," *American Mercury* 88 (March 1959): 93–96.

17. Richard Gid Powers, *Not without Honor: The History of American Anticommunism* (New York: Free Press, 1995), 290; Ernest Dunbar, "The Plot to Take Over the PTA," *Look,* 7 Sept. 1965; "The Movement to Restore Decency," *John Birch Society Bulletin,* Jan. 1969, both in folder 46, accession 73–150–81, MCP; Movement to Restore Decency, "Special Bulletin—

Feb. 1969," Motorede folder, box 3, John Birch Society Papers, John Hay Library, Brown University.

18. "How to Start a Motorede Committee," "MOTOREDE BASIC ACTIVI-TIES," "Possible Questions," all enclosed with Movement to Restore Decency, "Special Bulletin—Feb. 1969"; *Motorede Newsletter* no. 1 (May 1969), "Motorede" folder, box 3, Birch Society Papers; "Sex-Ed Flare-ups Would Ban Courses, Materials," *Library Journal* 94 (15 Nov. 1969): 4188; Drake, *Is the Schoolhouse the Proper Place,* 173; "Radio Tape of a Personal Attack against Reverend William Genne and Dr. Isadore Rubin" (Terre Haute, Ind.: WWVR Radio, 18 March 1969), folder 46, accession 73–150–81, MCP; "Suggested News Release," enclosed with *Motorede Newsletter* no. 1.

19. See, e.g., "Congress Ducks Sex Education Hassle," *Berkeley Daily Gazette,* 17 July 1969, reel 9, Women and Health Collection; Mackintosh et al., "Sex Education in New Orleans," esp. 48; MC to "Dear Friend," 6 March 1969, enclosed with *Motorede Newsletter,* no. 1.

20. Powers, *Not without Honor,* 312, 356; Mike Royko, "The New Peril: A Red in Bed," *Chicago Daily News,* 24 Feb. 1969, folder 46, accession 73–150–81, MCP; "Sex Education in the Schools," *JAMA* 203 (12 May 1969), "PPFA Subject—Sex Ed General-Lit" folder, box 111, PPFA.

21. "Sex Education in the Schools"; "Why the Furor over Sex Education," *U.S. News and World Report* 67 (4 Aug. 1969): 45; "Radio Tape of Personal Attack against SIECUS" (Inglewood, Cal.: KTYM Radio, 20 March 1968), folder 47, accession 73–150–81, MCP.

22. "Radio Tape of Personal Attack against SIECUS"; "Playboy Interview: Dr. Mary Calderone," 63; Mrs. R. E. Morgan to Paul Todd, 17 April 1969; Miriam Garwood, "Attacks against Sex Education—Southwest Region/PPWP" (ms, April 1969), both in "Sex Ed—Corresp—From 1963" folder, PPFA; "Public Schools: Sex in the Classroom," *Time* 94 (25 July 1969): 50; Carl T. Rowan and David M. Mazie, "Sex Education: Powder Keg in Our Schools," *Reader's Digest* 95 (Oct. 1969): 73; "Sex Education in School Upheld in Stormy Session," *Phoenix Gazette,* 30 Oct. 1968, folder 47, accession 73–150–81, MCP.

23. See, e.g., William and Victoria Schoenster to CEC, 29 March 1969, "Sex Ed" folder, box 1, NYSASCE; Mrs. Wellington Drexler to James G. O'Hara, 24 May 1969, "Sex Education" folder, box 13, James G. O'Hara Papers, Bentley Historical Library; Mrs. Edward C. Thedens to Office of the Gen-

eral Assembly, 31 Oct. 1970, "Responses to Sex Report" folder, package 1, UPCC.

24. _____ to MC, n.d. (rec. 25 Nov. 1974), "Correspondence, 1974" folder, accession 73.150, MCP.

25. Breasted, *Oh! Sex Education*, 119–120; Allyn, *Make Love, Not War*, 138–140; S. S. Retzer to United Presbyterian Church of the USA, 8 Sept. 1970, "Responses to Sex Report," package 1, UPCC.

26. Willard B. Thomas to Council on Church and Society, n.d. [1970], "Responses to Sex Report," package 1, UPCC; _____ to James Lincoln Collier and Lester A. Kirkendall, 20 June 1968, "Crank Corresp, 1968" folder, MCP; Max Rafferty, "The Dropout Parents: How Americans Got on a Sex Binge" [1969], in *Sex, Schools, and Society*, 225–226; idem., *Max Rafferty on Education* (New York: Devin-Adair, 1968), 149.

27. Planned Parenthood—World Population, "Sample Release" (ms, 12 May 1969), "PPFA Subject—Sex Ed, General-Lit" folder, PPFA; "Parents Not Teaching Sex to Children," *Berkeley Daily Gazette*, 29 Aug. 1969, reel 9, Women and Health Collection; Jacqueline Bezselich to William Ford, 28 June 1969, "Sex Ed" folder, box 7, Ford Papers; "Statement of Benjamin F. Lewis, Executive Director of Planned Parenthood Association Chicago Area . . ." (ms, 26–27 July 1971), "Sex Ed—1970" folder; Merle W. Zirkle, "A Rationale for a Program in Sex Education" (ms, Sept. 1969), "PPFA Subject—Sex Ed, General-Lit" folder, both in box 111, PPFA.

28. Letter by Mrs. Stephen Jordan, *Schenectady [N.Y.] Gazette*, n.d. [April 1969], enclosed with R. E. Morgan to Paul Todd, 17 April 1969, "Sex Ed—Corresp—From 1963" folder, PPFA; Moran, *Teaching Sex*, 161; Breasted, *Oh! Sex Education*, 227–232; Committee on Family Life, "Fellowship Dinner" (ms, 4 Oct. 1963), folder 15, box 27, RG 9, NCC.

29. Shirley Turpin to William P. Thompson, 22 June 1970; "Presbyterians Accept Liberal Sex Report, But . . ." *National Catholic Reporter*, n.d. [1970]; R. Norman Herbert, "Something Sacred Was Missing at General Assembly," *Presbyterian Layman*, Sept. 1970; "Evaluation Study of the Committees of the Pioneer and Pleasant Grove United Presbyterian Churches, Ligonier, Pennsylvania" (ms, n.d. [1970]); Elaine Tourier to Department of Church and Society, 31 May 1970, all in "Responses to Sex Report" folder, package 1, UPCC.

30. Testimony of Marjorie G. Lemlow, House Assembly Interim Committee on Education, Sensitivity Training Hearings (transcript, 5 Dec. 1968), 228,

LP 48:12, Legislative Papers, California State Archives; Nola Meredith to Howard Day, 3 Jan. 1970, folder 441, CDER.

31. Testimony of Nola Meredith, ST Hearings, 107–108; "Supplementary Evaluation of Curriculum Guides on Family Life and Sex Education and an Overview of the Guides" (ms, 6 March 1969), enclosed with Marilyn A. Angle, "Open Letter to California Parents and Taxpayers," 10 March 1969, folder 11, box 91, LCCP.

32. H. Edward Rowe, "Statement Concerning 'Moral Guidelines' Rough Draft" (ms, 24 July 1972), folder 442, CDER; Ellen Herman, *The Romance of American Psychology: Political Culture in the Age of Experts* (Berkeley: University of California Press, 1995), 284–285; *Guidelines for Moral Instruction in California Schools* (Sacramento: State Dept. of Education, 1969), 55, folder 438, CDER.

33. *Sex/Family Life Education and Sensitivity Training: Indoctrination or Education?* (San Mateo, Cal.: C.I.E. Information Center, 1969), 42–43, 52–53; American Education Lobby, *Sex Education: Assault on American Youth* (n.p., n.d. [1969]), 3–4, folder 11, box 91, LCCP; Breasted, *Oh! Sex Education,* 243–244; _____ to MC, 29 Sept. 1971, "Crank Corresp, 1968" folder, MCP.

34. Angle, "Open Letter to California Parents and Taxpayers"; form letter by David L. Bartlett, n.d., enclosed with Bartlett to Max Rafferty, 2 Sept. 1969, folder 747, CDER; American Education Lobby, *Sex Education,* 1; "Parents Thrash Out Sex Ed Dilemma," *Star Free Press,* n.d. [Sept. 1969], enclosed with Bartlett to Rafferty, 4 Nov. 1969, folder 747, CDER; _____ to MC, 20 April 1969, "Crank Corresp, 1969–75" folder, MCP.

35. Mrs. Mitchell J. Hochberg to CEC, 19 March 1969, "Sex Ed" folder, box 1, NYSASCE; _____ to MC, n.d. (rec. 25 March 1969), "Crank Corresp, 1968" folder; "Parents' School League Fights 'Permissiveness,'" *Oregon Journal,* 9 Sept. 1971, "By or about Dr. Calderone" folder; "Newsletter of Parents of New York United," no. 2 (Jan. 1970): 6, enclosed with _____ to MC, 11 Feb. 1970, "Letters" folder, all in accession 73.150, MCP; letter from Rudolph Morin, *Albany Knickerbocker News,* n.d. [April 1969], enclosed with Mrs. K. Fitzpatrick to Mrs. Allen D. Foster, "Sex Ed—Corresp—From 1963" folder, PPFA; _____ to SIECUS, 22 June 1969, "Crank Corresp, 1969–75" folder, MCP.

36. Breasted, *Oh! Sex Education,* 64; Antonio J. Lafata to James G. O'Hara, 19 July 1969, "Sex Ed" folder, box 13, O'Hara Papers; Shirley A. Giorgio to CEC, 25 March 1969, "Sex Ed" folder, box 1, NYSASCE.

37. Lydia Gleason to CEC, n.d. [March 1969], "Sex Ed" folder, box 1, NYSASCE; Mr. and Mrs. Herbert Gardzella to William Ford, 13 Feb. 1974, "Sex Ed" folder, box 16, Ford Papers.

38. Testimony of W. B. Woodard, 16 April 1969, LP 175:231, Legislative Papers, Cal. State Archives; Mrs. Carl Paratore to James G. O'Hara, n.d. [June 1969], "Sex Ed" folder, box 13, O'Hara Papers; "Sex Education in School Upheld in Stormy Session," *Phoenix Gazette*, 30 Oct. 1968, folder 47, accession 73–150–81, MCP; "Parents Thrash Out Sex Ed Dilemma."

39. Sandra Gardner, "New Jersey Journal," *NYT*, 21 Feb. 1982, 3.

40. Constance Horner, "Is the New Sex Education Going Too Far?" *NYT Magazine*, 7 Dec. 1980, 138, 142, 144; "Sex Ed 101 for Kids—and Parents," *Newsweek*, 1 Sept. 1980, 50–51; Dale Vree, "Public School Blues," *National Review*, 22 June 1979, 811; Ernest van den Haag, "Birds, Bees, and Bathroom Tours: Sex Education Revisited," ibid., 7 Dec. 1979, 1555–57; testimony of Thomas Walsh, "Transcript of Public Testimony on Family Life Education, State Board of Education," Session A (20 Feb. 1985), 44–45, folder 5a, accession 1997.025, NJSBE; Atta T. Blackwell, "School Sex Films 'Corrupting,'" *Ambler [Pa.] Gazette*, n.d. [March 1977], "Newsclippings—Sex Education" folder, box 8, Planned Parenthood of Southeastern Pennsylvania Records, Urban Archives, Temple University; Sandra Gardner, "Sex Education: A National Controversy," *Senior Scholastic* 113 (6 March 1981): 14–15.

41. Moran, *Teaching Sex*, 200–201; Horner, "Is the New Sex Education Going Too Far," 148; "New Jersey Board Mandates Sex Education," *Phi Delta Kappan* 61 (June 1980): 723; testimony of James Leck, Minutes of State Board of Education Hearing, 8 April 1980, II: 45; _____ to *60 Minutes*, n.d. (rec. 5 Nov. 1981), folder 1, box 1, accession 82-m129, MCP.

42. "Film Borrowers' Names Sought by Moral Majority," *NYT*, 8 Feb. 1981, 24; "Moral Majority Halts Lawsuit on Sex Education Film," ibid., 24 Feb. 1981, 14; "Dirty Old Woman," *60 Minutes*, 25 Oct. 1981 (produced by Elliot Bernstein), film 7, MCP.

43. Testimony of Catherine Denk, Minutes of State Board of Education, 6 Aug. 1980, I: 98; II: 15; testimony of Helen Foley, Minutes of State Board of Education Hearing, 8 April 1980, III: 45, both in accession 1997.025, NJSBE.

44. Testimony of Mary Flunn, Minutes of State Board of Education Hearing, 8 April 1980, II: 146; _____ to *60 Minutes*, n.d. (postmarked 31 Oct.

1981), folder 3, box 1, accession 82-m129, MCP; testimony of Rita Mahon, Minutes of State Board of Education Hearing, 8 April 1980, II: 78. On *Our Bodies, Ourselves,* see Allyn, *Make Love, Not War,* 183.

45. See, e.g., "'Sensualists' Said behind Sex Education Movement," *Stockton [Cal.] Record,* 10 Dec. 1968, folder 47, accession 73–150–81, MCP; *Guidelines for Moral Instruction in California Schools,* 37, 43–50; Marilyn Angle to Howard Day, 2 April 1969, folder 11, box 91, LCCP.

46. Testimony of Jean Belsante, Minutes of State Board of Education Hearing, 8 April 1980, II: 61; testimony of Preston Smith, ibid., III: 29. For similar charges, see Vree, "Public School Blues"; Blackwell, "School Sex Films 'Corrupting'"; Michael Lienesch, *Redeeming America: Piety and Politics in the New Christian Right* (Chapel Hill: University of North Carolina Press, 1993), 82–83.

47. Testimony of Mary DeCillis, Transcript of Public Testimony on Family Life Education, session B, 20 Feb. 1985, 38, folder 5b, accession 1997.025, NJSBE; testimony of Mary Baird, Minutes of State Board of Education Hearing, 8 April 1980, III: 7.

48. Moran, *Teaching Sex,* 213–215, 204; William T. Martin, *With God on Our Side: The Rise of the Religious Right in America* (New York: Broadway Books, 1996), 249–252; C. Everett Koop, *Koop: The Memoirs of America's Family Doctor* (New York: Random House, 1991), 213–214.

49. Bonnie Nelson Trudell, *Doing Sex Education: Gender Politics and Schooling* (New York: Routledge, 1993), 18, 3; Moran, *Teaching Sex,* 214.

50. "Sex Education: Three Choices," *NYT,* 25 Aug. 1985, Long Island Weekly Section, 1, 14; "Battle Lines Being Drawn over Sex Education," *Los Angeles Times,* 23 Dec. 1968, folder 47, accession 73–150–81, MCP.

Epilogue: Searching for Common Ground

1. James Davison Hunter, "Reflections on the Culture Wars Hypothesis," in *The American Culture Wars: Current Contests and Future Prospects,* ed. James L. Nolan Jr. (Charlottesville: University Press of Virginia, 1996), 253; idem., *Culture Wars: The Struggle to Define America* (New York: Basic, 1991), 42–43; idem., "The American Culture War," in *The Limits of Social Cohesion: Conflict and Mediation in Pluralist Societies,* ed. Peter L. Berger (Boulder: Westview, 1998), 3.

2. Hunter, "Reflections," 253; idem., *Before the Shooting Begins: Searching for Democracy in America's Culture War* (New York: Free Press, 1994), 8; idem., *Culture Wars,* xii, 174, 198.

3. For the skeptical view, see Randall Balmer, *Blessed Assurance: A History of Evangelicalism in America* (Boston: Beacon, 1999), 109; Michael Lind, *The Next American Nation: The New Nationalism and the Fourth American Revolution* (New York: Free Press, 1995), 252. For a more positive reading, see Christian Smith, *A Christian America? What Evangelicals Really Want* (Berkeley: University of California Press, 2000), esp. 147–148.

4. Allan S. Miller and John P. Hoffmann, "The Growing Divisiveness: Culture Wars or a War of Words?" *Social Forces* 78 (Dec. 1999): 721; Margaret S. Hrezo and Melinda Bollar Wagner, "Civility or the Culture Wars in Politics and Religion: Case Study of Oliver North in Virginia," in *Culture Wars in American Politics: Critical Reviews of a Popular Myth,* ed. Rhys H. Williams (New York: Aldine De Gruyter, 1997), 160; Balmer, *Blessed Assurance,* 98.

5. See Gary B. Nash, Charlotte Crabtree, and Ross E. Dunn, *History on Trial: Culture Wars and the Teaching of the Past* (New York: Knopf, 1997).

6. See, e.g., Mark Gerson, *The Neoconservative Vision: From the Cold War to the Culture Wars* (Lanham, Md.: Madison Books, 1996); Gertrude Himmelfarb, *One Nation, Two Cultures* (New York: Knopf, 1999); John J. Miller, *The Unmaking of Americans: How Multiculturalism Has Undermined the Assimilation Ethic* (New York: Free Press, 1998).

7. Compare Robin D. G. Kelley, *Yo' Mama's Disfunktional! Fighting the Culture Wars in Urban America* (Boston: Beacon, 1997), and Todd Gitlin, *The Twilight of Common Dreams: Why America Is Wracked by Culture Wars* (New York: Henry Holt, 1995).

8. See Nathan Glazer, *We Are All Multiculturalists Now* (Cambridge, Mass.: Harvard University Press, 1997), esp. 9, 81.

9. Nash, Crabtree, and Dunn, *History on Trial,* 197, 39–46, 268, 235.

10. Alan Wolfe, *One Nation, After All* (New York: Viking, 1998), 276; Balmer, *Blessed Assurance,* 105; Robert Booth Fowler and Allen D. Hertzke, *Religion and Politics in America: Faith, Culture, and Strategic Choices* (Boulder: Westview, 1999), 239; Douglas Jacobsen and William Vance Trollinger, "Introduction," in *Re-Forming the Center: American Protestantism, 1900 to the Present,* ed. Jacobsen and Trollinger (Grand Rapids, Mich.: Eerdmans, 1998), 8; and esp. Smith, *A Christian America?*

11. Nash, Crabtree, and Dunn, *History on Trial,* 217; James W. Fraser, *Between Church and State: Religion and Public Education in a Multicultural America* (New York: St. Martin's, 1999), 204, 208–215; Barbara G. Gaddy, T. William Hall, and Robert J. Marzano, *School Wars: Resolving Our Conflicts over Religion and Values* (San Francisco: Jossey-Bass, 1996), 191.

12. "Without a Prayer," *Time* 142 (20 Dec. 1993): 41; "A Principal's Troubling Prayer," *Newsweek* 122 (20 Dec. 1993): 107. The local school board later overrode the superintendent who had fired the principal. "Principal Who Allowed School Prayer Reinstated," *Jet* 85 (10 Jan. 1994): 32.

13. Fraser, *Between Church and State*, 206–208.

14. Louise Adler, "Curriculum Challenges in California," *Record in Educational Administration and Supervision* 13 (Spring–Summer 1993): 10–20; Gilbert T. Sewall, "Religion and the Textbooks," in *Curriculum, Religion, and Public Education: Conversations for an Enlarging Public Sphere*, ed. James T. Sears with James C. Carper (New York: Teachers College Press, 1998), 82.

15. "Is There a Common Moral Framework That Schools Can Embrace?" in Sears and Carper, eds., *Curriculum, Religion, and Public Education*, 131; Richard Rorty, "Religion as a Conversation-Stopper," *Common Knowledge* 3 (Spring 1994): 1–6.

16. Stephen L. Carter, *The Culture of Disbelief: How American Law and Politics Trivialize Religious Devotion* (New York: Basic, 1993), 207.

17. See, e.g., Sewall, "Religion and the Textbooks," 73–84; Paul Boyer, "In Search of the Fourth 'R': The Treatment of Religion in American History Textbooks," in *Religious Advocacy and American History*, ed. Bruce Kuklick and D. G. Hart (Grand Rapids, Mich.: Eerdmans, 1997), 112–136.

18. Sewall, "Religion and the Textbooks," 81; Joan DelFattore, *What Johnny Shouldn't Read: Textbook Censorship in America* (New Haven: Yale University Press, 1992), 88.

19. Arthur M. Schlesinger Jr., *The Disuniting of America: Reflections on a Multicultural Society*, rev. ed. (New York: Norton, 1998), 83–84, 133; Richard Bernstein, *Dictatorship of Virtue: Multiculturalism and the Battle for America's Future* (New York: Knopf, 1994), 54; Frances Fitzgerald, *America Revised* (New York: Vintage, 1979), 94; DelFattore, *What Johnny Shouldn't Read*, 158–159.

20. Benedict Anderson, *Imagined Communities*, rev. ed. (New York: Verso, 1991), 201, 204; Yael Tamir, "Theoretical Difficulties in the Study of Nationalism," in *Theorizing Nationalism*, ed. Ronald Beiner (Albany: State University of New York Press, 1999), 71–72.

21. David Miller, *On Nationality* (Oxford: Oxford University Press, 1995), 36–37; David Archard, "Myths, Lies and Historical Truth: A Defence of Nationalism," *Political Studies* 43 (Sept. 1995): 472–481.

22. William McNeill, *Mythhistory and Other Essays* (Chicago: University of Chicago Press, 1986), 14.

23. See Rogers M. Smith, *Civic Ideals: Conflicting Visions of Citizenship* (New Haven: Yale University Press, 1997); Gary Gerstle, *American Crucible: Race and Nation in the Twentieth Century* (Princeton: Princeton University Press, 2001).

24. Gerald Graff, *Beyond the Culture Wars: How Teaching the Conflicts Can Revitalize American Education* (New York: Norton, 1992), 8.

25. Linda M. McNeil, *Contradictions of Control: School Structure and School Knowledge* (New York: Routledge, 1986); James W. Loewen, *Lies My Teacher Told Me: Everything Your American History Textbook Got Wrong* (New York: Touchstone, 1995), 287–288.

26. Warren A. Nord, *Religion and American Education: Rethinking a National Dilemma* (Chapel Hill: University of North Carolina Press, 1995), 260.

27. On how such instruction might work, see ibid., ch. 9; Nel Noddings, *Educating for Intelligent Belief or Unbelief* (New York: Teachers College Press, 1993), ch. 8.

28. Kenneth T. Jackson, "Is History Flunking as a Profession?" *OAH Newsletter* 28 (Aug. 2000): 9; Diane Ravitch, "The Educational Backgrounds of History Teachers," in *Knowing, Teaching, and Learning History: National and International Perspectives,* ed. Peter N. Stearns, Peter Seixas, and Sam Wineburg (New York: New York University Press, 2000), 143; Linda S. Levstik, "Articulating the Silences: Teachers' and Adolescents' Conceptions of Historical Significance," ibid., 297–298; Richard J. Paxton, "A Deafening Silence: History Textbooks and the Students Who Read Them," *Review of Educational Research* 69 (Fall 1999): 316, 320–321.

29. Christopher J. Lucas, *Teacher Education in America: Reform Agendas for the Twenty-First Century* (New York: St. Martin's, 1997), 86, 118–119, 194; Richard J. Paxton and Sam Wineburg, "Expertise and the Teaching of History," in *Routledge International Companion to Education,* ed. Bob Moon, Miriam Ben-Peretz, and Sally Brown (New York: Routledge, 2000), 859–860.

30. Walter Lippmann, *American Inquisitors* (New Brunswick: Transaction, 1993 [1928]), 22, 64–65.

31. George Marsden, "The Meaning of Science for Christians: A New Dialogue on Olympus," in *Evangelicals and Science in Historical Perspective,* ed. David N. Livingstone, D. G. Hart, and Mark A. Noll (New York: Oxford, 1999), 334–335.

32. George M. Marsden, *The Outrageous Idea of Christian Scholarship* (New York: Oxford, 1997), 46.

Acknowledgments

This book required me to visit more than forty archives in twenty states. I could not have researched or written it without the financial support of several generous institutions: the Indiana Historical Society, the North Caroliniana Society, the Arthur and Elizabeth Schlesinger Library, the Bentley Historical Library, and the Oberlin College Library. The Spencer Foundation provided a Small Research Grant during the early stages of the project, then awarded me a National Academy of Education/Spencer Foundation Post-Doctoral Fellowship that allowed me to complete it. I am especially grateful to Ellen Condliffe Lagemann, the president of the Spencer Foundation, for her friendship and dedication.

At New York University, I've worked under four department chairs: Neil Postman, Ellen Lagemann, Floyd Hammack, and Richard Arum. All of them have been unfailingly supportive of this book and of its author. Thanks also to Lucy Frazier, the best administrative assistant in the world, as well as to several graduate students who helped me mine material for the project: Michelle Boule, Carley Moore, and Holly Epstein Ojalvo. The Interlibrary Loan staff at NYU's Bobst Library tracked down each of my arcane requests with competence and good cheer. I'm also indebted to Charlie Sprague for helping me win internal grants from the New York University Research Challenge

Fund as well as the NYU School of Education Research Challenge Fund, whose support I gratefully acknowledge here. Thanks, finally, to the students in my Education and the Culture Wars course at NYU, who let me test many of the ideas in this book. I hope they learned as much from the course as I did from them.

Most of all, I appreciate the intrepid colleagues who plowed through the different incarnations of this book and offered wise critiques: Barbara Beatty, Robby Cohen, Joan DelFattore, Elisabeth Hansot, Victoria Hattam, Elizabeth Knoll, Ellen Lagemann, Jeffrey Mirel, Doug Rossinow, Joyce Seltzer, Camille Smith, Ronald Walters, and especially David Tyack. David's career has been a model of scholarship and friendship, making all of us better historians and—more important—better people. I wish him health and happiness in his retirement.

How can you thank the people who love you the most? You can't. Susan Coffin has stood by me at every step of this project, and at every juncture of our lives. Her steadfast love and friendship have been the anchor of my world, keeping everything else from drifting out to sea. During all of my research trips, there wasn't a moment when I didn't think of Susan and our two delightful daughters, Sarah and Rebecca. Together, they made Van Morrison's "Coming Home" the sweetest song of all.

Index

Harvard University Press is a member of Green Press Initiative
(greenpressinitiative.org), a nonprofit organization working to
help publishers and printers increase their use of recycled paper
and decrease their use of fiber derived from endangered forests.
This book was printed on 100% recycled paper containing
50% post-consumer waste and processed chlorine free.

BD/O